JOHN GAY, Ed.D.

Assistant Professor, Health Science Department
Towson State University, Towson, Maryland

MOLLY WANTZ, Ed.S.

Assistant Professor, Department of Physiology and
Health Science, Ball State University, Muncie, Indiana

HAROLD SLOBOF, Ed.D.

Associate Professor, Department of Health Sciences,
Mankato State University, Mankato, Minnesota

CAROL HOOPER, M.P.H.

University of Maryland School of Medicine,
Baltimore, Maryland

WARREN BOSKIN, Ed.D.

Associate Professor, Department of Health Science and Safety,
San Diego State University, San Diego, California

ILLUSTRATIONS BY DENISE LAUDERDALE

CURRENT HEALTH PROBLEMS

1979   **W. B. SAUNDERS COMPANY**   Philadelphia · London · Toronto

W. B. Saunders Company: West Washington Square
                           Philadelphia, PA   19105

                           1 St. Anne's Road
                           Eastbourne, East Sussex BN21 3UN, England

                           1 Goldthorne Avenue
                           Toronto, Ontario M8Z 5T9, Canada

Library of Congress Cataloging in Publication Data

Main entry under title:

Current health problems.

Includes index.

1. Health.   I. Gay, John E. [DNLM: 1. Medicine
— Popular works.   2. Mental health — Popular works.
WB120.3 G285c]

RA776.C94   613   77-72798

ISBN 9-7216-4057-5

Cover painting is "Opus 1972" an enamel on steel painting by Virgil Cantini

Current Health Problems   ISBN 0-7216-4057-5

Last digit is the print number: 9   8   7   6   5   4   3   2   1

INTRODUCTION

The basic premise of this text is that, in addition to the presentation of basic cognitive and affective information, health education should go one step further by assisting students in developing decision-making skills. The authors feel that it is not enough for a student to acquire information and clarify feelings, attitudes and values. The student must be able to apply this information and make intelligent decisions concerning his or her own life.

Each chapter presents basic health information. Included in some chapters are exercises to assist the reader in clarifying attitudes and values. Each section concludes with exercises designed to develop decision-making skills.

The text begins by offering the student a basic foundation of what is meant by health and how this meaning applies to the world, the nation and the individual. It is followed by a discussion of the many modes used in the solution of a health problem and then establishes a specific model for solving health-related problems. This model presentation is followed by "walking the student through" a realistic problem.

The chapters on mental health focus on decision-making and assist students to move in a positive, growing direction. The aim is to aid the student in realizing that life, while a challenge, can be both meaningful and fun. As students go through these chapters they are asked to examine their own self-concepts and to explore ways of changing, growing and becoming. Emotions, crises, problem-solving and mental illness are also discussed.

The total combination of drugs, personality and society is considered in Section Four, Assimilated Substances and Our Culture. These chapters present factual information that is examined in conjunction with the decision-making skills of the reader. Alcohol, tobacco and drugs are dealt with as separated entities in some respects and as a conglomerate in others. The sociological aspects of American drug-taking are also explored.

The chapters on sexuality are designed to present scientific information about the social, emotional and physical elements of sex, sexuality and sexual relations. Throughout the chapter, students are asked to examine themselves as total sexual beings and ultimately are asked to make decisions concerning their own sexual behaviors. The topics discussed include sex roles, perceptive and pleasure systems, psychosexual development, sexual attitudes and values, coitus, sexual behavior, sexual dysfunction and birth control.

Before discussing chronic and communicable diseases, the concepts of body perception and reactions to illness are explored. The reader is asked to apply these concepts by reflecting on his or her own health behavior and sick role patterns. In the discussion of chronic and communicable diseases, the author not only describes the diseases but also emphasizes preventive actions.

The final section, dealing with health and aging, employs many of the concepts developed in previous chapters. If a person is to achieve a relatively healthy old age, then he must, at a young age, identify and maintain positive health behaviors. This section identifies the three ways an individual ages: biologically, psychologically and sociologically. It investigates the dimensions of aging in terms of normal changes, nutrition, exercise and disease, and it looks at the various health agencies that provide services by and for the elderly.

Although this text emphasizes only five major aspects of health education, it is felt that the information presented in each section can easily be correlated with many other areas in health. The decision-making skills developed by the student, as a result of participating in the exercises included in this text, can be carried over into all aspects of health and life.

JOHN GAY, ED.D.

CONTENTS

SOLVING HEALTH PROBLEMS

CHAPTER 1

SOLVING
HEALTH PROBLEMS

We live in a world of rapid changes—changes in all scientific fields, changes in technology, and social and psychological changes. At no time in the history of mankind have these changes been so rapid and so far-reaching. We have moved by leaps and bounds from a society of farmers clustered together in small communities to a highly industrialized, mobile, urban society.

These changes have allowed greater self-fulfillment than was ever thought of by prior generations; but if we are to achieve this level of fulfillment, we must learn to deal with the changes in our environment in a positive way. Only through positive interaction with the environment can we avoid creating new and perhaps more serious problems as well as seek satisfactory solutions to existing problems.

The question of primary importance is, How does one go about solving the problems that plague each one of us? How does one maintain some degree of equilibrium in an ever-changing society? In short, how can the individual reach the level of fulfillment that most closely approximates his or her potential?

This question is not easily answered. To be sure, if we are to reach our fullest potential, we must have the ability to solve problems that would decrease our sense of fulfillment. Some of these problems may be physical, whereas others are emotional. Only healthy individuals will be capable of developing their lives to the greatest extent.

CONCEPT OF HEALTH

Throughout history, the concept of health has changed drastically. Inevitably, it will continue to change as new methods are found to meet the needs of the individual and society. There seems to be no one definition of health that is universal. To the average person, health may mean freedom from any disease. To a secretary, the definition of health might include the ability to carry out a day's work and still have some reserve strength to meet personal needs. The college student may look at

3

health as a condition that allows him to engage in any activity to the utmost of his ability.

All these views of health have at least one thing in common, namely that all individuals seem to consider themselves healthy when they feel a positive sense of well-being, or as the World Health Organization has stated, a state of complete physical, mental and social well-being and not merely the absence of disease or infirmity.

This dynamic concept of health is also brought out in The School Health Education Study, which states that "health is a quality of life involving dynamic interaction and interdependence among the individual's physical well-being, his mental and emotional reactions and the social complex in which he exists." We see, therefore, that health is not an abstraction that exists only in the minds of philosophers but is really a specific and concrete condition that describes the interaction among our physical, emotional and social states.

However, even though health is concrete, we must keep in mind that the state of one's health is a dynamic process that changes from day to day and from hour to hour. Thus, an infinite number of factors influence health, and therefore, decision-making for one's own health and well-being is essential.

DECISION-MAKING
FOR HEALTH-RELATED PROBLEMS

How do we go about making our health behavior decisions? Assuming that we have some choices as to how we interact with our environment as a physical, mental and social being, it is essential that we be able to make decisions regarding this interaction. Can this be done merely on the basis of intuition or how we "feel" about something or someone? Must we always experience something before we decide its merits and demerits? Do we use only information that we have acquired through our own experiences, or should we include the experiences of others or writings on the subject?

The fundamental aim of this first section is simply to present new tools and skills that enable innovation in solving health problems and making health-related decisions. These tools may be viewed as the instruments for "do-it-yourself thinking." Today, in most of our education as well as in our daily lives, we are generally given detailed instructions that tell us to do A and B in order to get C. These "recipes" tend to obviate any use of creative thinking in solving a problem or coming to a decision. It is this "following the bouncing ball" that tends to deter our ability to deal with day-to-day problems, let alone make long-term decisions regarding our health and well-being.

We are going to develop a system to assist you in your decision-making skills. Just as the do-it-yourself books provide a detailed set of instructions, so do the following pages and worksheets. In contrast to traditional "how-to" instructions, however, our instructions outline a step-by-step method for dealing creatively with any health problem in a flexible rather than a rigid framework.

The first time you use this system, you will probably find it advantageous to follow each procedure rather explicitly, as in learning any new system or skill. After gaining a thorough understanding, you will be able to adapt each procedure to your own problems without necessarily following every step. In solving most everyday problems, you will find that you can use this method almost subconsciously.

The worksheets at the end of this chapter are designed to demonstrate how creativity can be applied at *each* stage of a logical, methodical approach to problem-solving. The main emphasis is on piling up alternatives and applying weighted evaluation at every stage — in finding the facts, identifying the problem, searching for ideas, finding the solution, and accepting the results. At the same time, the worksheets provide exercise, or practice, in using your imagination. Recent research has demonstrated that practice substantially develops creative decision-making skills.

Keep in mind that this system is completely flexible, since a completely rigid structure for so dynamic a process would be impossible. These steps provide only a guide and do not represent a fixed formula for the solution of a problem. For example, identifying the problem may call for additional fact-finding, and so it is with each of the suggested steps. You should continually review the system to find how to make it work best for you and your particular problem.

A suitable solution may actually be found at any stage of the process. For a particular problem, some of the steps may be academic. However, if at least some thought is given to each, refinements in the solution of the problem are often possible. Obviously, there is rarely a best solution — only the best alternative. By probing each of the steps, you are more likely to find an alternative that is closer to the perfect solution and to obtain much greater insight into your problem.

THE MODEL

Now that we have laid the groundwork for our decision-making model, let's see how it works. Problem-solving can be approached in a number of ways. Some methods are scientific and logical, others are emotional, and still others are a combination of both. Rather than logic and reason, our model uses emotions as the source of data.

The process we will use in our decision-making scheme is really quite simple. It involves six steps: (1) perceive the problem, (2) define the problem, (3) get ideas about the problem, (4) evaluate the ideas, (5) act, and (6) react.

Perceive the Problem. This step seems to be simple at first glance, but just for a moment reflect on your own life and past problems that required a decision. How many times have you been asked, "What's wrong?" or "What's bugging you?" and your only response was, "I don't know"?

Perception of the problem is essential if it is to be solved; and true perception of the problem requires both divergent and convergent approaches. That is, an individual must look outward, beyond himself, and at the same time screen out irrelevant data. Through this process, the individual explores his feelings and begins to focus on the specific problem.

Problems may center on any type of situation, such as dating behavior, drug usage, or selection of a life style or even a type of dress. Whatever the problem may be, this first step is essential in order to work toward a solution.

Define the Problem.   Once the general problem has been identified, it must be defined in rather specific terms. The individual must narrow the scope of the problem so that it is workable and he has some sense of direction. For example, if the general problem concerns dating behavior, it is now necessary to focus on the specific aspect of the problem. Is it related, for example, to physical needs, financial concerns, or time problems? Where does the specific problem lie?

Get Ideas about the Problem.   This step begins the "nuts and bolts" process of our decision-making scheme. Here we begin to generate as many solutions as possible to the problem at hand. Write them down without any evaluation—no solution is right or wrong at this point.

In this step the creativity of problem-solving begins to come to the forefront. With the mind totally open and with no right or wrong solutions, the free flow of alternatives is possible. Perhaps others may be brought in to offer ideas and possible decisions, but again, it is a "brainstorm" session in which no idea is too bizarre or too simple.

Evaluate the Ideas.   Now that a number of ideas have been generated, the problem-solver must begin the task of evaluating alternatives to determine which is best for his needs at this time. One method of doing this is through a system of paired weighting.

Paired weighting is nothing more than a method of comparing a number of items (in this case, alternative solutions to problems) and measuring them in relation to each other. It is particularly useful when the items are extremely different or to detect small variations in very similar items.

Figure 1–1 shows a paired weighting chart. Each number on the chart represents an alternative solution generated in the previous step, and each pair of numbers is a guide for comparing. In order to compare the alternatives, the decision-maker simply decides which one of each pair is more important and circles it. When he has done this with all the pairs, he totals the number of times each alternative has been circled to obtain a comparative weight for each of the possible solutions.

Figure 1–2 presents a completed paired weighting chart in which the choices have been circled and then counted. To take an accurate total score for each number, remember this method: one is the *only* number that goes straight across in a single horizontal row; 20 forms the only

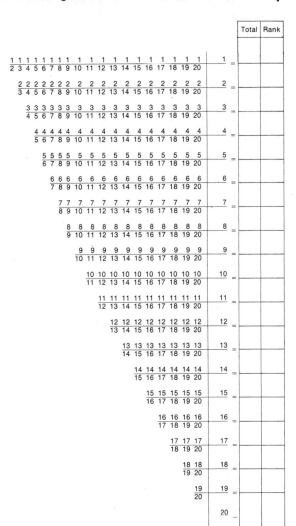

Figure 1–1   Paired weighting chart.

single vertical column. All other numbers follow an L shape, having both a vertical column and a horizontal row.

For each total, begin at the top line, and proceed down the vertical column. Then continue along the horizontal row, from left to right. For instance, in getting the total score for criterion 15, you would go to the top line where 15 appears under 1, count downward until reaching the horizontal 15 row, and then complete your total.

It is interesting to note that this method of evaluating alternatives allows the individual to take into account his personal value system as well as the prevailing social value system.

Act.   Now that ideas have been generated and evaluated, some action must be taken. At this point the decision-maker has chosen the solution and acts accordingly. This stage is really the application of the entire system to the problem at hand.

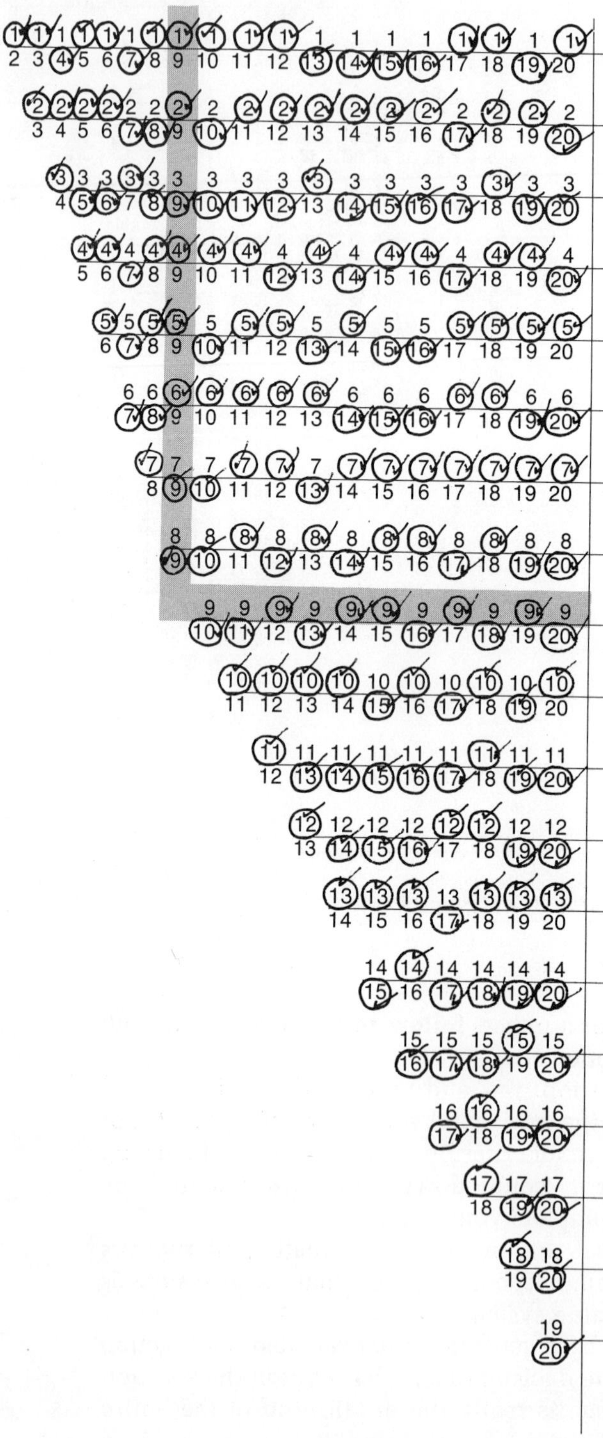

	Total	Rank

1 = 12

2 = 13

3 = 4

4 = 12

5 = 11

6 = 8

7 = 15

8 = 8

9 = 8

10 = 13

11 = 4

12 = 6

13 = 11

14 = 8

15 = 9

16 = 9

17 = 11

18 = 4

19 = 10

20 = 14

Figure 1-2 *See legend on opposite page.*

React. The individual now stands back and attempts to perceive reactions to his decision in an unbiased (as far as possible) manner. He observes the responses of others, processes his own feelings and thoughts, and attempts to evaluate his decision. If he is satisfied, he continues this behavior. If he is dissatisfied, he may choose to repeat the entire process, using the knowledge acquired during the first attempt as a source of data.

One thing must be kept in mind at all times: in order to make an intelligent decision, the decision-maker must have as much information as possible to "play into the system." Paired weighting, for instance, serves no useful function unless there is enough information to allow intelligent choices between alternatives. The remainder of this book will provide some factual information to assist in those choices.

Figure 1-2 Completed paired weighting chart. Each pair of alternatives is weighed, and the preferred choice is circled. In totaling the score for each alternative, follow an L-shaped pattern, as shown for #9. Check off each time 9 is circled and enter the total in the appropriate column. The rank is based on the number of times each alternative is chosen. In this chart, the highest ranking alternative is #7 (score of 15), which should be the likely solution to this problem.

EXERCISES FOR THOUGHT

ACTIVITY 1:
TYPICAL HEALTH-RELATED PROBLEMS

Add five other health-related problems to the following list:

1. Physical appearance
2. Pet peeves
3. Anxiety
4. Peer approval
5. Heterosexual behavior
6. Money
7. School
8. Parental discipline
9. Allergies
10. Chronic diseases
11. Acute diseases
12. Acne
13. Homosexuality
14. Identity of self
15. Drug-taking behavior

16. _____

17. _____

18. _____

19. _____

20. _____

ACTIVITY 2

Choose one problem from Activity 1 and define it for yourself. What, specifically, is the problem?

ACTIVITY 3

Dealing only with the problem as defined in Activity 2; list at least 20 possible solutions or decisions. (Remember: include no evaluation, and be creative.)

1. _____

2. _____

3. _____

4. _____

5. _____

6. _____

7. _____

8. _____

9. _____

10. _____

11. _____

12. _____

13. _____

14. _____

15. _____

16. _____

17. _____

18. _____

19. _____

20. _____

ACTIVITY 4

On the following chart, pair weight the alternatives you listed in Activity 3.

	Total	Rank

$$\frac{1\ 1\ 1\ 1\ 1\ 1\ 1\ 1\ \ 1\ \ 1\ \ 1\ \ 1\ \ 1\ \ 1\ \ 1\ \ 1\ \ 1\ \ 1\ \ 1}{2\ 3\ 4\ 5\ 6\ 7\ 8\ 9\ 10\ 11\ 12\ 13\ 14\ 15\ 16\ 17\ 18\ 19\ 20} \qquad 1 =$$

$$\frac{2\ 2\ 2\ 2\ 2\ 2\ 2\ \ 2\ \ 2\ \ 2\ \ 2\ \ 2\ \ 2\ \ 2\ \ 2\ \ 2\ \ 2\ \ 2}{3\ 4\ 5\ 6\ 7\ 8\ 9\ 10\ 11\ 12\ 13\ 14\ 15\ 16\ 17\ 18\ 19\ 20} \qquad 2 =$$

$$\frac{3\ 3\ 3\ 3\ 3\ 3\ \ 3\ \ 3\ \ 3\ \ 3\ \ 3\ \ 3\ \ 3\ \ 3\ \ 3\ \ 3\ \ 3}{4\ 5\ 6\ 7\ 8\ 9\ 10\ 11\ 12\ 13\ 14\ 15\ 16\ 17\ 18\ 19\ 20} \qquad 3 =$$

$$\frac{4\ 4\ 4\ 4\ 4\ \ 4\ \ 4\ \ 4\ \ 4\ \ 4\ \ 4\ \ 4\ \ 4\ \ 4\ \ 4\ \ 4}{5\ 6\ 7\ 8\ 9\ 10\ 11\ 12\ 13\ 14\ 15\ 16\ 17\ 18\ 19\ 20} \qquad 4 =$$

$$\frac{5\ 5\ 5\ 5\ \ 5\ \ 5\ \ 5\ \ 5\ \ 5\ \ 5\ \ 5\ \ 5\ \ 5\ \ 5\ \ 5}{6\ 7\ 8\ 9\ 10\ 11\ 12\ 13\ 14\ 15\ 16\ 17\ 18\ 19\ 20} \qquad 5 =$$

$$\frac{6\ 6\ 6\ \ 6\ \ 6\ \ 6\ \ 6\ \ 6\ \ 6\ \ 6\ \ 6\ \ 6\ \ 6}{7\ 8\ 9\ 10\ 11\ 12\ 13\ 14\ 15\ 16\ 17\ 18\ 19\ 20} \qquad 6 =$$

$$\frac{7\ 7\ \ 7\ \ 7\ \ 7\ \ 7\ \ 7\ \ 7\ \ 7\ \ 7\ \ 7\ \ 7\ \ 7}{8\ 9\ 10\ 11\ 12\ 13\ 14\ 15\ 16\ 17\ 18\ 19\ 20} \qquad 7 =$$

$$\frac{8\ \ 8\ \ 8\ \ 8\ \ 8\ \ 8\ \ 8\ \ 8\ \ 8\ \ 8\ \ 8\ \ 8}{9\ 10\ 11\ 12\ 13\ 14\ 15\ 16\ 17\ 18\ 19\ 20} \qquad 8 =$$

$$\frac{9\ \ 9\ \ 9\ \ 9\ \ 9\ \ 9\ \ 9\ \ 9\ \ 9\ \ 9\ \ 9}{10\ 11\ 12\ 13\ 14\ 15\ 16\ 17\ 18\ 19\ 20} \qquad 9 =$$

$$\frac{10\ 10\ 10\ 10\ 10\ 10\ 10\ 10\ 10\ 10}{11\ 12\ 13\ 14\ 15\ 16\ 17\ 18\ 19\ 20} \qquad 10 =$$

$$\frac{11\ 11\ 11\ 11\ 11\ 11\ 11\ 11\ 11}{12\ 13\ 14\ 15\ 16\ 17\ 18\ 19\ 20} \qquad 11 =$$

$$\frac{12\ 12\ 12\ 12\ 12\ 12\ 12\ 12}{13\ 14\ 15\ 16\ 17\ 18\ 19\ 20} \qquad 12 =$$

$$\frac{13\ 13\ 13\ 13\ 13\ 13\ 13}{14\ 15\ 16\ 17\ 18\ 19\ 20} \qquad 13 =$$

$$\frac{14\ 14\ 14\ 14\ 14\ 14}{15\ 16\ 17\ 18\ 19\ 20} \qquad 14 =$$

$$\frac{15\ 15\ 15\ 15\ 15}{16\ 17\ 18\ 19\ 20} \qquad 15 =$$

$$\frac{16\ 16\ 16\ 16}{17\ 18\ 19\ 20} \qquad 16 =$$

$$\frac{17\ 17\ 17}{18\ 19\ 20} \qquad 17 =$$

$$\frac{18\ 18}{19\ 20} \qquad 18 =$$

$$\frac{19}{20} \qquad 19 =$$

$$20 =$$

MENTAL HEALTH

CHAPTER 2

I AM

IALAC—I Am Lovable And Capable. Once each of us comes to the realization that we all have good personal qualities and competencies, then living with ourselves and others becomes much easier and more fulfilling.

The most important word to deal with in the context of mental health is "I". There has been a long-standing taboo regarding selfishness, so perhaps you need permission to focus your attention primarily on yourself. Who am I? is a primary question in life, and it is vital for each of us to spend time developing an answer.

Part of the chore in answering the question Who am I? is recognizing the fact that each of us has a set of characteristics that makes us unique. No other being is exactly like you (at least not until cloning may become a reality). At the same time, we have qualities that are common to a certain group of individuals and other qualities that are universal. So, while you are unique, you are also like all others and in certain regards like some others.

The "I" has a special feeling to the particular being we are. It is the me of my perceived body, personality and memories. It is limited by the sum total of our experiences. It is the point of view from which we see the world, but it goes beyond awareness. The word "I" connotes a meaning that is special to us. There is only one "I," although there are millions of "you."

Try carrying on a conversation with another person, beginning each sentence with the word "you." Then begin each sentence with "we," "they" and finally "I." Notice how different and more satisfying it will be to finally communicate about yourself. From our perceptual base, we are each the center of our own universe.

Albert Camus began his essay The Myth of Sisyphus with the statement,

There is only one truly serious philosophical problem, and that is suicide. Judging whether life is or is not worth living amounts to answering the fundamental question of philosophy.

This is a choice that is constantly with us, and we reinforce our decision to continue living every moment of every day until we die. To attain a high level of spiritual (and therefore total) wellness, it is vital that each of us consider why we should continue life—For what purpose?

Each one of us is both lovable and capable.

The process of searching for purpose is as important as discovering "the answer," for there is no set answer. Furthermore, these partial answers are always changing or evolving. Occasionally, people commit suicide for existential, philosophical reasons, but that is probably the rarest rationale for suicide. Camus's statement has probably never driven anyone to suicide.

The usual, expected and certainly hoped for response to Camus is that we do have a reason to exist. A significant goal of the mentally well person is to say, "I feel good about who I am." One of the hazards of an LSD trip (or a similar intense mind trip) is that we've been given the opportunity to examine hidden aspects of ourselves, and the possibility exists that we won't like what we see. This is acceptable when we are able to change what we don't like about ourselves, but it may be disastrous when we are unable to change and are forced to live with this threatening self.

Black is beautiful! But if I am black and I am good, it is not because of my blackness but because I Am. A person may be proud to be black and may feel good about it, but that is not the only reason for such a positive self-concept. Being able to identify with that racial group may be supportive, but it cannot be the only rationale for feeling good. I am, therefore I am good!

René Descartes said "I think, therefore I am," meaning that the power of knowing and perceiving establishes our existence. This concept, while true, is based on rationalization and logic, rather than emotional response. This human quality may best be expressed as, "I love, therefore I am." The truly aware person also operates on a feeling level, not only taking in physical stimuli, but synthesizing and manipulating this information so that it adds to his or her emotional reservoir.

It is therefore important for us to develop the feeling part of ourselves. In meeting each situation, we first react on a "gut" level (first impressions) and then put our higher thought processes to work to analyze and compute the data. So, part of determining who we are is to become as aware as possible of our environment, which includes ourselves. We need to develop abilities that will enable us to reach a high level of awareness. In this regard the ultimate is what has been called the state of "cosmic consciousness," in which everything in the universe is known and felt at once, in some manner. Obviously this is a controversial, if existent, state, but the concept of cosmic consciousness is a useful extreme, showing us a direction to move in. The senses we use to see, smell, taste, hear and feel cues in our environment, which seems to be infinitesimal, are underdeveloped, to say the least. We are just beginning to create techniques for increasing awareness on all levels.

Working on increasing one's awareness and opening up to the stimuli of the environment leads to two seemingly unrelated but actually complementary conditions: *Unity* and *infinity*. They deal with the whole and its parts. The universe, including us, can be perceived as one united entity. At the same time it consists of a seemingly endless number of parts. We cannot understand all these working parts, nor can we entirely grasp the immensity of the whole, except on some abstract intellectual plane.

While we are contemplating the realm of the universe, we might consider the ideas of transcendence, whether they be in the novel *Jonathan Livingston Seagull* by Richard Bach or in the karmic law of Hinduism or Buddhism. If everything is "one," then so are life and death, even though they might be two opposite halves.

However, it is not satisfying to look only outward, for we must also look inward, into ourselves. A fuller understanding of self is achieved through self-reflection and introspection. How much time does each of us spend truly alone? Very little. We are usually with people, or if alone, we have television, radio, stereo or some other distraction that competes with our private thoughts. Time to be completely alone is a necessity, and if you haven't had much, try isolating yourself and thinking only of yourself for at least 30 minutes. Try doing it while looking at yourself in a mirror, either dressed or naked. If you have never done something like this before, you may find it an enlightening experience.

At the same time we should be cautioned against overreflecting. We must balance this intentional concern with ourselves with everyday living. Life can become a drag if taken too seriously.

SELF-CONCEPT

When two people meet, there are actually six selves present simultaneously. There is myself as I perceive me, as the other perceives me and as I actually am. Then there is the other person as she/he perceives herself/himself, as I perceive her/him and as she/he actually is. R. D. Laing writes in Knots[1]:

Narcissus fell in love with his image, taking it to be another.

Jack falls in love with Jill's image of Jack, taking it to be himself.
She must not die, because then he would lose himself.
He is jealous in case any one else's image is reflected in her mirror.

Jill is a distorting mirror to herself.
Jill has to distort herself to appear undistorted to herself.

To understand herself, she finds Jack to distort her distorted image in his distorting mirror.
She hopes that his distortion of her distortion may undistort her image without her having to distort herself.

How we develop and perceive ourselves is obviously very tricky and complex, but it is all the more complicated when others are involved. Not only do we all cover up our real selves to others, but we hide parts of our "selves" from ourself. The purpose of traditional (Freudian) psychotherapy is to bare the real self, or unconscious mind, through a combination of analyses of dreams, errors, associations, reactions and so on.

Freud sees three categories of self: The id or innate self reacts without concern for the future or fear of censorship. The ego is the "I" or self of personality; the feeling of who we are. Finally, the *superego* is the social self, or the actions that are taken to satisfy society; it is the conscience that is learned from the complex socialization process. Our concerns in mental health are with the ego (one's feelings about oneself) and then with the superego.

A differentiation must be made between self and self-concept. The self has hidden aspects that we have not brought to consciousness. Some of this is so threatening that we will never bring it to the level of awareness. Although the basic self or ego is relatively stable, it does undergo certain minute changes every moment as we live through each experience. As a matter of fact, it is the total of all our experiences.

The self-concept, on the other hand, is what we picture ourselves to be. Portions of this picture are realistic, while other parts are entirely fantasy. Much of what we label as mental illness is actually a gross unrealistic self-concept. In order to live a happy life, we must have a positive self-concept. Sometimes we tell ourselves that we are good in one way or another that is untrue. We may think of ourselves as good-looking, intelligent or having a good singing voice, for example. Usually we are put on the tract of accurate perception by the cues of others around us, particularly close friends and relatives, people whose judgment we trust and have confidence in. These cues may be very direct or subtle. Sometimes we pick up on them; at other times we may choose to ignore them.

At times, though, we are unable to be our real selves for a variety of reasons. Consider the boy who is afraid of animals and cries when approached by a barking dog. His father or mother may comment that men aren't afraid of such small animals. What a quandary! The developing or evolving self and self-concept are dependent upon what others will or will not allow us to be.

Reactions of others, however, are not always responses to what we are doing as much as they are responses to how *they* are handling the situation. A dying person, for example, is usually very angry but may not know how to express the anger or at whom to direct it. Frequently, the nurse, being the most available person, may bear the brunt of this emotional expression.

It takes a strong and perceptive individual to recognize when she or he is not the target and to be able to restrain from striking back. In her book *You Are Not the Target*, Laura Huxley described an array of "recipes" designed to assist people in utilizing their physical and psychological capacities to deal with others. When people show hostility or aggression toward us, it is rarely a simple attempt to harm us but rather a primary attempt to bolster their own levels of self-worth. This is not to say we should always turn the other cheek, but we need to place our reactions in the proper perspective.

Self-concept has much to do with our physical beings. We usually look out at the world, not at ourselves in a mirror, so we usually don't know how we look at a particular moment. Some people, therefore, have a more or less accurate perception of how they appear. Generally, however, we strive to appear as we want ourselves to look in fulfilling a role. Motorcycle gang members wear their denim or leather jackets and club emblems to portray a certain image to themselves and others. Part of the physical image, then, is not only the appearance of the body but also the manner of dress. When we meet someone for the first time, we react not only to their body and face but also to the clothes they wear.

When changes in the body occur too rapidly for us to adjust our self-concept accordingly, we become frightened. This happens to accident or war victims or patients who undergo radical surgery and lose parts of their bodies or are severely disfigured. Severe psychological trauma frequently results, since many cannot cope with the shock of this sudden change in their bodies. In this case, the body image does not keep up with the actual body appearance. An example that most of us can relate to concerns the physical changes that accompany pubescence. Do you remember the feeling as a young man of the facial stubble after the first shave, or the realization as a young woman that your breasts were developing? How did you feel when your pubic hair first appeared? These images of our bodies are as important to our mental health as our psychological self-concept is.

Each of us wears many masks or roles that we move into and out of. Generally, we maintain a certain set of roles, and other persons expect us to act consistently within these roles. But occasionally we act out of character, and that can present problems for everyone. Nevertheless, we have a constant, ongoing need to alter our roles or try new ones. The growing individual continually probes his or her potentials, including all the possible functioning roles. Usually these changes are minor, involving such things as hair style, clothing or friends.

The hardest part of the task of venturing into different roles is that our social environment fosters getting and keeping a fixed role. We are forced into a certain identity, beginning with the expectations of basic sexual and cultural roles and moving quickly into employment roles. The usual first question when meeting a person is, What do you do? This necessitates a role answer—I'm a student, doctor, dancer, salesperson—with all the accompanying stereotypes. Even the answer "nothing" conjures up stereotypical images such as loafer, hippy, unambitious, incompetent and the like.

People are simultaneously parts of many larger groups. Others see us as having sexual, racial, and religious roles; living in a certain geographical area; working at a particular job; being married or not; and so on. It is impossible to be so objective that we can immediately put all biases aside and see the real persons we encounter. Perhaps one of the most difficult tasks of the helping professions is enabling people to overcome the stifling aspects of role playing and to focus on true identity or self-concept.

Eric Berne has worked extensively in structuring a role-playing theory of personality development called *transactional analysis*. Briefly, the theory states that we interact with others in the role of Parent, Adult or Child. Being in the role of Parent is to act as your parent did in the past in terms of oral and body language and feelings. Since everyone has had a parent or parent substitute, we have all observed how to act as Parent, how to set rules, protect and teach. The Parent role may be played directly, as our own parents acted, or indirectly, as parents generally influence children.

Everyone likewise plays an Adult role, which begins during the first year of life, in that we are all capable of some independent, autonomous thinking and self-determinant actions. This is the part of ourselves that must be present for survival. It takes in external data, processes it and makes decisions leading to correct, objective responses. The Adult role also has the function of balancing or regulating the Parent and Child activities.

The Child role is also present in each of us. We were all cared for during early life and are still cared for in various ways from time to time,

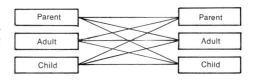

Figure 2–1 Transactional analysis model: a relationship diagram. (From Berne, Eric: *Games People Play.* New York, Grove Press, 1964, p. 32.)

even if it is a simple thing like being served in a restaurant. Whereas the Adult processes external data, the Child records internal reactions to external stimuli. The Child may then respond either naturally (creatively) or simply as the Parents direct. How any role exhibits itself is dependent upon the many complex factors that make up personality, as well as the specific situation.

In the transactional analysis model, when two people interact there are nine possible "transactions" that can take place. Any one of the three roles (Parent, Adult, Child) of one person may interact at one time with any of the three roles of the other (Fig. 2–1). The games people play, then (and we all play these life games), are based on the types of roles in which we respond to each other. This response is determined not only by our Parent-Adult-Child role but also by the kind of Parent-Adult-Child we are at the time.

OPENING

> *Jack can see that he sees*
> > *what Jill can't see*
> > *and that Jill can't see Jill can't see it*
>
> *Jack can see that he sees*
> > *what Jill can't see*
> *but Jack can't see*
> > *that Jill can't see*
> > *that Jill can't see it*
>
> *Jack tries to get Jill to see*
> > *that Jill can see*
> > *what Jack can't see*
> *but Jack can't see*
> > *that Jill can't see that Jill can't see it*
>
> *Jack sees*
> > *there is something Jill can't see*
> *and Jack sees*
> > *that Jill can't see she can't see it*
>
> *Although Jack can see Jill can't see she can't see it*
> > *he can't see that he can't see it himself.*[2]

Portions of ourself are known and unknown, to us and to others. This combination of knowns and unknowns is best described in the Johari

	Known to others	Not known to others
Known to self	1 OPEN	2 BLIND
Not known to self	3 HIDDEN	4 UNKNOWN

Figure 2-2 Johari window.

window developed by Luft and Ingraham.[3] Their model (Fig. 2–2) presents four quadrants, each representing a level of awareness of behavior, feelings and motivation based on who preceives it. The *open* quadrant is known to self and others, the *blind* is known to others but not to self, the *hidden* is known to self but not to others, and the *unknown* is not known to either self or others.

The objective of *opening* is to increase that part of us known to self and others and to reduce all other unknown qualities. Any change in one quadrant affects all others; thus, as the open quadrant increases, quadrants 2, 3, and 4 decrease. The more we open to self and others, the less there is that is blind to us, hidden from others or unknown to all. Conversely, of course, the more that is unknown, the less that is known by self or others.

Sidney Jourard[4] defines *self-disclosure* as "the act of making yourself manifest, showing yourself so others can perceive you." It is not only an act but also an art that requires a certain amount of confidence, assertiveness and creativity, especially if you consider that decisions are constantly being made as to how much to disclose, to whom and in what circumstances.

It is a matter of being transparent to oneself as well as to others. When we wear clothes, we hide our bodies from the world. When we choose not to disclose in other ways, we hide the real self. We may or may not be transparent with friends, family, lovers, teachers, self and others.

To self-disclose, to be transparent, to open is to achieve a certain degree of freedom, that is, to be free enough to take chances of baring our selves and not be overly concerned with the consequences. This comes about not through a "laissez faire" approach of doing *whatever* you want *when* you want but rather through an arduous process of growing in a supportive environment, being nurtured by caring parents and being allowed to experiment under somewhat controlled circumstances. It is very much like the freedom acquired by a performer, such as a dancer, who has learned a high degree of motor skills through long hours of practice, adhering to a rigorous practice schedule. In time that dancer may develop real freedom of movement, achieving an array of physical expressions and skills. This mastery is developed through discipline and a degree of conformity. It creates an awareness of the body and of the potential as well as limitations of that body. A greater appreciation of others' physical expressions accompanies one's own accomplishments and attempts.

This freedom is linked to another aspect of opening — acting with spontaneity. It is a comforting feeling to be at ease enough to behave without continual censorship. All too often, fears, particularly fear of failure; inhibit spontaneous behavior. It should be an acceptable standard to try and not succeed, for we may learn as much from failure as from success. To fail frequently implies that we are failures. Because of this failure-success syndrome, we must continue to try, thus proving that we can achieve certain tasks. Another common predicament is to compare our abilities with others around us, usually with those who are more capable at the particular skill.

Being open means allowing others to be open also. Acceptance of others, not being overly judgmental, is as much a part of opening as self-reflection of building one's ego. A common reaction to another's behavior is to ask *why* rather than *what*. Rather than evaluate, accept; rather than ask *why*, think about *what* has happened. It is more productive to interact on a direct feeling level with friends, rather than as someone to merely accept or reject. Children, for example, need to know that no matter what, their parents will accept and love them.

However, we must maintain a certain balance between what to disclose and what to keep private. Everyone has a need for privacy, a need not to disclose all. Not all opening can be done with others. Sometimes it is difficult to find private places and moments, but we all need to take the time to look at ourselves, in the mirror in the privacy of our own rooms perhaps, just to try on new faces. The concept of self-disclosure does not include keeping no secrets; rather, it is a matter of appropriate disclosure.

To whom, then, do we open? That is a dilemma. Usually we are more open to those closest to us and those we love, or *significant others*. They are the ones we know best and trust. We can more accurately predict their reactions, and their judgments are highly valued. Nevertheless, there are some occasions when we would open more readily to strangers than to intimate friends.

In his book *Values Clarification*, Sidney Simon describes an interesting and useful exercise, called the privacy circle, in which a model of the people in our lives (Fig. 2–3) is used to reflect with whom we would share various feelings, behaviors and facts about ourselves. For example, if you shoplifted some merchandise from a department store, whom would you tell? With whom would you discuss your sexual experiences? When you cried? With whom would you cry? If you wanted to make love with your mother or father, could you admit it even to yourself?

As you can see, there are numerous sides to our selves, with varying levels of privacy about them. One of the guidelines to this disclosing behavior is our values. According to Raths,[6] the process of valuing involves (1) *choosing*, freely, from a variety of alternatives after considering carefully the consequences of each alternative; (2) *prizing*, or cherishing the choice and publicly affirming it; and (3) *acting* consistently and in a patterned way. A value is not only a readiness to act (the definition of an attitude) but actually performing the action, verbally or physically.

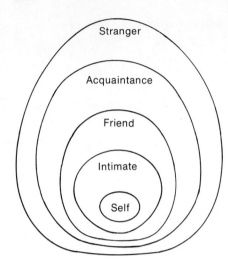

Figure 2-3 Privacy circle.

This entire focus on opening, self-reflection and self-disclosure can be summed up as trying to be oneself and being happy about that self. It is what Jourard[7] calls an *authentic being*. To be honest with self and others leads to more open communications between people. The pervading attitude in this utopian way of thinking is the feeling of "us" rather than "me and them." It is a step in closing gaps between people, regardless of their basis. As John Lennon sings,

Imagine all the people sharing all the world
You may say I'm a dreamer
but I'm not the only one
I hope someday you'll join us
and the world will be as one.[8]

ENDNOTES

1. Laing, R. D.: *Knots*. New York, Vintage Books, 1970.
2. *Ibid.*, p. 57.
3. Luft, Joseph: *Of Human Interaction*. Palo Alto, National Press Books, 1969, p. 13.
4. Jourard, Sidney: *The Transparent Self*. New York, D. Van Nostrand Co., 1971, p. 19.
5. Simon, Sidney B.: *Values Clarifications*. New York, Hart Publishing Co., 1972, p. 184.
6. Raths, Louis E., Merrill Harmin, and Sidney B. Simon: *Values and Teaching*. Columbus, Ohio, Charles E. Merrill Publishing Co., 1966, p. 30.
7. Jourard, *op. cit.*, p. 133.
8. Lennon, John: *Imagine*. New York, Marlen Music, Inc., 1971, pp. 3–4.

BIBLIOGRAPHY

Berne, Eric: *Games People Play*. New York, Grover Press, Inc., 1964.
Harris, Thomas A.: *I'm Okay, You're Okay*. New York, Harper & Row, Publishers, 1969.

Hayakawa, S. I.: The self-concept — why we reject some ideas and accept others. *Journal of Dental Medicine*, 15:3, 1960.

Huxley, Laura: *You Are Not the Target*. North Hollywood, California; Wilshire Book Company, 1963.

Jourard, Sidney: *The Transparent Self*. New York, D. Van Nostrand Company, 1971.

Laing, R. D.: *Knots*. New York, Vintage Books, 1970.

Luft, Joseph: *Of Human Interaction*. Palo Alto; National Press Books, 1969.

Raths, Louis E., Merrill Harmin and Sidney B. Simon: *Values and Teaching*. Columbus, Ohio, Charles E. Merrill Publishing Company, 1966.

Samples, Bob, and Bob Wohlford: *Opening*. Reading, Mass., Addison-Wesley Publishing Company, 1973.

CHAPTER 3

BECOMING

CHANGING AND GROWING

Throughout life, each person continues to change. These changes may be significant and observable or minor and hardly noticeable. It is all part of the evolutionary process, progressing perhaps at the proverbial snail's pace but always proceeding.

It is hoped that this change will be largely in a positive, meaningful direction, which then fulfills our definition of growth. Healthy growth is that which is allowed to develop with freedom, leading to independence, progress and maturity. It is a matter of reaching forward, toward achievement of potential, and in time further expanding that potential. Growing involves acting from healthy spontaneity rather than from fear of the repercussions, whether physical or psychological, of one's behavior.

Change, however, is not so easily accomplished, for it must be accepted not only by oneself but also by other people—particularly, significant others. They must allow these changes to take place. Otherwise, they may invalidate these new aspects of self. Many people may resist changing and growing because of the pressures put on them to stay the same. This may be particularly true in a marriage relationship when one partner moves into different areas of interest. If the marriage is to remain intact, one partner must accept the change or grow with the other. A long-term, satisfactory marriage involves, among other things, a continuous process of moving and catching up, of changing, adjusting, changing again and readjusting.

One characteristic of a mentally unhealthy person is changelessness, or a lack of growth. Jean Paul Sartre, in his play *No Exit*, tells the story of a group of people who are condemned to a hell of changelessness. They must exist in the same room with the same people and furnishings and the same social status for eternity. This is, of course, an extreme situation, but it serves to illustrate that many people allow few changes in their lives and consequently enjoy little growth.

The phenomenon of growth may be carried beyond random changes to a more directed or self-determined process of becoming. This does not mean that we strive to become a particular person but that we are constantly evolving into whatever we will be in the next future moment. We are simultaneously being and becoming. Becoming, a more complete concept of growing, involves not merely being manipulated by, coping with or adjusting to the environment but having an independent, intentional way of living.

Another term used to characterize a person who is changing, growing and becoming is "maturing." Probably the most important part of the word *maturing* is the suffix -*ing*; which implies an ongoing process. It begins, perhaps, with the idea that the human mind at birth is like a *tabula rasa*, or smooth tablet, with no impressions on it, to be etched or molded throughout life. The mind is therefore never completed or "mature."

In addition, there are many dimensions of maturity. We mature professionally, physically, psychologically, socially and philosophically, as a speaker, writer, mover, lover, parent or child. We also mature within the cultural criteria of maturity.

Maturation is a time-consuming process that is based upon undergoing experiences, both positive and negative. We must be involved in a variety of situations and must try out various tactics or behaviors for ourselves before we can meet any criterion for maturity. The truism "there is no substitute for experience" bears repeating. No amount of reading or simulation can ever truly replace involvement, although obviously, many situations are too dangerous to experience firsthand. We cannot experiment with all types of drugs, for example, in order to know their effects. We need to depend upon others for information about them. Likewise, we may safely sit in a driver simulator to practice reacting to emergency traffic situations. Even so, the process of doing is an irreplaceable necessity to becoming a mature individual.

Although some experiences may be painful, we ought to approach new experiences with an attitude of challenge and enjoyment, for they promote growth and sustain the process of becoming. Jourard[1] talks about not only growing experiences but also the experience of growing. A constant regeneration of energy and matter is necessary for change and growth. Not only do experiences add to our capabilities to develop, but there is joy in merely experiencing the maturing process.

Seeking growth experiences involves taking risks, more or less so depending on set and setting. Imagine a hurdle racer who is quite advanced in this racing skill. When running at top speed, the hurdler is in a state of controlled, forward-leaning unbalance. Each hurdle will seemingly come up to the hurdler, rather than the hurdler running up to it. The successful hurdler need only lift the forward leg, and momentum will carry him or her over each barrier, as opposed to having to jump over. If we are in control of our psychological growth and development, we meet each experience as the capable hurdler meets each hurdle. Running at a high speed may increase the consequences of a spill, but it significantly reduces the possibilities of falling and simultaneously increases the satisfaction of more fully achieving potential. Likewise, we add to meaning in life by seeking new experiences.

All these experiences involve restructuring or evaluation of previously held beliefs and values. They are risky to both us and those

TABLE 3-1 SOCIAL READJUSTMENT RATING SCALE

Rank	Life Event	Mean Value
1	Death of spouse	100
2	Divorce	73
3	Marital separation	65
4	Jail term	63
5	Death of close family member	63
6	Personal injury or illness	53
7	Marriage	50
8	Fired at work	47
9	Marital reconciliation	45
10	Retirement	45
11	Change in health of family member	44
12	Pregnancy	40
13	Sex difficulties	39
14	Gain of new family member	39
15	Business readjustment	39
16	Change in financial state	38
17	Death of close friend	37
18	Change to different line of work	36
19	Change in number of arguments with spouse	35
20	Mortgage over $10,000	31
21	Foreclosure of mortgage or loan	30
22	Change in responsibilities at work	29
23	Son or daughter leaving home	29
24	Trouble with in-laws	29
25	Outstanding personal achievement	28
26	Wife begins or stops work	26
27	Begin or end school	26
28	Change in living conditions	25
29	Revision of personal habits	24
30	Trouble with boss	23
31	Change in work hours or conditions	20
32	Change in residence	20
33	Change in schools	20
34	Change in recreation	19
35	Change in church activities	19
36	Change in social activities	18
37	Mortgage or loan less than $10,000	17
38	Change in sleeping habits	16
39	Change in number of family get-togethers	15
40	Change in eating habits	15
41	Vacation	13
42	Christmas	12
43	Minor violations of the law	11

Source: Holmes, T. H., and Rahe, R. H.: The social readjustment rating scale. *Journal of Psychosomatic Research, 11*:213, 1967.

around us because their consequences may involve such changes as leaving old friends and acquaintances, living in new environments and, most important, altering life styles. Drs. Thomas Holmes and Richard Rahe hypothesize that large or significant alterations in life styles can contribute to illness. They have developed a Social Readjustment Rating Scale (Table 3–1), which compares changes in an individual's life with disabling conditions. Their findings show that a correlation exists between change and illness. Such events as divorce, death of a significant other, change of jobs and moving, alone or in combination, may be stressful enough to produce actual physical illnesses.

PAST, PRESENT, FUTURE

The process of becoming has been discussed in terms of past experiences and future direction. Although both are valid and necessary considerations in regard to the quality of an individual's life, the most important time in every person's life is *now*. We can live only in the present, not in the already foregone past or in the unpredictable future. In the strictest philosophical, existential definition, the present can never really be experienced, since it is an immeasurably short moment, spearating past and future. But in the practical sense, *now* is the moment we always live in, and it holds the greatest motivational force. It is the meshing of past and future into present behavior.

Even though we recall and reminisce about the past and fantasize

We live in the *now*, moving toward the future and coming from the past.

about the future, we are always present-oriented. Now behavior is to live here, not in an absent environment; to taste, see and hear, not only to intellectualize; to express, rather than to explain or manipulate; and to act spontaneously and freely, not out of fear. This present-oriented attitude is seen in many people who are faced with a terminal illness and impending death. They may tie up emotional and social loose ends, express their previously repressed desires, frustrations, angers and requests, and live from day to day, fully and without fear. These people almost universally describe this "mind cleansing" as a sense of relief.

It should be added that living for the present is not a hedonistic, sensory satisfying approach but rather a realistic, fulfilling one. It does not rule out planning for the future or learning from past experiences.

The influence of the past on our present lives is probably more vital and deeper than we can imagine or measure. Although each of us is unique, we are all the product of millions of years of evolution, sharing the same origin and the same anthropological history. All this takes place through genetic storage and transmission of knowledge and skills. Slow, imperceptible genetic changes are shaped by the total social and physical environment. Plants, animals and insects are all affected by, and in turn influence, the species *Homo sapiens*. Certain survival characteristics, such as two front-centered eyes, body temperature and the sexual drive, remain stable through genetic coding. On the other hand, there are certain less stable qualities that are better served by adaptation to environmental changes.

C. G. Jung explains the concept of universally inherited characteristics as the *collective unconscious*, which is the inborn psychological make-up of humankind; it is purely objective and all-encompassing. It is distinguished from the *personal unconscious*, which is made up of once-conscious material that we experienced but have since forgotten or repressed. The collective unconscious consists of *archetypes* as old as the human race itself. The archetype is the original form on which all other representations are based. It is shared by primitive as well as modern human beings.

Therefore, we are products of a collective past, influenced by our prenatal environment and most immediately by a socialization process. Socialization begins at birth with physical contact, or lack of such contact; with other human beings.

Margaret Mead, in *Culture and Commitment*, describes three patterns of transference of culture from generation to generation. The first, which she calls *postfigurative*, is a culture in which children learn primarily from their parents, grandparents and elders. It is dependent upon three generations living simultaneously. Change in such a culture is almost imperceptible; it is assumed that the existing life style will be preserved and that the children's future life will be like that of their ancestors.

The *cofigurative* society begins with a break from the previous postfigurative culture. The break may be caused by a population-wide disaster, the development of a new technology, migration to a new culture, being conquered or certain other kinds of revolution. Leadership

In this new world, we have much to learn from children.

changes, and contemporaries become the models for behavior. These models may be young people or elders not of one's own immediate ancestry. Frequently, in cofigurative societies, grandparents are not present.

Mead sees the emergence of a new, third from of cultural transference, called *prefiguration,* in which things are so new or unknown that all generations must learn together. Many adults, for example, grew up in a world without television, atomic energy and the H-bomb, computers, and space travel. These advances are all very significant factors in the world today, and the younger generations take them for granted. It is similar to being first generation pioneers, reared in a totally new land. This may be the basis for the generation gap, in which those of one generation do not fully understand, empathize with or really know those of another.

Richard Farson,[2] like Margaret Mead, thinks that young people really may know more than older people do today. He calls this phenomenon a *reverse transmission of culture* and suggests seven reasons why youth—particularly college students—may threaten the established order:

1. There exists a crisis of incongruity. We talk peace and see war; talk honesty and see cheating as the norm; retain sexual and other double standards.

2. Young people have discovered powerful means of disrupting the system and forcing change.

3. Youthful sexuality and sexual attitudes have changed.

4. The deepest values of youth — education, military, work — are no longer the same.

5. Parents no longer control youth; outsiders such as peers, mass media, schools and other community institutions do.

6. Young people are more comfortable with temporary systems.

7. Young people see the world differently from the older generation.

Being educated, then, is a matter of somehow dealing with the ancestral past and with behavior in the present. But what the educated individual is depends upon who is defining the term "educated." Being educated is part of the process of becoming, but schools — the institutions supposedly structured to perform this task — seem to be functioning more as an instrument for indoctrination. Some feel that this is perpetuated by relegating students to a secondary role of "just" student. Faculty, staff and student alike may view the student's role as passive, to receive and spew back units of information. Students are seen by many as "them," not to be trusted to act correctly on their own. They may not determine their own curriculum in most cases, although there is some trend toward open-ended general education requirements, community involvement, independent study and pass-fail grading. At the present, however, most colleges still function in the traditional manner.

Jerry Farber, in his writings *The Student As Nigger* and *The University of Tomorrowland*, eloquently describes this controversial point of view. He claims that school is a "master-slave" situation in which students have no part in deciding what they will learn or how they will learn it. Having to live in the "student's role" means, for example, eating in a cafeteria separated from a faculty dining room, parking in a separate lot and having to follow other rules separate from other members of the campus community. The important point, however, is not what the role of student really is, but how one feels about it. Whether each student feels as if she or he is *just* a student, and whether others perceive and treat him or her as *just* a student, is important in how one goes about becoming an educated person.

Carl Rogers sees the educated person as one who is able and allowed to experience the gamut of feelings, sift through evidence from all sources, engage in self-discovery and, therefore, become completely involved in the process of being and becoming. Rogers calls such a person a "fully functioning organism." The teacher of such an individual is not only a model but also a helper who allows learning to take place. That teacher is available for consultation when assistance is requested, not only during class time and within the four walls of the classroom.

One inhibitor to becoming fully functioning or an educated person is the presence of others who may try to exploit or control us in some way. This exploitation may happen on a personal level, when it is usually very obvious, or it may be exploitation by a group we are part of. In the book

The Greening of America, Charles Reich describes the present consciousness of the United States that created the Corporate State, in which institutions and organizations become dominant over the individual and individual will. The individual fits into this system of meritocracy through the competitive struggle for success. Through rule and organization, the Corporate State can administer and control both work and domestic life. The people in this state are role-players, taking their behavioral cues from advertising in one medium or another, rather than being authentic, self-motivated people. They are other-controlled. According to Reich, the Corporate State is so encompassing and overwhelming that no one person or even one company, no matter how large, can turn this system around. A revolution of sorts, involving a new discovery of self or consciousness, is what he perceives in the future.

Another description of the dynamics of control has been written by a leading community organizer, Saul Alinsky, who worked actively with unions and other community groups from the 1930's to the mid-1970's, when he died. According to Alinsky, there exists a sort of power triangle consisting of those in power, the *haves*; those without power, the *have-nots*; and the group to which most of us belong, the *have-a-little, want mores*.

Those with power, money, food, security, access to medical care and luxury spend most of their time keeping their power and wealth. Therefore, the haves oppose change and foster the status quo. The have-nots, as typified by poverty, sickness, hunger, unemployment and underemployment, lack of education, poor housing, political disenfranchisement and so on, actually outnumber the haves, who may be their only source of power. The have-a-little, want mores are torn between maintaining the status quo to keep what little they have and wanting change to increase their status and material possessions. Although the have-a-little, want mores may vacillate or wear two hats. Alinsky thinks that it is within this group that creative change is spawned. However, no matter what, there will exist conflict that must somehow be dealt with, and it is hoped that this can be accomplished directly, openly and with dignity.

After looking at the effects of the past and influences of the present, a discussion of the future is the logical next step. Although there has always been an interest in contemplating and predicting the future, an upsurge of interest in futuristic activity was recently spurred by Alvin Toffler's *Future Shock*. His major hypothesis is that just as there is a shock effect when we travel into a new and different culture with a strange language and customs, so too can we find ourselves in a drastically alien future.

Probably the key to the future shock is acceleration, and we are already seeing a turnover that occurs at shorter and shorter intervals. Appliances, for example, are made with more plastic and throw-away parts and contain a high degree of built-in obsolescence. The average American family changes houses every five years. The ultimate example of this acceleration is the population explosion, with its geometrically progressing doubling time. Another way in which acceleration contributes to future shock is the shortening of travel time. Travel time from coast to coast has been cut in half in the past 20 years and will become shorter yet with new high-speed trains and supersonic transports. The advent of communications satellites has made round-the-world instant contact almost taken for granted.

Perhaps the most difficult adjustment to make in the future will be to the tremendously increased amount of available information and stimuli. The increase in the amount of words put out in the mass media through books, magazines, newspapers, television, radio and even taped telephone messages leaves the individual with the difficult task of organizing and using all this data input.

Whatever shape the future takes on a societal level, we must still deal first with the immediate and personal future. Aside from basic life style, including marriage, family and living partners, the biggest consideration in a person's life is work, whether it involves building a career; earning a salary, working for mere subsistence or passing the day away.

Work involves a whole set of expectations — by oneself, others and society — and reflections of values. There is, in fact, a "work ethic" that seems to imply that work must be difficult and unpleasant to be worth while. It is almost as if someone who enjoys work should not get paid as much as one who works "hard" and hates it. This school of thought reflects the value that something attained without hard work and suffering isn't valuable. For example, there are those who believe that college students should put in long, laborious hours studying for a class for it to be a truly academic learning experience. The courses that do not require memorization of long lists, reading of many books or writing of papers may be considered "sliders," and have a low status despite the learning that occurs or the long enjoyable hours spent on various involvement projects. So education, or at least educational institutions, may perpetuate this ethic of work being unpleasant.

Furthermore, the kinds of experiences higher education provides determine, to some extent, the student's self-concept. Perhaps more important are those experiences that are omitted from the learning process; that is, activities involving the development of independent research and decision-making skills. Extended further is the demeaning idea of the student as an irrelevant person who is magically transcended into a knowing role upon completion of a course of study or degree. Joe or Jane Student doesn't receive nearly the attention or credibility as does Joe or Jane College Grad. The educational system is a model of the work system that believes only certain "credentialed" professionals can make decisions.

DEVELOPMENT OF PERCEPTION

The way in which we come to perceive things is quite interesting. How do we gain the ability to differentiate between meaningful and trivial information? How do we come to process information so that we use only what is relevant? Or why do some people crowd their thoughts with extraneous matter not pertinent to the task they are working on? How do we become feeling or not? Why are some people more empathetic than others?

Our first impressions are basically acquired through the eyes of others. As infants, we watched others in our environment react to various stimuli. Through observing and imitating we learned not only basic skills, such as language, but also the parts of our environment that demand the most attention and reaction.

An example of the observe-imitate basis for learning is the Suzuki method of music education. In this method, the student listens to the sounds (songs) made on the musical instrument being learned and repeats those sounds. The first skills are not note reading, which comes much later, but listening and copying sounds. In a similar manner, we learn appropriate behaviors by modeling after certain exemplars; such as parents, friends, teachers, and relatives.

Although there are many exemplars available, we choose particular people. Often these choices are based on our emotional attachment to the model; this is obvious when it comes to people with whom we have daily or regular contact. In choosing other models, however, the emotional attachment is secondary. Thus, we may copy the behavior of someone we do not know (e.g., television or sports personalities) because it is likely to please those with whom we are emotionally close.

Nevertheless, most of the specific origins of our information and motivations are lost. There is a *sleeper effect*, which postulates that we forget where we learned most specific pieces of data that we believe to be true. Often the source is not highly reliable. The information may have been learned from a movie, from a newspaper article or by word of mouth

We learn appropriate behavior by modeling after certain exemplars.

but not from a scientifically accurate source. Still, we hold onto these "truths" and find them difficult to shake. However, they become just as important as a basis for decision making as if they had come from a highly renowned scientific journal.

Figure 3–1 illustrates a communications model that is useful in partially explaining how information is sent and processed for immediate and future use. For example, when two people are talking to each other, the speaker, or sender of the message, is the *information source* and *encoder*, or *transmitter*. In other words, this person has the information and must put it in some form or code so that it can be transmitted to another source. The other ultimate source, or *destination*, must *decode* the information into usable form. This is done by the *receiver*. The unsual signal used in transmission between two people is voice, and the code is language. Occurring simultaneously with the intended signal are extraneous stimuli or potential disturbances (*noise*), which may interfere with the ability of the receiver to "hear" the signal. In some instances, the noise source may be stronger or more attractive than the primary signal, and the intended message is lost. It should be noted that there is one important element missing from the original model—*feedback*. For communication to be accurate, the receiver must inform the sender as to whether the message was perceived. When this does not occur, we have no way of knowing whether any learning has taken place.

There is also a psychophysiological component in deciding what is most important to admit into our functional consciousness from our environment. Many people simply do not have the neurological capability to differentiate between relevant and irrelevant material. A common neurological manifestation is the inability to filter out background noise (traffic sounds, other voices in the distance) from the primary or relevant source; this is a perceptual handicap.

One definition of perception is "the more complex process by which people select, organize and interpret sensory stimulation into a meaningful and coherent picture of the world."[3] It is a matter of making sense out of experience. Human beings are complex information systems capable of choosing, problem-solving and decision-making. How we behave and what choices we make are dependent upon an interaction between our interval state (memory, values, goals) as determined by previous learning

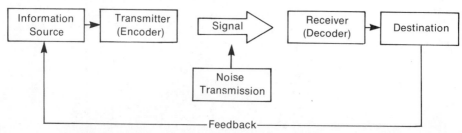

Figure 3–1 Shannon-Weaver communications model. (Adapted from Shannon, C. F., and W. Weaver: *The Mathematical Theory of Communication.* Urbana, Ill., University of Illinois Press, 1949, p. 98.)

and the environment. Environments are not exactly the same for all people, since we each have individual perspectives. Not only does the environment differ, however slightly, but each individual's reaction to the same stimulus differs. *Set*, the readiness of a person to act in a certain way, is the unique, active part of one's internal state that causes one person to respond differently from another. Therefore, accurate perception of reality is quite complex and varies from person to person. Consequently, accurate prediction of individual behavior is also difficult to accomplish.

How we perceive things is also dependent upon the temporary state of mind and body and our awareness at the moment, or what is called state of consciousness. Someone in a chemically altered state of consciousness—through use of marijuana, mescaline or LSD, for example—may see objects in quite a different way from when she or he is not under the influence of these chemicals. Such qualities as the texture, color, and size may appear to be altered. After climbing a mountain, you would obviously see things from a different physical and psychological perspective.

A term that might describe a more permanent condition of perception is *sense-ability*, or the ability to use one's senses. It means that an individual can be open to utilizing all senses of touch, sight, sound, smell, taste and space. It is the freedom to use these senses to the fullest, without fear of ridicule or other inhibiting factors.

Much of achieving accurate perceptual skills involves intentionally allowing certain messages to be filtered into our consciousness, and blocking those that may be inconsistent with our values. One example of the *selective perception* is the magazines, newspapers and books we choose to read. Politically left-leaning people tend to read more liberal or radical literature, while conservatives prefer conservative authors. We allow ourselves to recollect only certain experiences of our past, and imagine possible future happenings that are soothing, although sometimes we imagine unpleasant possibilities. Reality—or at least what we perceive as real—is therefore in the eyes of the beholder. Of all the continuous and overwhelming amount of sensory and factual input available to us in a variety of codes, we select relatively few to decipher and incorporate into our perceptual being. The accuracy of the decoding is, of course, dependent to some extent upon how we wish things were.

Another mode of experiencing or perceiving, is fantasy. It is more available to us under special conditions, such as in dreams, although we can have true fantasies even in awake states. Some daydreams, for example, are freely associated fantasies, whereas others are based on actual events. It is interesting to speculate further as to the reality of fantasies, to wonder whether perhaps the dream itself is indeed real and everything else—what we call consciousness—is the fantasy.

It is believed that perception is limited by the boundaries of an individual's *life space*, or psychological field. It may be large and expanding or narrow and static, depending upon the variety of human experiences and how "open" the individual is. Of course, the bigger one's life space, the greater the opportunity for personal freedom and growth and development. The individual with a large life space is usually involved in actively testing reality by evaluating personal perceptions to find out how true they are under different circumstances.

LOVE AND TRUST

Loving is risky and scary, but not as scary as the alternative — not loving. To love truly and without qualification involves deep commitment, a basic trust and authentic caring for another person. It is reciprocal in that we are lovable as well as loving. We give as well as take.

Gibran says of love:

> Love gives naught but itself and takes
>   naught but itself;
> Love possesses not nor would it be
>   possessed;
> For love is sufficient unto love.[4]

Love almost defies definition, since its meaning needs to be qualified over and again. To whom or what is love limited? What are its conditions? How must it be transferred or communicated? Are there exceptions to any of the criteria that make up this definition?

Perhaps the best discussion of love is presented by Erich Fromm in his book *The Art of Loving*. He says that "love is the only satisfactory answer to the problem of human existence."[5] Nearly every definition of the mentally healthy individual contains love as one of its criteria.

One of the most useful concepts put forth by Fromm is that there are five basic kinds of love or objects of love. The first, and most fundamental, is *brotherly love* — a love of the world. It is the loving feeling we get when we are together with a mass of people and our skin tingles from being with others. This love for all human beings is a love of equals in that we are all people and share a common humanity.

Motherly love is an unconditional affirmation of a person's life. I exist, therefore I am loved. It is in one sense passive, since the child need not do anything overtly to earn this love. A love that must be earned by deed is tenuous and unstable, since it may disappear whenever the desired behavior is withdrawn. As a child grows, this more or less one-way love becomes reciprocal, beginning at about age eight to ten years. Unlike brotherly love, this relationship is based on inequality, in which one fulfills the other's needs. A difficulty in motherly love occurs when the child passes infancy, and parents expect the child to show a reciprocating appreciation. If the child does not respond as the parent expects, all kinds of conflict arise that may or may not be satisfactorily resolved. Eventually, this love should grow into a mature motherly/fatherly love, transferring not only to the father but to others as well. As an adult, the person then develops a motherly or fatherly conscience.

Fromm's five kinds of love.

Erotic love, according to Fromm, involves the desire for complete union with another person. Unlike motherly or brotherly love, it is not universal in nature but is aimed at completing a relationship physically as well as "spiritually" with another. It is a sexual fulfillment that extends beyond immediate gratification. Although erotic love is exclusive, involving two people, there may also be present an element of brotherly love, since it is a love involving equals.

To love others as human beings is to love oneself as a human being. Thus, *self-love* and love of others are inseparably connected. It has been a normal value that to love oneself is sinful, but self-love is not synonymous with selfishness. A selfish person is incapable of loving himself or herself and therefore is unable to love others. A common fear is that narcissism may be carried to extreme so that love of self becomes an obsession. It is normal and healthy, however, to go through the narcissistic stage; it is only when someone returns to it later in life that it can interfere with functioning.

Fromm's final object of love is *love of God*. Love of God is the realization of that which "God" represents to oneself. It is dependent upon the individual's spiritual perceptions of what is best for that person, and is not universal for all people. It emanates from the desire to overcome a separateness and find union within the universe. In the Western religions, love of God is a thought experience, but for Eastern religions it is a feeling of oneness. This Eastern philosophy seems to be becoming more prevalent in the Western hemisphere.

Merely describing love objects does not say anything about the quality of a loving relationship or the complexity of various kinds of love. For example, we may feel both erotic and brotherly love for the same person; and different people may love us in many ways. One important characteristic of love between two people is that each fits into the life space of the other. Take, for instance, the following poem by R. D. Laing:[6]

> *Jill and Jack both want to be wanted*
>
> *Jill wants Jack because he wants to be wanted*
> *Jack wants Jill because she wants to be wanted.*
>
> *Jill wants Jack to want*
>   **Jill to want*
>   *Jack's want of her want*
>   *for his want of her want of*
>
> *Jack's want that Jill wants*
>   *Jack to want*
>   *Jill to want*
>   *Jack's want of her want*
>   *for his want of*
>   *her to want Jack to want**
>
> **repeat sine fine*

Jack and Jill have equal and reciprocal needs that each other can fulfill, and the meeting of these needs, or wants, forms the basis of a loving relationship, although it is certainly not enough for a lasting, mature love. A relationship of only meeting wants (e.g., a simple motherly love relationship), would be only temporary and not unconditional.

There is a distinction between a symbiotic union, in which each partner feeds the wants and needs of the other, and mature love, in which a desired union occurs simultaneously while preserving individual identity. The symbiotic union may be passive, in which one partner submits to the dominance of the other. In clinical psychological terms, this is a masochistic role in that the subdominant person copes with separateness by becoming part of the other person's personality. There is also an active role, which is the antithesis of the passive type. It is the dominant (sadistic) partner who makes the "weaker" one part of himself or herself.

Mature love requires a high degree of giving and taking. It is virtually impossible in a practical sense for both partners to be constantly and completely equal. Dominance may swing from one person to the other, depending upon the circumstances. Each may have a set of strengths and weaknesses; each may have greater or lesser desires and motivation in particular realms of interest. Mature love brings with it a fusion of two strong and equal but complementary individual personalities. Both must be able to give as well as receive.

Love also incorporates the elements of care, responsibility, respect and knowledge. Care is the genuine concern for the life and well-being of those we truly love. Responsibility is a completely voluntary readiness to act in the best interests of another. Respect is the ability to see loved ones as unique individuals and to allow them to grow and develop at their pace and style. Knowledge is the accurate perception of the partner's individual identity aside from oneself. All these elements constitute the prerequisites to mature love.

Another way of distinguishing between what is and is not mature love has been developed by Abraham Maslow. Love is one of the basic human needs; if not met, the individual is, of course, deficient and must strive to overcome this deficit. Maslow calls this love need D-love, or deficiency-love, which is a selfish love. On the other hand, the person (child or adult) whose love need is being fulfilled has B-love, or love for the being of others, which is an unselfish and giving love.

B-love is enjoyed completely for itself rather than as a means to achieve some goal. It is an end in itself and yet has no ending, since it continually grows. B-lovers are less demanding, feel less threatened or jealous, and act more independently and autonomously than D-lovers. B-love is open; partners disclose more of themselves, drop their defenses, act with spontaneity and need not depend upon living a role to protect themselves. This may seem to involve a higher degree of risk-taking, but there is actually more security in the relationship. B-love is obviously a more complete, richer, worthwhile and enhancing experience. It allows the optimum development for each person.

Similar to Maslow's B-love is Martin Buber's I-You (or I-Thou) relationship. I-You is not two single words, but a word pair; thus, it describes not two beings but the relationship of one to the other. This relation may involve the sphere of nature, other human beings or spiritual beings. Buber uses another word pair, I-It, to describe our attitude toward another person or an object. The I of I-It is different from the I of I-You, just as the I-You relationship differs from the I-It attitude.

I-You centers on people (including ourselves) and things as part of the whole. They are not objects to be experienced or explained. It is like a song that we hear in its entirety, rather than listening to one note at a time. I-It analyzes and perceives each note of the song as a separate entity. I-It encounters and sees objects. I-You is an association; I-It is a differentiation.

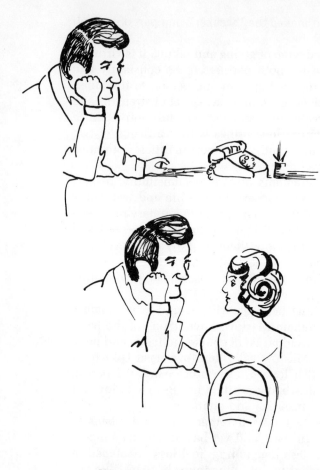

I-You/I-It: Both kinds of relationships are necessary.

We react to the world on two levels. On the one hand, we meet everything and everyone as being and becoming. This is a cosmic existence that defies measurement. On the other hand, we perceive our physical boundaries, we see things and record them in terms of time and space. This is an ordered and logical world, which is relatively reliable, has definable physical properties, and constitutes what we know to be tested truths.

In practical terms related to the process of living the best life, we each need to reach a happy medium of I-You and I-It perceptions and relationships. This is not to say that everyone has to achieve the same absolute balance of I-You and I-It, but both are necessary for optimal functioning. Not with everyone we meet can we establish strong I-You connections, although there are some who mistakenly think they are able to do this on the personal level. The I-You love situation is only occasionally effectuated, and these peak experiences, in order to happen, must be tempered with I-It perceptions. The I-It world sets up the I-You relationships and makes it possible.

The I part of the word pairs I-You and I-It should be qualified, since it is certainly not the same from person to person or from situation to situation. Some people hardly have an I at all, and may see the world as It-It. Students who approach their education in this way study for the sake of study itself, rather than for its connectedness with their lives. Others may have an I-I attitude, which is a sort of vegetative existence that closes out the world. If the world is acknowledged, it is certainly only on the I-It level, never becoming "emotionally" involved. There are also other perceptions involving We, He, She and Them, but not I. Each one has its own particular drawbacks to becoming a psychologically healthy person.

An I-You relationship, then, is the goal of loving. It is the implicit trust that allows and leads to the communion (or co-union) of two people as one. Lovers may be parent-child, brother-sister, man-woman or any two people. Communion between two people can take an infinite number of symbolic and actual forms.

PERSONALITY DEVELOPMENT

As one goes through the developmental process of becoming a mature, healthy individual, there are an infinite number of paths possible. Why do we choose one particular set to become who we are? How does personality develop, and what components are important? These and similar questions are continually being examined, so much so that there are almost as many theories as there are theorists. Who, then, to believe? The most useful solution would be to pick and choose from each and organize one's own theory, as long as it is most functional and open to change.

The most logical place to start is with Sigmund Freud, since most modern psychologies are based upon his tenets to one extent or another. Although it is common to find fault with some of Freud's theory, or at least his emphasis on certain psychological underpinnings, his basic ideas are still quite valid today.

The first core characteristic of personality that Freud attributes to human beings is the presence of a number of universally inherent and stable *instincts*. The three instincts believed to be present at birth are the life, death and sexual instincts. Taken together, they compose the id concept. The life instinct, or *eros*, is the drive for self-preservation, that is to obtain food, water and air. The death instinct, or *thanatos*, stems from a deterministic philosophy that all events have rational causes. Since a basic predicament of life is the eventual biological deterioration of the body, the psyche or mind manifests that somatic process in a death wish. It operates antagonistically to the life wish. Finally, the sexual instinct, or *libido*, is the most controversial of Freud's postulates and the one that consumed most of his attention. Although this instinct has origins in the preservation of the species, it is not only limited to the genitalia but involves other related actions and secondary sex areas, such as the anus, mouth and breasts.

All these instincts have a common general form in that they all have a *biological source*. The instinct is a psychic representation of the somatic process. Freud's theory, therefore, is biological in nature, as opposed to psychosocial theories of personality development. Second, all instincts contain a *driving force*—energy—that is based upon the deprivation of need. The instinctual reaction is to satisfy needs. This satisfaction of needs, or *aim*, is the reduction of tension caused by deprivation. Finally, all instincts have an *object*, usually external but sometimes internal, which serves as a focus for the tension reduction or need fulfillment. Therefore, instincts or drives have a biological origin that eventually is psychologically expressed as temperament or personality.

While the id is self-centered and selfish in nature, the superego seeks to follow the order and laws of society. Where the id functions to reduce metabolically produced tension (Freud calls this gratification the pleasure principle), the superego functions to reduce culturally produced *anxiety*. In the evolutionary process, society has set up a series of restrictions and rules. Not to follow these laws is to be punished in a number of ways, usually by other members of society who serve as representatives of the common good. For example, children, acting primarily on the pleasure principle, are punished frequently by their parents, who are teaching them the social rules. The punishment is usually not harsh, often consisting of verbal reprimands. In an effort to avoid punishment and the guilt association with breaking social laws, people learn to conform to greater or lesser degrees. Guilt is actually the internalized form of punishment.

The functional objective of personality, therefore, is to maximize instinctual gratification while minimizing punishment and guilt, and thus relieve tension and anxiety. In order to do this, we develop mechanisms of defensiveness. These *defense mechanisms* enable us to deal with the conflict arising from wanting to express instincts fully but not wanting to experience any punishment or guilt. It is a way of compromising between the demands of instinct and society. Defenses are aroused when the instinct-society conflict becomes strong enough to cause an anxiety reaction in anticipation of punishment and guilt. Freud believed that defensiveness is always present, since instincts are never completely dormant. Hence, all behavior is so motivated.

The whole process of handling instinctual demands so that they may be acceptably and maximally expressed is the function of the ego. This ability to differentiate between appropriate and inappropriate is called *reality principle functioning*. The ego functions to filter out the real (acceptable) from fantasy (unacceptable), the instinctual self from the rest of the world. Defense mechanisms are generally unconscious; to be aware of them would not protect us from guilt, although it might insulate us from punishment. The ego functions through defense mechanisms to keep any information from the consciousness that will harm us (through guilt and anxiety). The common defense mechanisms are listed and explained in Chapter 4.

Perhaps as important as Freud's explanation of the id, ego and superego as the skeleton of personality is his theory of the five psychosexual stages of development. Any failure to satisfactorily complete or deal with each stage, except the last, will result in a fixation at that stage and an adult personality type characteristic of that stage. The most important are the first three stages, which last to about five years of age.

During the first year of life, the mouth, which is involved in the two activities of receiving (passive) and then taking (aggressive) is the infant's primary erogenous zone. The conflict that arises during this *oral* stage is based on the child continually wanting gratification and the parent not being able to give constantly. The most important focus of this conflict is food or nourishment. The *anal* stage, in which the erogenous zone is the anus, occurs during the second and third years of life. Here, giving (expulsive) and withholding (retensive) are the primary activities, and bowel training is the source of conflict. In the *phallic* stage, as you might expect, the genitals are the erogenous zone. The major conflict lies in the Oedipus complex, in which the child competes with the parent of the same sex for the attention of the other parent. During this stage, according to Freud, boys may have castration fears or anxieties, and girls may have penis envy; however, this concept has been altered to a more generalized form by later Freudian psychoanalysts. The phallic stage occurs from about the third through the sixth years.

Perhaps the most controversial and least accepted theory of Freud is his fourth developmental stage, called *latency*, in which the sexual instinct is actually dormant from about age six until puberty. It is more likely, however, that the dictates of society and culturally based learning would cause an apparent lack of sexual interest or drive, and that it is not metabolically initiated. The last, or *genital*, stage is the sexually mature individual who incorporates all that was learned during the previous stages into the expressions of intercourse and orgasm.

One neo-Freudian, Erik Erikson, explains how personality develops through a series of eight stages, during which conflicts are encountered that are either successfully or unsuccessfully traversed. Each stage is built upon the preceding stage in a sequential order. His stages are similar to Freud's psychosexual stages, but Erikson emphasizes the psychosocial rather than the biological sources. How each stage is fulfilled is manifested in the accumulation of the individual's character traits (Fig. 3–2).

During the first stage of life, infancy, we are more dependent and helpless than at any other time. This stage is comparable to Freud's oral stage. A person whose nurturing and protection need is met in infancy will develop a general sense of trust—trustfulness of others as well as a feeling of one's own trustworthiness. Basic mistrust in adults may be expressed by separating onseself from others or at least not establishing close or lasting relationships.

Erikson's second stage is synonymous with Freud's anal stage. As a child gains muscular control, not only of the anus but in talking, sight discrimination and other more complex muscular coordination, a conflict surfaces between holding on and letting go. If a child learns to retain or eliminate at will in an acceptable, appropriate manner, then autonomous

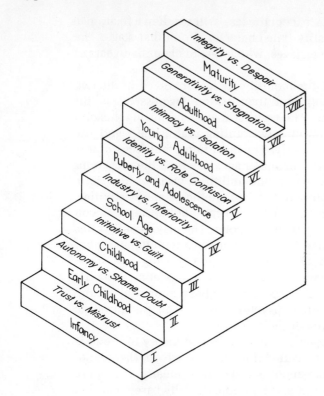

Figure 3–2 Erikson's eight stages of personality development. (Adapted from Erikson, Erik: *Identity: Youth and Crisis.* New York, W. W. Norton & Co., 1968, p. 94.)

behavior will follow. Otherwise, traits of doubt in acting and shame in one's own conduct and the conduct of others will be expressed. During this stage, children learn to deliberate the boundaries of themselves and the world outside.

Erikson's third stage, the preschool years, is marked by a great increase in gross motor ability, (general physical coordination) and the child can more freely experiment in becoming the kind of person she or he will be. Locomotion and language develop and these allow a greatly expanded imagination, which can be frightening to the child. Since Erikson is a neo-Freudian, this stage naturally includes the Oedipus conflict, but the child must ultimately fail in the competition with his or her same sexed parent. The way in which this is resolved, as well as how related growth is handled, will determine that person's initiative and responsibility in adulthood. If excess punishment is given, then guilt and resignation will result.

During school age, youngsters learn about task identification and how well they are able to make things. Erikson calls this a sense of industry; if not properly developed, then the feeling of inferiority will develop. These accomplishments vary from construction in crafts to construction of a poem, story or song, for example. This stage is chronologically similar to Freud's latency period.

The main accomplishment of puberty and adolescence is the molding and solidifying of one's identity or role. As the play age was marked by imagination, so adolescence is marked by turning the imagined, changing self into something more stable or permanent. This is not to say that no changes will occur or that growth ceases, but ego identity becomes strong. If this is not accomplished, then that adult will have the character trait of role diffusion.

Although Erikson has not studied the last three stages as thoroughly as those before adulthood, he does describe general characteristics of young adulthood, adulthood and maturity. After adolescence, when youth are expected to begin to live independently and separately from parents, they will need to learn how to become intimate with others, or to function more of less in isolation. This involves sexual intimacy, of course, but also includes intimacies of friendship and fellowship. During the seventh stage of development, the focus is on working toward establishing and helping the next generation, called generativity, or else stagnating in this sense. Generativity is achieved not by merely wanting or having children, but by truly caring for them. The final stage, in late adulthood, is the achievement of integrity, or what Erikson defines as the acceptance of one's life cycle and the togetherness of all things and people. Not to have this ego integrity is to despair that there is no purpose in life. The emergence of a person's personality, therefore, is formulated by the manner in which she or he moves through each stage.

There is another school of humanistic psychologists who explain personality development on the basis of fulfillment of a hierarchy of human needs, and the ability, therefore, to actualize one's potential. Carl Rogers puts forth the idea that the actualizing tendency is a positive direction in which we move, and that there is a need for positive regard and positive self-regard. In other words, we want to have social approval from other people plus a sense of self-worth. Rogers says that we are born with a set of inherent potentialities (Freud's instincts) and a consequent actualizing tendency, which is actually biological. How we display personality, then, is the manner in which the inherent potentialities and actualizing tendencies interact in the process of living. The fully actualized person would have a childhood of unconditional positive regard and minimal need for defensiveness. This leads to openness of experience, so that new experiences are freely sought, and a self-concept that is congruent with what the person truly and fully is.

Another humanistic psychologist of importance in structuring a theory of personality development is Abraham Maslow, who bases his human motivation theory on fulfillment of five basic needs. This hierarchy, in which one need must be satisfied before the next level can be expressed, progresses from the physiological to the more psychological.

The most basic drive involves satisfaction of *physiological* needs. This is the survival instinct whereby the cells of the body require nourishment to live and grow. One important part of this need is the existence of *homeostasis*, or the automatic and constant process of maintaining the normal state of the blood stream. The second important process is the presence of appetite, by which the body hungers for a chemical that is lacking. Given a variety of foods, a child will choose the correct foods as needed by the body, based on specific appetites for certain missing nutrients.

Once physiological needs are satisfied, the *safety* needs, including security, structure and laws, a strong protector and stability, may be attended to. This can be seen in the child's need for some orderly routine, and can result in unwarranted fears. For example, it is common for children to have great fears of losing their parents, if only because they provide protection and safety.

The need for *belongingness and love* is the longing for intimacy and identification. This is not a sexual need, but a social one. It is more psychological than the two preceding needs are, and when gratified, it opens the way for the fulfillment of the *esteem* needs. Just about everyone has the need to feel worth while, to have a sense of self-respect and self-esteem. The esteem need consists of a desire to achieve, to be capable, to master certain tasks and to possess strength. It also includes another subsidiary set of wants; to attain status, prestige (respect from others), fame, recognition, dignity and appreciation. Satisfaction of these needs leads to a strong, self-confident and adequate personality.

The greatest fulfillment of needs, according to Maslow, is achieved by the optimal use of one's capabilities, or what he calls *self-actualization*. He also refers to this process as growth toward full-humanness. Like Rogers, Maslow recognizes the instinctiveness of human nature, that this inner nature is in essence a not yet finalized or actualized potential, and that inner nature is good (or at least neutral) rather than evil. He also mentions a *cognitive* or understanding need, but this is a condition for the satisfaction of other needs. It is the universal impulse to know, explain and satisfy curiosity.

Another explanation of personality development is expressed in the theories of *behaviorism*. Although certain tenets are common to all behaviorists, there are extremes, from early, moderate behaviorism to more recent and radical behaviorism. The primary focus has been upon the stimulus-response action, the principle that every stimulus an individual encounters necessitates some response. As the same stimulus and response occur regularly, an S–R (stimulus-response) bond is formed. This bond is strengthened when the response is rewarded, and it is weakened when followed by punishment.

As a basis for response, there are a number of *primary drives* (hunger, thirst, sex, activity, curiosity and pain) that we continually attempt to satisfy. The goal is to reduce the tension caused by these primary drives through the use of *primary reinforcement*. Hence, the primary reward corresponding to the primary drive of thirst is water or liquid, and the reward for hunger is food. There is also a *general drive* or tension produced by the total accumulation of the primary drives.

As a particular S-R bond gets very strong, a person's behavior will become habit, and once learned, habits maintain a strong resistance to change. A set of personality characteristics is formed when stimulus-response becomes generalized, and a similar response is triggered by similar but not identical stimuli. The S–R action is not a simple one,

Self-actualized people?

however, and usually contains intervening variables operating between the stimulus and the response, so that the behavioral diagram looks like this: S–O–R. The O represents the intervening variable, or the organism. These organismic variables involve the intellectualization process and may vary considerably, according to transiency (as with temporary emotional or motivational states), relatively fixed values or constitutional predispositions. The learning process is a matter of the organism's (person's) responding to secondary reinforcement by repeating the rewarded behavior in a variety of similar circumstances.

Responses are usually dependent upon the condition of the organism and its environment, and are therefore controllable. For the behaviorist, *operant conditioning* is easily achievable by manipulating the stimulus or response. It is a matter of bringing a voluntary response under stimulus control. The response may be *unconditioned* when it is not the result of previous experience, or it may be a *conditioned* response when prior experience elicits a response to a previously "neutral" stimulus. When a certain stimulus serves to cue a particular response, it is a *discriminative stimulus*, and learning has taken place. This is the basis of the techniques used in *behavior modification*, which attempts to use mostly positive reinforcement to cause a desired response. By providing the appropriate cues, we elicit the desired response. For example, people in the habit of smoking, when provided with such cues (discriminative stimuli) as a morning cup of coffee, alcohol at a party or a tense situation, will immediately light up a cigarette. Their response is conditioned.

An interesting, although not as useful, theory of personality development has been evolved by William Sheldon. It is a constitutional theory of temperament that classifies personalities as congruent with one of three body types or *somatotypes*. By studying hundreds of individuals, Sheldon was able to identify traits that were common to or at least predominant in one type or another. On a 7-point scale, the somatotype of a person is expressed by three numbers, each designating the strength of one of the characteristics. The first numeral refers to the degree of *endomorphy*, the second to *mesomorphy* and the third to *ectomorphy*. Thus, the most extreme endomorph is 7–1–1, an extreme mesomorph is 1–7–1 and an extreme ectomorph is 1–1–7.

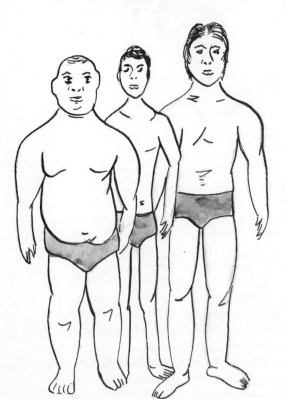

Stereotyped examples of Sheldon's three basic somatotypes: endomorph, mesomorph and ectomorph.

A predominant endomorph has highly developed and massive viscera and is often fat. The temperament correlating to the endomorph is *viscerotonic,* characterized by relaxed posture and movement, slow reaction, deep sleep, real love of eating, high degree of socialization, enjoyment of physical comfort, tolerance and complacency. A viscerotonic individual is really into food, sleep and comfort. These individuals are very relaxed and people-oriented.

A mesomorphic physique is hard, firm and tough. This individual is muscular and probably athletic. The accompanying temperament is *somatotonia,* which characterizes a personality that is assertive or aggressive, adventurous, risk taking, bold, direct, active, dominant and boisterous. Of course, not many people are 1–7–1, and it would be hard to find such a stereotype. The somatotonic person does crave action and motion, though, and has a high energy level.

The ectomorph is thin and frail, with little visceral or somatic development. This individual is lean, though poorly muscled, and has delicate bones. *Cerebrotonia* is the corresponding temperament, which means that such a person is restrained, seeks privacy, is hypersensitive, sleeps poorly and is inhibited. A cerebrotonic person, being tense, is likely to be susceptible to heart disease. Jung would classify such a person as *introverted.*

According to Sheldon, personality stems from an inherited body and metabolic type and resultant temperament. This temperament, although mainly present at birth, is also influenced by expectation. As people react to our body builds, we act as they expect us to. Thus, the jolly fat person stereotype becomes a self-fulfilling prophecy. Body types are static (we can do nothing about it), but temperament is a dynamic component of the individual.

PURPOSE IN LIFE

While it is relevant and helpful to study the various theories of personality development, at the root of it all is always the question, Why should people become what they are? Or perhaps more important, What should we become? The most meaningful question for a person to confront is, What is my purpose in life?

An ancient Greek story tells of Sisyphus, who was condemned by the gods to roll a large rock to the top of a mountain, whereupon the rock would roll back down to the bottom. Sisyphus would then have to begin rolling it back up, only to have it roll down again when it reached the top. This process continued for eternity as punishment for his scorn of the gods, his hatred of death and his passion for life. What meaning could there be to this eternal toiling? The analogy here is that we each must consider the purpose of our life.

Rollo May talks about the hollow people who do not know what they want or what they feel. This modern-day emptiness seems to stem from the knowledge that what these persons want is really what others want or

The major philosophical question in life is, What is the meaning or purpose of our being?

expect of them. The problem then arises of people who are not authentic, or *inner directed* (to use the term of sociologist David Riesman), but are apathetic, passive and directed by others. May refers to this as emptiness.

The Austrian psychiatrist Viktor Frankl bases his theory of *logotherapy* on the search for the meaning of human existence. To be able to deal with the question of the purpose of life, to "know" some of the reasons for existence, will enable one to endure the hows, or problems, of living. The meaning of life cannot be defined in a general way, however; it consists of responding to each unique situation, and thus evolving a conglomerate answer. Nevertheless, the meaning of life is very concrete and real, not a vague abstraction. Just as situations do not exactly repeat themselves and responses vary accordingly, so the destiny of each person differs.

Frankl tested and developed much of his theory as a prisoner in the Nazi concentration camp at Auschwitz. In this environment, in which every material possession and aspect of human dignity were taken away, people were stripped to their barest nakedness, literally and figuratively. Despite this environment, or perhaps because of it, certain discoveries about the human condition were made. No matter how limited, people do have a choice of action. Apathy and emptiness can be overcome, and spiritual freedom attained. In even the most barren, lacking environment there are choices to be made, even if it is only the decision to submit to power or to assume power.

Another important lesson learned in the concentration camp was the value of suffering. According to Frankl, without suffering (and death), human life cannot be complete; without suffering we would know no pleasure. Nietzsche said, "That which does not kill me, makes me stronger." All experiences, if regarded as useful and as opportunities for learning, add to the growth of an individual. They give direction to life.

A psychological view of suffering has been described by the psychologist David Bakan, who relates, on a primary level, suffering and human understanding. Suffering is manifested on the biological level as disease, on the psychological level as pain and on the existential (spiritual) level as sacrifice.

In dealing with suffering, there are two possible reactions: oblivion (physical or mental unconsciousness) or understanding. Management of suffering through human understanding is undoubtedly the superior choice, although there are times when the option of partial oblivion is useful. Complete oblivion is the same as death, and is usually not considered as satisfactory an answer as understanding, a human endowment that should be cultivated. In order to cope with suffering and learn from it, a level of awareness must be reached. However, suffering often serves to diminish awareness, and only a mature person can see beyond the immediate source of suffering to find meaning in it all.

Pain is perhaps the most prominent of human experiences, along with its antithesis, pleasure. Not only is it important as a motivator, that is, to initiate certain behaviors in order to avoid pain, but it demands an explanation for its existence, even though it almost defies definition. For example, one of the toughest aspects of diagnostic medicine is for the patient to describe the pain symptoms accurately to a physician or nurse. Therefore, each person must define pain for himself or herself. It can be understood only in relative terms, and is based upon previous pain or pleasure experiences.

At the very least, to know pain communicates to us that we are alive. It gives some direction and growth to life. But it is certainly not enough of an impetus to stimulate continual growth. Growing and becoming, to be an ongoing process, must involve discipline and maturity if intrinsic and active participation in this constant procedure is to be achieved. Additionally, such preconditions as creativity, energy and purpose in life are required. John Gardner speaks of the mature society or individual as that "system or framework within which continuous innovation, renewal and rebirth can occur."[7]

The first prerequisite for self-renewal is awareness that we are in need of renewal. It is easy to continue renewal when young, since the initial growth period is in progress, but people become narrower in their interests and more specialized in their skills. There is great comfort and security in participating in activities that we have done many times before and for which we know the limits of our capabilities. This is true for an entire society as well as for an individual. There is a tendency to protect the past and resist change.

Self-renewal is not the accumulation of more skills however; it is more the actualization of the potential already possessed. In this sense, then, Gardner's thinking is similar to that of Maslow and Rogers. The self-renewing individual does not leave this exploration to chance, but systematically and knowingly engages in it. The educational system is one institution of society that should help remove the barriers to fulfillment and self-renewal. Education also has the responsibility for helping develop a person versatile enough to be constantly self-renewing.

The concept of continual growth and self-renewal is not aimless, but has an organized direction toward some individual and societal meaning. The self-renewing person has made a commitment to certain goals. Frequently, this goal is spoken of as happiness; but happiness—at least the happiness defined as a state of gratification, comfort, ease, entertainment and achievement of goals—is a static no-growth state. Unless happiness involves striving toward meaningful goals, purposeful effort, full use of potential and a capacity to love, then it is not a part of the self-renewal process or self-renewing person. Self-renewal, then, returns us to the fundamental questions of, Who am I? What is my function in life? What directions should I take? It is a future-oriented concept that functions in the present.

ENDNOTES

1. Jourard, Sidney: *The Transparent Self*. New York, D. Van Nostrand Co., 1971, p. 125.
2. Farson, Richard: The reverse transmission of culture. In Marshall, Bernice (Ed.): *Experiences in Being*. Belmont, Calif., Brooks/Cole Publishing Co., 1971.
3. Berelson, B., and G. A. Steiner: *Human Behavior: An Inventory of Scientific Findings*. New York, Harcourt Brace, and World, 1964, p. 88.
4. Gibran, Kahlil: *The Prophet*. New York, Alfred A. Knopf, 1923, p. 17.
5. Fromm, Erich: *The Art of Loving*. New York, Harper & Row, Publishers, 1956, p. 6.
6. Laign, R. D.: *Knots*. New York, Vintage Books, 1970, p. 49.
7. Gardner, John W.: *Self-Renewal*. New York, Harper & Row, Publishers, 1964, p. 5.

BIBLIOGRAPHY

Alinsky, Saul D.: *Rules for Radicals*. New York, Vantage Books, 1971.

Bakan, D.: *Pain, Disease and Suffering, Toward a Psychology of Suffering*. Chicago, The University of Chicago Press, 1968.

Brill, A. A. (Editor and translator): *The Basic Writings of Sigmund Freud*. New York, Random House, 1938.

Buber, Martin: *I and Thou*. Translated by Walter Kaufmann. New York, Charles Scribner's Sons, 1970.

Dubos, Rene: *So Human an Animal*. New York, Charles Scribner's Sons, 1968.

Erikson, Erik: *Identity: Youth and Crisis*. New York, W. W. Norton & Company, 1968.

Farber, Jerry: *The Student As Nigger*. North Hollywood, California, Contact Books, 1969.

Frankl, Viktor E.: *Man's Search for Meaning*. New York, Washington Square Press, 1963.

Fromm, Erich: *The Art of Loving*. New York, Harper & Row, Publishers, 1956.

Gardner, John W.: *Self-Renewal*. New York, Harper & Row, Publishers, 1963.

Huxley, Aldous: *The Doors of Perception*. New York, Harper & Row, Publishers, 1954.

Jourard, Sidney: *The Transparent Self*. New York, D. Van Nostrand Company, 1971.

Jung, C. G.: *The Archetypes and Collective Unconscious*. Princeton, Princeton University Press, 1959, 1969.

Maddi, Salvatore R.: *Personality Theories*. Homewood, Illinois, The Dorsey Press, 1968, 1972.

Marshall, Bernice (Ed.): *Experiences in Being*. Belmont, California, Brooks/Cole Publishing Company, 1971.

Maslow, Abraham: *Motivation and Personality*. New York, Harper & Row, Publishers, 1970.

Maslow, Abraham: *Toward a Psychology of Being*. New York, Van Nostrand Reinhold Company, 1968.

Mead, Margaret: *Culture and Commitment*. Garden City, New York, Doubleday & Company, 1970.

Overstreet, H. H.: *The Mature Mind*. New York, W. W. Norton & Company, 1949.

Patton, Bobby R., and Kim Giffin: *Interpersonal Communications*. New York, Harper & Row, Publishers, 1974.

Reich, Charles: *The Greening of America*. New York, Random House, 1970.

Sheldon, William: *The Varieties of Temperament*. New York, Hafner Publishing Company, 1970.

Terkel, Studs: *Working*. New York, Pantheon Books, 1974.

Toffler, Alvin: *Future Shock*. New York, Random House, 1970.

CHAPTER 4

EMOTIONS, CRISIS AND PROBLEM SOLUTION

MENTAL WELLNESS

As we have seen, there is purpose to everything, and all experiences give meaning to life. Not only does each experience contribute to personal growth but it contributes in a progressive way. We build one experience onto another in a manner that enables us to transcend previous states. This transcendence is a matter of upgrading individual potential as an ongoing condition.

Halbert Dunn,[1] in defining high-level wellness, includes three aspects of functioning as follows:

1. a direction in progress forward and upward toward a higher potential of functioning;

2. an open-ended and ever-expanding tomorrow, with its challenge to live at a fuller potential; and

3. the integration of the whole being of the individual, of the total individual—body, mind, spirit—in the functioning process.

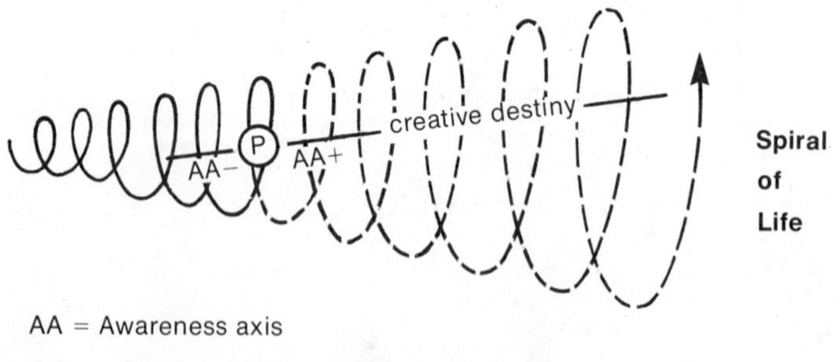

AA = Awareness axis

AA+ = Creative pole of the awareness axis

AA− = Negative pole of the awareness axis

Figure 4-1 Conceptual model of high-level wellness. (Adapted from Dunn, Halbert: *High Level Wellness.* Virginia, R. W. Beatty, Ltd., 1961.)

In this conceptualization, the person (P) is a body of organized energy, which can be abundant and creative (AA+) or deficient and negative (AA−). The spiral moves forward and upward, open-endedly encompassing the person. Although there may be fluctuations in the level of human wellness, both the lowest (sickness) and highest (wellness) potentials are increasing. This conceptualization can be argued with and should not be looked upon as the last word, but it should be taken to make the point that growing and maturing are or can be totally positive fulfilling processes.

Some other features of human nature should be stressed in supporting this concept of the total person as a potential fulfilling and expanding being.

1. People function as *total personalities*, not separate physical, mental and spiritual aspects. Every change or action in one part of the person affects all other parts to some degree, no matter how small. Not only is there an ecological balance between humans and the environment, but there is the same sort of ecosystem operating in the person.

2. Each human being is unique. The manifestations of our physicalness, psychological character and spirituality are different from those of all others, and their interactions produce further differences that make individuals unique.

3. We are made of energy, and the way in which it is manifested determines the kind of person we are and our level of wellness. Our tissues amount to an organized energy source to be utilized in some way. It can be put to creative use or it can be turned inward to function negatively or adversely. Our energy must be continually replenished by air, food, water, psychological stimuli and spiritual or philosophical ideas.

4. We all live in an inner and an outer world. We take in and process various psychological and physical elements, using some immediately, rejecting or eliminating others, and storing the rest for possible future use. We must coordinate the exchange between our inner selves and the outer world in which we function.

5. The final point of human nature to be considered here is the interrelationship of self-integration and energy use. Our organized body energy functions to help our integrated body, mind and spirit operate to the fullest potential.

Being positively directed does not exclude the existence of potentially negative or disabling occurrences. Within the psychological domain, these usually take the form of crises and emotional stress. Both crisis and stress are normal situations that must be expected, and one means of measuring mental growth may be through our approach to the daily problems we encounter. Each problem met successfully adds to our growth. In terms of wellness, it further increases individual potential, because it adds to our confidence to know we are capable of solving a problem through our personal resources. It is a reinforcing experience that shows us the reaches of our skill.

In a similar way, each of us learns to use a set of emotions. The term "emotional control" signifies not that emotions are suppressed or restrained but that a full range of emotions is used appropriately. Thus, emotional control means judicious use rather than limited use. Another key word is "appropriately," which can be defined only in terms of societal expectations, for displays of emotions must be manifested in a culturally acceptable manner. Otherwise, behavior is labeled "out of control." To have full use of one's emotions is a matter of both self-satisfaction and acting within the frame of reference of others.

EMOTIONS ARE GOOD

Trying to find a satisfactory definition of the term emotion is almost impossible. There is no definition that has been widely accepted in the psychological literature, although much has been written about the characteristic states of emotion. Most definitions, however, seem to include the quality of intensity and accompanying bodily changes that are a disruption from the homeostatic condition. Remember, this disruption is not necessarily bad, although it may interfere with desirable functioning. In modern conversation the word emotions is frequently used interchangeably with feelings, but there is a difference between them. First of all, feelings are experiences of mild intensity, whereas emotions are strongly moved reactions. Therefore there is a distinction of degree. More important, though, there is a qualitative difference. Feelings are a first-person experience and consequently are truly known only to oneself or me. Only I know how I feel. Emotions vary in kind (anger, fear, love, hate and so forth) and are directed at some object. Feelings are reactions to a particular aspect of the object or situation, indicating degrees of attractiveness or unattractiveness.

Feelings not only describe the state we are experiencing ("I feel tired") but also say something subjective about it ("I feel pleasantly tired"). Feelings take into account whether the object is pleasant, eliciting an approach response to the stimulus, or unpleasant, eliciting a withdrawal response. In this way feelings are more descriptive than emotions, even though emotions are accompanied by significant body changes. Further, when we speak of values and attitudes we refer to the larger category of feelings.

Before any emotional response is aroused, there is a series of events that must occur (Fig. 4–2). First, there must be an object or event to which to respond. Not only do we experience, but something or someone occasions that experience; one particular object or a group of objects (people or things) may be involved in such a setting. In order to evoke emotional response, this object (or situation) must be perceived in a way

Figure 4-2 Chain of emotional response.

that relates to us personally, within our frame of reference. In simplest terms, it must be distinguished (perceived) as a separate object, and then meaning must be attached to it (appraisal). Appraisal is an evaluation of the stimulus, whereas the emotional response proceeds beyond that stage to an action. This action (reaction) may express a wish to either attract or repel the object, depending upon its appraised threat or worth. The appraisal that arouses emotion is immediate, direct and intuitive.

Although the study of emotions has engaged psychologists and philosophers, such as Aristotle and St. Thomas Aquinas, for a long time, it is only within this century that scientific theories have evolved. For example, Charles Darwin, in *The Expression of the Emotions in Man and Animals*, proposed that emotions evolved from a physical and purposeful expressive action originally meant to relieve or gratify certain desires and sensations. Eventually, as the same action was repeated, it became habit and was genetically passed from generation to generation. Darwin hypothesized that certain bodily changes took place for functional purposes and eventually became innate.

The first scientific and popularly accepted theory of emotion was presented by the psychologists William James and Carl Lange. They claimed that certain physiological changes occur directly from perception of the stimulus and that this bodily change is the emotion. However, whereas James saw the physiological changes as primarily visceral, Lange emphasized circulatory changes.

Walter Cannon, who disagreed with the James-Lange theory, developed an emergency theory, which states that emotions involve autonomic nervous system changes that serve emergency action—fight or flight. As a result of adrenal secretion and sympathetic excitation, the body is prepared for struggle. Emotion, according to Cannon, is an energizer. Whereas James was visceral and Lange vascular, Cannon was neurological in explaining the psychophysiology of emotions.

Emotions, then, affect how we function and act continuously in response to the world around us. Preceded by immediate and intuitive appraisal, the spontaneous resultant emotion must then be expressed or put into action, partially as an attempt to restore homeostasis. The most obvious and visible emotional expression is muscular tension and posture, or body language. This, of course, includes facial expressions and body carriage, but we may also observe changes in skin tone. Sometimes we are more conscious about controlling our muscular expression, but at other times it may be so automatic and less consciously intentional that it gives us away. Emotional expressions therefore act as another vehicle for communications by which we tell others what we are feeling and thinking. However, unless others are accurately reading our body language, communication will break down. The student sitting in class with a bored facial expression may be truly bored with the professor's lecture, tired, preoccupied or just hostile about being in a classroom.

Emotions also help us to achieve our goals. "Negative" emotions direct us away from certain goals, just as "positive" emotions attract us toward goals. Emotions begin to hinder us when they are acutely intense (e.g., being unable to act when presented with a real threat), when they become excessive (uncontrollable anger) or when they are chronic (such as fear of fear itself).

Emotions are sometimes in conflict with each other, and this can be destructive. For example, suppose you want to present a speech to a class or some other group. You may get "psyched up" to do well, but your fear may be so powerful that you become "tongue-tied." The basic conflict is whether to approach or withdraw from the situation. We frequently withdraw—decide not to take the risk—rather than face possible embarrassment or the discomfort of the accompanying nervousness. At other times we persevere, using our intelligent, decision-making processes to measure the possible good and bad consequences.

Emotional control is important for adequate personality development and good mental health because it is a way of handling inevitable conflict. Of course, such control is not synonymous with restraint, since it should help, not hinder. To control fear of public speaking by not participating at all restricts one's functioning. The solution to overcoming negative emotions is to increase the desirability of pursuing our goal to the point where it weighs more heavily than possible resultant failure. To further ensure success, one must anticipate possible problems and prepare accordingly to reduce both the possibility and the consequences of failure. However, once emotions have become too strong, they may interfere with any rational solutions. Over a period of time, emotional reactions can become so ingrained as to become habit.

An investigation of any English language thesaurus will reveal that there are over 400 names for emotions. From time to time we feel all these emotions, but some occur more frequently or have a greater impact on our lives. However many emotions there are, they do not usually express themselves as simple, isolated processes. Rather, they are complex, often involving a number of other emotions. For example, a feeling of jealousy may simultaneously consist of love, anger, loss and frustration; or it may lead to other emotions, which may be more intense, such as hatred.

In handling emotions, it is important to recognize their presence and the mode in which they are expressed. This is the first requisite for having a full range of emotional expression. Furthermore, we need to be comfortable about the manifestations of emotions that have become common to our individual personalities.

The one basic emotion, which has been discussed at length in the preceding chapter, is *love*. One aspect of love not covered in the previous discussion is its intensity. A strong emotion of love for someone is accompanied by various bodily reactions, which all add up to a desire to externalize this feeling. We frequently want to hug, kiss and share things with a loved one. A variety of changes, such as "butterflies," skin flushes and tingling, or even crying for joy, are not uncommon. A person in love also wants to spend much of his or her time with the other.

Whereas love energizes, the opposite, equally intense emotion, *hate*, possesses the quality of negative energy. Hate inhibits the fulfillment of an actualized life, since it is so reactive. Feeling true hate toward someone is

Love energizes; hate saps energy.

to focus on detractive extremes. We are repelled by such forces and must spend time and energy dealing with them by withdrawal, destruction or giving in. Nevertheless, hate, like all emotions, has a function, which is to protect us from external threats to ourselves and our value systems. An intense feeling of hatred is based upon a reaction to a threatening force, whether it be a distasteful food, a source of pain or a cruel person.

The emotions of joy and sadness represent the extremes of our high and low points in daily living. The objects of joy can be sensual, aesthetic, spiritual, pastoral or whatever. Joy can be quiet or loud, rowdy glee; it can be solitary or shared. However, it is not synonymous with *happiness*, although they certainly are similar. Joy is an inward satisfaction, a good feeling that things have gone well; it stems from the knowledge that things are right. Happiness is a more transient and superficial gladness, but joy involves a sense of fulfillment that we grow on, and it remains part of our strength.

Sadness, although a negative and often unwelcome emotion, is necessary for a full range of experience in living. It is the valley that makes possible the peaks of happiness and joy. This is particularly true of sadness due to loss, since we could never possess either feelings or material goods if they were not ultimately losable. Furthermore, it is a desirable quality to be able to express sadness at appropriate times, shed tears and then resume living. The problem is, however, that we are encouraged to withhold expressions of sadness (e.g., "men don't cry" or "big girls don't cry"); we are told not to be sad or are allowed to feel sad only in culturally acceptable contexts. An extension of the prolonged sad state is depression, which may be considered an emotion by some, but is also thought of as a prolonged psychological state carrying with it a set of possible symptoms. The depressed state is extremely draining and negative, whereas sadness is more meaningful.

Probably the most difficult emotion to express is anger, because society does not readily accept it. Whereas hatred is chronic, anger is an acute form that falls into the general category of aggression. The other emotion that accompanies aggression is hostility, which is more long term than anger; hostility, in fact, comes more from hatred than from anger. The whole aggression response may stem from frustration of not being able to achieve goals, either directly or because of an intervening emotional reaction (generalized anger). Frustration does not always lead to anger and aggression, but depends upon perception of the situation and how a person is used to acting in such circumstances.

Anger is the immediate response to a present threatening force. It is a reaction to an already existing obstacle to the goal, and if not satisfactorily overcome, it leads to despair and depression. However, caution must be taken to manifest anger in such a way that it does not lead to further blockage of goals. A direct display of anger may result in a counterreaction that causes greater anger as well as other negative emotions and reactions. Anger must be directed toward the source of anger only, and not at the general object or situation. When I am angry with another person for a particular behavior, then it should be made clear that I am angry only with the specific behavior and not with any other part of the person.

Anger may sometimes be displaced or directed at an entirely unrelated object. Although this may occasionally be helpful, its use is limited. Eventually the sources of anger must be directly confronted. We can punch boxing bags or hit tennis balls only for so long before the anger turns inward to become a self-destructive force (e.g., ulcers). Moreover, it is even more harmful to release the emotion of anger only toward some targets and never toward the real or more important sources. In any case, showing anger is risky, for it may necessitate a retaliatory response that can be more difficult to handle then the initial source of the anger, or it may really hurt the other person.

If we not allow our anger to be vented because we are afraid of the consequences, then it can be replaced by fear. For example, we may have been frustrated and annoyed by our parents but never allowed ourselves to be overtly angry because of the fear of repercussions. This resentment could then become a generalized fear of people like our parents, such as any authority figure.

Fear is a basic emotion that on a chronic, diffuse level leads to anxiety. A certain amount of anxiety is natural and is usually helpful to superior functioning, but intense and chronic anxiety can inhibit normal functioning. Frequently, if we are somewhat aware of our body and its changes, we can feel anxiety as muscular tension or marked increase in circulation. This anxious energy must be dealt with, perhaps by stress reduction through dispersion or transference or by using it in a highly physical activity. It is difficult, at best, to calm the nervously anxious state by intellectualization.

However, fears can be intellectualized away or at least analyzed and worked out. Perhaps the biggest prerequisite to overcoming fear is to realize that it exists. Fear is such an uncomfortable emotion that it is frequently repressed and later manifests itself in a way that is harmful to oneself. We run away from what we fear rather than face its possible consequences. Sometimes the destructive consequences are obviously very painful, but at other times we preclude significant growing experiences because of our withdrawal. Ironically, a large category of fear is that which stems from the unknown; by succumbing to it we avoid all activities aimed at discovery. For example, because of possible rejection, we may have great fears about approaching another person to whom we feel affectionate. However, if we never approach that person, we cannot possibly achieve the objective of spending time with him or her.

LONELINESS, DEPRESSION AND CRISIS INTERVENTION

LONELINESS

There are psychological "down" states that are universal and must be dealt with. The ultimate expression of these low states is suicide as a way out, and the two conditions most often linked with terminating one's life are extreme loneliness and depression.

Loneliness takes two forms, one that stems from and can be termed as societal loneliness and the other a personal feeling of separation. Socially bred loneliness is equal to a kind of estrangement from others in the culture. In this country it might be called the "isolated American."

Philip Slater,[2] referring to loneliness on the social level, points to three human desires that are inhibited by American culture and thus lead to loneliness. First is the desire for community, or the longing to live in harmony and trust with all other human beings. This desire is frustrated by the value our culture places on competition at the expense of actions of cooperation, which are viewed as relatively weaker. Even when we cooperate it is often with the goal of doing better than another group.

Second is the wish for engagement with social and interpersonal problems, which is frustrated by the culture's encouragement of the tendency to avoid unpleasantness and long-term involvement. It is the same as the tendency to resist change that Toffler and others warn about.

The third frustrated desire is for dependence. We are rewarded continually for being independent and not having to ask others to do "favors" for us. It begins at birth by such practices as early weaning (breast feeding is unusual after six months of age) and premature toilet training. The United States has a traditional unwritten committment to individualism—and rugged individualism at that. This value may be the combined result of capitalism and pioneerism (imperialism?). We are taught to make it on our own and outdo all competitors.

Slater points to yet another concept of culturally inflicted loneliness. It is that individual human worth is valued less than the social good. This is manifested in a number of ways, and one of them is war, in which deaths of thousands of people are justified by the need to maintain a "nation." Easy killings devalue human life. In industry the hiring and firing of employees depends upon economic conditions; people will be replaced by machines if machines increase profits.

Loneliness is also spawned by such cultural practices as sexism, racism and all other divisions that separate people by inborn or other distinctions. Belonging to one group means exclusion from another, a definition of alienation. We may be split into such dichotomies as male/female, black (et al.)/white, liberal/conservative, and humanist/scientist. At present it seems almost as if two separate cultures are operating: the old system, predicated on technology, property rights, competition and the importance of production and characterized by violent secret striving, is opposed by the new system, in which human needs, personal choice, cooperation, consumer's rights, openness and gratification of desires take precedence. Of course there are many overlaps between the two, but a pattern can be seen. The important point is that the differences tend to separate and alienate people.

As interesting and widespread as cultural loneliness may be, we must deal on a daily basis with personal loneliness and alienation. The primary consideration in the predicament of loneliness is that as completely unique individuals all human beings must live and die alone. We are alone in our bodies, separated from each other by the cells and tissues that compose them. As infants and children we all have felt the basic fear of abandonment, of having to travel through the unknown without mother or father. This is another reason why it is so important to give children, early in life, the security and affection they need and ask for.

As frightening as loneliness may be, and as isolated as we may feel, we must learn to cope with it. We are all we've got, so we had better learn to like ourselves and be in touch with who we are. Loneliness is not to be equated with physical aloneness; it is a mental state. It is possible to be lonely in the midst of a crowd; in fact it is a common feeling. Alienation and loneliness can occur as well in school with peers, at home with family or in bed with a lover. Conversely, loneliness may be overcome in solitude.

Everyone is lonely to some extent at certain times. The point is not to flee from loneliness by surrounding oneself with friends and other people, as many do, but to come to terms with it and learn about living as a separate person. One way to do this is by being alone—completely alone—for periods of time. Thoreau sought physical aloneness at Walden

Loneliness is a feeling, not a physical situation.

Pond and became less lonely for it. This aloneness of choice brought him closer to nature, enabling him to investigate his self and the world around him and to place things in proper perspective. Being free, at least periodically, from the judgments of other people allows us the time we need to get to know ourselves and find purpose in life.

Certain conditions are more likely to foster loneliness. Some are natural but most are human-made. Traveling, for example, increases the feeling of separateness by placing the person in an alien environment. This is particularly true when one travels to a place where another language is spoken, because not knowing the language makes it difficult to know what others are feeling and thinking. The elderly have come to know loneliness just by living in a youth-oriented culture; many of them feel almost like aliens in a strange land. People who have power are frequently lonely because they cannot trust others if they are to maintain their power.

DEPRESSION

Loneliness, particularly when it is very intense or when we are unable to cope with it, is at the heart of despair and depression.

Depression is something we all feel at one time or another, although it cannot be accurately described. Such terms as "bummed out," "down" or "in the dumps" just do not communicate how a person feels. There are different levels of intensity for the depressed state; some are easy to cope with, whereas others are overwhelming.

Knowing that everyone gets depressed or that we have been depressed like this before does not ameliorate our depression. However, it does help us through this temporary state of mind and body. Experience is a wonderful teacher, and each period of extreme sorrow or depression helps teach us to judge its transiency and to see that things can work out and get better. It also helps to establish a firm philosophy of life so that in despair life does not seem completely meaningless. It is almost like traversing the hills and valleys, knowing that every depth will be followed by a peak. We can control our lives so that the valleys are not too drastically low and the peaks rise higher and higher. This is part of what Dunn refers to as a higher level of wellness and what Maslow calls self-actualization. Otherwise, each time we hit a peak we would have only the depths of depression to look forward to. Realistically, we have to expect times of depression, but we can do so with the knowledge that the depression will not be too intense and that we will be in control of our actions.

Sometimes it is difficult to overcome depression on our own, and professional helpers—counselors, psychologists and psychiatrists—are needed. In such cases, we depend upon their experiences to help show us the way or to analyze the depression so that we can consciously cope with it. Frequently, we rely upon nonprofessionals (e.g., friends) to help us reflect upon our depression and work through it. However, as families become smaller, more dispersed and less close knit and as friendships become more transient, there are fewer close friends and relatives readily available.

CRISIS

As problems become too great to handle, we move into crisis situations. A crisis is any hazardous event or crucial time in life that cannot be managed with tools that previously worked. It is a problem that has become unsolvable, at least temporarily. This leads to further anxieties that hamper our ability to think through solutions, and we are unable to take independent action.

Crisis, then, is an upset in the steady state, an imbalance between the level of difficulty of the problem (for that individual) and the available set of coping skills. This imbalance persists until some alternative is found. It is generally agreed that intense crises usually last from one to about eight weeks.

Figure 4–3 shows how crisis progresses from normal stress to a continued state of disequilibrium and crisis. Once the source of stress is present and the homeostatic condition is upset, there is the need to restore

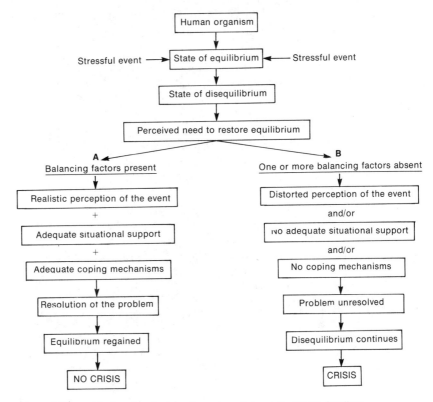

Figure 4–3 Paradigm: Effect of balancing factors in a stressful event. (From Aguilera, Donna C., Janice M. Messick, and Marlene S. Farrell: *Crisis Intervention.* St. Louis, The C. V. Mosby Co., 1970, p. 52.)

balance; this is the first step in the problem-solving process. From this point, any of a number of factors can lead to either successful solution or eventual crisis.

The first factor is the person's level of awareness of the event and its relationship to the feeling of stress. If we do not know where tension comes from, it is difficult to deal with it, although various tension-reducing techniques may alleviate discomfort. For example, aspirins may reduce tension headache, but unless the source of the tension is understood, the headache cannot be dealt with permanently.

The second factor in crisis development is the support available from close friends, relatives or anyone else involved in the problem. Adequate situational support consists of any empathetic, listening person who can assist, in any way, in coping.

Finally, each one of us has a set of mechanisms that help us reduce tension and cope with anxiety and depression. Although everyone has the same available mechanisms, we each develop certain ones that fit our personalities. Those that were tried and proved successful in the past will be used again. If our coping skills are not developed, however, our stressful events are likely to escalate into crises. Problems will remain unsolved, and disequilibrium will continue.

The level of individual crisis, then, is somewhat dependent upon past stressful experiences and how successfully they were resolved. For example, suppose you are out of money and are going to school full time. How to get money for food, clothing, entertainment and other needs may be a problem you never faced before and could easily lead to overwhelming frustration and depression. But if you had worked out similar problems in the past, you would be able to follow many paths to possible solutions. You could cut down on school hours, increase work hours (you would need to learn how to get an adequate job), cut down on some expenses (such as rent), investigate student loans and so on. The intensity of crisis may therefore run the gamut from a very temporary controlled situation to a "can't cope" neurosis.

Crisis can be divided into two types: situational (environmental) and developmental (maturational). *Situational*, or *environmental*, crisis occurs when an acute stressful event becomes overwhelming and causes disequilibrium. The event is not perceived as an ego threat, purposeful problem-solving energy is not mobilized, and great anxiety eventually occurs. These stressful events are quite individualistic in the sense that a situation that overwhelms one person might seem normal to someone else and easy to handle for another. Some common situational crises are death and grief, divorce, change of role status, physical illness, birth, and relocation of job or residence.

Developmental, or *maturational*, crisis is associated with moving from one stage of growth to another. In this sense, it is more long term than environmental crisis, since it is not precipitated by a relatively unexpected stressful event. Nevertheless, it follows the same pattern of equilibrium imbalance, perception, support and coping. Attending college, for example, is a normal time of crisis, since it has the stressful ingredients of being in a new environment, being away from home, family and close friends (often for the first time) and having to face a future of independence and responsibility. It is always somewhat frightening to wonder about how one will make it on her own or his own for "the rest of my life." Examples of other developmental crises are parenthood, marriage, puberty, entry into kindergarten, and old age.

There is also a phenomenon of anticipatory crisis that occurs before many events and can be just as disabling as crisis produced by the stressful event. It occurs because the stress is perceived as very great before the actual event. Anticipatory crisis may happen prior to any big decision-making, before important examinations or at Christmas and other holidays. Usually it is a matter of gearing up for coming events in order to be prepared to experience them; this is a useful, energy-gathering mechanism. However, for some it can get out of hand and mushroom into a crisis; this is commonly seen in the panic reaction to final examinations or the post-holiday depression, when suicides and other self-destructive actions occur.

Common Intervention Techniques*

Technique	Description
Assertive Training	Reducing anxiety through affirmative statements and action
Confrontation	Presenting the client's problem and feelings directly to him/her
Environmental Manipulation	Removing or changing certain disorganizing elements from the environment in order to deal with the emotional disturbance
Feedback and Interpretation	Adding to the client's awareness of the psychological processes in operation by interpreting their responses and pointing out why they act as they do
Modeling	Showing others successful behavior in similar situations
Reassurance	Letting the person know that, no matter what, he or she is okay
Relaxation Training	Not a solution to the problem but a way of getting physical and mental relaxation so that other methods can work more easily
Self-Disclosure	Both the counselor and client disclose certain appropriate personal material as a way to opening
Ventilation	Allowing for a release of emotions in an acceptable, nondestructive manner; getting things off one's chest

*From Getz, William, Allen E. Wiesen, Stan Sue and Amy Ayers. *Fundamentals of Crisis Counseling.* Lexington, Massachusetts: D.C. Heath and Company, 1974, pp. 32–41.

CRISIS INTERVENTION

In recent years, there has been a rapid expansion of intervention clinics or centers to help people cope with crises. The purpose of crisis intervention is simply to reestablish equilibrium, not to engage in any long-term therapy. Crisis intervention provides the necessary situational support and helps the person utilize appropriate coping skills to solve problems. Crisis counselors can also help the person to gain a realistic view of the situation.

Crisis centers with such acronyms as HELP, WE CARE, FRIENDS and LIFELINE had their origin as suicide prevention centers and expanded their services to handle drug crises and other acute conditions. They use a variety of techniques, either alone or in combination, depending upon the skills of the counselor and the requirements of the client.

DEATH: THE ULTIMATE LOSS

What is death? Is it truly inevitable? Why, then are we constantly seeking immortality? Is death just a thought, a conceptualization or intellectualization? Or is it more involved, with gut level feelings—emo-

"Ring around the roses," an old children's game played during the great plague in Europe to mock death.

tions? Is death like pre-birth? What were you before you were born? What is your concept of death—and of time?

The list of wonderments and questions goes on and on, but they are unanswerable, because death has a uniqueness based on our inability to experience it and still live. Some claim to have "died" and returned to life, but these deaths have been so few and lasted for such a short time, that no conclusive reports about afterlife exist.

The concept of death is relative and depends upon the developmental level of the individual. The child's view of death is different from the adult's. According to Kastenbaum and Aisenberg,[3] infants up to two years old have no real concept of death other than that things may be present one moment and gone the next, as when they play peek-a-boo. From age two to five years, death is recognized but is not understood as being permanent; death may seem synonymous with sleep. From age five to about nine years, children see death as a personification, such as an angel, a skeleton or perhaps a "death-man." After age ten years, children know death as final and inevitable. They understand their own mortality.

The concept of death is predicated not only on chronological development but also on our spiritual and psychological orientation. Therefore, it is constantly and gradually being altered and depends upon time, place and social context. In this sense, then, our attitudes and feelings about dying and death are situational. Certainly our feelings when discussing death in a classroom, on an intellectual, detached level, are different from those we have about it with close friends and family. Sometimes we feel ready to die, but at other times death anxiety is quite high.

The primary phenomenon of death is that it represents the final separation. Although it is a loss that is greater than any we can know, we have experienced its qualities and characteristics when we have cherished something and lost it. Death may involve the loss of ego, body,

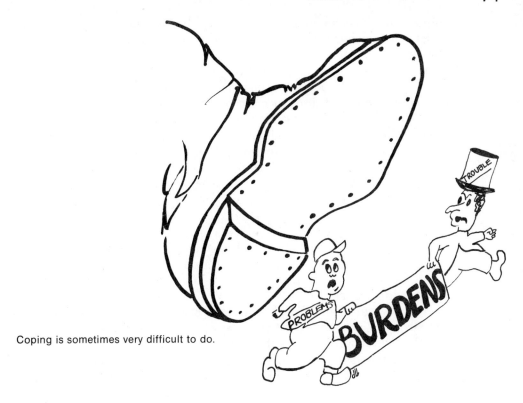

Coping is sometimes very difficult to do.

others or the opportunity for experience. Although loss is usually an unwanted experience, eventually we must lose everything we possess. The quality of having necessitates not having, since nothing is permanent. Loss is necessary for growth, and death may be seen as the final stage of growth.[4] In order to grow, you continually die and are reborn. Each time we go through the process of losing something or someone, we grow and become more ready to experience our own dying. Therefore, loss is ultimately a beneficial learning experience, even though it is undoubtedly painful.

Elisabeth Kübler-Ross has worked with hundreds of dying patients and their families in an attempt to understand the psychological changes that take place when a person learns she or he is terminally ill and about to die. The stages she describes are the same as those we all experience when faced with the loss of a prized object or loved one. Not all people go through these steps in textbook fashion; everyone proceeds at an individual pace and style. However, Kübler-Ross does identify the important processes. Remember, they are only a guideline to understanding the dying process, not a rigid, fixed format.

Denial is the initial reaction to any loss. If your bicycle were stolen, your immediate response would be something like, "Where else could I have parked it?" A person who learns that cancer will soon kill him or her first entertains thoughts that it was misdiagnosed, it will be easily cured, or it will not be fatal. The initial denial is a feeling of isolation and helplessness. It is an attempt to avoid reality, like hoping we are in the midst of a dream and normal conditions will be resumed when we awake. The denial may take many forms; we may refuse to believe the illness actually exists, or we may deny mortality altogether.

Anger, the next coping mechanism, is the outlet of resentment over being the victim of death. Once the individual faces the reality of dying, then existing rage must be handled. The object of this anger may be whoever happens to be available. People suffering great loss do not always rationally manifest their anger. A nurse or orderly in the hospital may incur the patient's wrath only because that professional is well, energetic and able to function. It is the expression of envy that accompanies seeing everyone else alive and enjoying life.

Bargaining, not a major stage in dying, usually follows anger and is an unrealistic plea to go on living. This frequently takes the form of a religious prayer — if God will let me live longer, then I will repent, or some other promise is given. Patients may often put their physicians in the role of God by bargaining with them ("Doctor, if I stop smoking now, will you cure my lung cancer?").

Depression is the fourth stage. It may set in shortly after the knowledge of loss or it may be delayed; but it follows the feelings of isolation and loneliness. It is the depression of having to travel this path of death alone. It is at this point that those who come in contact with the dying person, whether in a personal or a professional capacity, physically touch or show other expressions of togetherness. A terminally ill person desperately needs the feel of another warm, human body to help overcome the isolation and subsequent depression.

Acceptance, the last stage of dying, is a reestablishment of contact with reality in a constructive way. Depression, although it also involves facing reality, leaves a person helpless. Acceptance allows action. The negative side of acceptance is resignation, and it may be that depression leads only to resigning oneself to the fate of death. It is hoped that people will advance to the acceptance stage so that they may participate in their dying actively and with full awareness.

Kübler-Ross identified another emotion operating throughout all the stages — hope. It is generally the hope that death will not come. Not all the stages may occur in sequential order, and some stages (e.g., bargaining) may be omitted altogether. In addition, people may go through one stage only to regress later. Many people die before they can reach the last stage because they do not have the skills, they do not have help or they die soon after learning about their terminal condition.

Besides looking at death as loss or separation, we can also examine possible styles of dying. A person may die passively as a nonparticipant, or actively, participating until the final moment of life. Death may be acute/violent or chronic/degenerative. Grieving is particularly difficult in the case of a sudden death, such as by accident, since there is no preparatory time for anticipatory grief. We may die knowingly, fully aware of the processes we are going through, or unknowingly, such as in a coma. Death may occur in the home, the hospital (the usual place) or anywhere; a common fear is that of dying in a public street, where everyone may observe this private act. Death may be personal (e.g., at home) or impersonal (in a hospital). Finally, from a cultural point of view, death may be natural or tragic.

In the death-denying culture of the Western world, most deaths are considered tragic, particularly when they occur prematurely. Most of all, though, we die according to the prevailing culture. Through literature, art, movies and television we have learned that the hero's death is admirable, to die like a martyr is noble, and to panic in the face of death is cowardly.

Causes of death may be classified into four general categories:

Natural — nonintentional deaths from old age or illness, considered a normal process

Accidental — may be truly accidental or involve a subconscious intentional self-destructive wish to some extent

Suicide — intentional or subintentional killing of oneself

Homicide — intentional killing of another, including war deaths, capital punishment and mercy killing

For obvious legal, medical and practical reasons, it is important to be able to determine the actual moment of death. Nevertheless, a universally accepted definition of death has not been found. Probably the most widely accepted definition is that of brain death. The Institute of Society, Ethics and the Life Sciences has defined death as "an irreversible cessation of spontaneous brain functions."[5] Biological death may be more broadly defined as the permanent cessation of every vital function. Until recently, the cessation of heart beat, or heart death, was the usual confirmation of death. There may also exist a condition of psychological death, in which the heart is still functioning and brain waves may be recorded but the individual is ostensibly in a vegetative state.

Criteria for determining when a person really is dead became more complex as it became more important to be precise. The advent of organ transplants has made it imperative to be able to pronounce a person dead as quickly as possible after she or he has actually died so that organs designated for transplant can be as fresh as possible. In addition, there is the possibility of keeping the body of a legally dead person functioning so that the organs can be used for transplant in the future. Medical schools may also use functioning cadavers for training and experimentation, such as to perform new surgeries or to test drugs. As we learn more about how to control the human body, we may be able to make more choices concerning the circumstances of where and how we die.

All this talk about the use of dead bodies and structuring our own dying is very new and therefore uncomfortable. It is uncomfortable also because our basic attitude toward death is fear, and it takes a great deal of conscious effort to overcome this fear.

Fear of death includes concern not only about one's own mortality but also about the effect someone else's death may have on our lives. For ourselves, we may feel apprehension about what afterlife may hold in store for us, we may be afraid of the physical and psychological pain of the dying process and we may fear loss of existence as a single, whole

Fear	Self	Other
1. After death	Fear of death as punishment (heaven-hell) Fear of the unknown Fear of what will happen to the body	Fear of retaliation (associated with guilt of wishing another dead)
2. Event of dying	Fear of pain and suffering Indignity of dying or psychological pain	Vicariousness—watching others suffering, seeing disintegration of body and mind
3. Cessation	I am not (nonbeing) Missing "good" times	Abandonment Self-vulnerability

Figure 4–4   Fear-of-death matrix.

entity. Some common fears of death and dying that people have are:

1. growing old—although this is not a death fear per se, it is related
2. the unknown—similar to fear of the future
3. decay—disintegration of the body to nothingness
4. what happens to the body after death—it may be eaten by worms or abused in some way
5. irreversibility—as far as we know, dead is dead
6. loss of pleasure—and, conversely, loss of suffering; both mean loss of feeling
7. losing time—time runs out on life; the clock never stops running
8. loss of self-control and self—the realization that the chemical constituents of our body are worth no more than one dollar (probably less than 90 cents by now)
9. cessation of thought—we can no longer enjoy experiences
10. the act of dying—helplessness, indignity of being weak and dependent
11. the future of those who depend upon us

All these fears, although they might not always manifest themselves overtly, are present to a lesser or greater extent. The intensity with which these fears are felt may be quite low or high enough to interfere with the ability to consider the subject of dying. Regarding the death of self, Kastenbaum has listed seven important facts in the realization that "I" will die.[6]

1. I am an individual with a life, therefore I will die.
2. I belong to a species with the characteristic of death.
3. Intellectually, I know death is certain.
4. There are many causes of death, I cannot evade them all.
5. Death will occur in the future, I do not know when.
6. Death is final and certain.
7. Death is the ultimate separation.

Perhaps it might bring some of these points home if you were to fantasize about the circumstances of your own death. What might be the

CERTIFICATE OF DEATH

STATE OF CALIFORNIA—DEPARTMENT OF HEALTH
OFFICE OF THE STATE REGISTRAR OF VITAL STATISTICS

STATE FILE NUMBER | LOCAL REGISTRATION DISTRICT AND CERTIFICATE NUMBER

DECEDENT PERSONAL DATA
1A. NAME OF DECEASED—FIRST NAME | 1B. MIDDLE NAME | 1C. LAST NAME | 2A. DATE OF DEATH—MONTH, DAY, YEAR | 2B. HOUR M.
3. SEX | 4. COLOR OR RACE | 5. BIRTHPLACE (STATE OR FOREIGN COUNTRY) | 6. DATE OF BIRTH | 7. AGE (LAST BIRTHDAY) YEARS | IF UNDER 1 YEAR: MONTHS, DAYS | IF UNDER 24 HOURS: HOURS, MINUTES
8. NAME AND BIRTHPLACE OF FATHER | 9. MAIDEN NAME AND BIRTHPLACE OF MOTHER
10. CITIZEN OF WHAT COUNTRY | 11. SOCIAL SECURITY NUMBER | 12. MARRIED, NEVER MARRIED, WIDOWED, DIVORCED (SPECIFY) | 13. NAME OF SURVIVING SPOUSE (IF WIFE, ENTER MAIDEN NAME)
14. LAST OCCUPATION | 15. NUMBER OF YEARS IN THIS OCCUPATION | 16. NAME OF LAST EMPLOYING COMPANY OR FIRM (IF SELF EMPLOYED, SO STATE) | 17. KIND OF INDUSTRY OR BUSINESS

PLACE OF DEATH
18A. PLACE OF DEATH—NAME OF HOSPITAL OR OTHER IN-PATIENT FACILITY | 18B. STREET ADDRESS—(STREET AND NUMBER, OR LOCATION) | 18C. INSIDE CITY CORPORATE LIMITS (SPECIFY YES OR NO)
18D. CITY OR TOWN | 18E. COUNTY | 18F. LENGTH OF STAY IN COUNTY OF DEATH YEARS | 18G. LENGTH OF STAY IN CALIFORNIA YEARS

USUAL RESIDENCE (IF DEATH OCCURRED IN INSTITUTION, ENTER RESIDENCE BEFORE ADMISSION)
19A. USUAL RESIDENCE—STREET ADDRESS (STREET AND NUMBER OR LOCATION) | 19B. INSIDE CITY CORPORATE LIMITS (SPECIFY YES OR NO) | 20. NAME AND MAILING ADDRESS OF INFORMANT
19C. CITY OR TOWN | 19D. COUNTY | 19E. STATE

PHYSICIAN'S OR CORONER'S CERTIFICATION
21A. CORONER: I HEREBY CERTIFY THAT DEATH OCCURRED AT THE HOUR, DATE AND PLACE STATED ABOVE FROM THE CAUSES STATED BELOW AND THAT I HAVE HELD ON THE REMAINS OF DECEASED AS REQUIRED BY LAW AN: (INVESTIGATION OR INQUEST)
21B. PHYSICIAN: I HEREBY CERTIFY THAT DEATH OCCURRED AT THE HOUR, DATE, AND PLACE STATED ABOVE FROM THE CAUSES STATED BELOW AND THAT I ATTENDED THE DECEASED: FROM (ENTER MONTH, DAY, YEAR) TO (ENTER MONTH, DAY, YEAR) AND I LAST SAW THE DECEASED ALIVE ON (ENTER MONTH, DAY, YEAR)
21C. PHYSICIAN OR CORONER—SIGNATURE AND DEGREE OR TITLE | 21D. DATE SIGNED
21E. ADDRESS | 21F. PHYSICIAN'S CALIFORNIA LICENSE NUMBER

FUNERAL DIRECTOR AND LOCAL REGISTRAR
22A. SPECIFY BURIAL, ENTOMBMENT OR CREMATION | 22B. DATE | 23. NAME OF CEMETERY OR CREMATORY | 24. EMBALMER—SIGNATURE (IF BODY EMBALMED) LICENSE NUMBER
25. NAME OF FUNERAL DIRECTOR (OR PERSON ACTING AS SUCH) | 26. IF NOT CERTIFIED BY CORONER, WAS THIS DEATH REPORTED TO CORONER? (SPECIFY YES OR NO) | 27. LOCAL REGISTRAR—SIGNATURE | 28. DATE RECEIVED FOR REGISTRATION BY LOCAL REGISTRAR

MEDICAL AND HEALTH DATA

CAUSE OF DEATH
29. PART I. DEATH WAS CAUSED BY: ENTER ONLY ONE CAUSE PER LINE FOR A, B, AND C
IMMEDIATE CAUSE (A)
CONDITIONS, IF ANY, WHICH GAVE RISE TO THE IMMEDIATE CAUSE (A), STATING THE UNDERLYING CAUSE LAST.
DUE TO, OR AS A CONSEQUENCE OF (B)
DUE TO, OR AS A CONSEQUENCE OF (C)
APPROXIMATE INTERVAL BETWEEN ONSET AND DEATH
30. PART II: OTHER SIGNIFICANT CONDITIONS—CONTRIBUTING TO DEATH BUT NOT RELATED TO THE IMMEDIATE CAUSE GIVEN IN PART IA | 31. WAS OPERATION OR BIOPSY PERFORMED FOR ANY CONDITION IN ITEMS 29 OR 30? (SPECIFY OPERATION AND/OR BIOPSY) | 32A. AUTOPSY (SPECIFY YES OR NO) | 32B. IF YES, WERE FINDINGS CONSIDERED IN DETERMINING CAUSE OF DEATH? (SPECIFY YES OR NO)

INJURY INFORMATION
33. SPECIFY ACCIDENT, SUICIDE OR HOMICIDE | 34. PLACE OF INJURY (SPECIFY HOME, FARM, FACTORY, FREEWAY, HIGHWAY, STREET, OFFICE BUILDING, ETC.) | 35. INJURY AT WORK (SPECIFY YES OR NO) | 36A. DATE OF INJURY—MONTH, DAY, YEAR | 36B. HOUR M.
37A. PLACE OF INJURY (STREET AND NUMBER OR LOCATION AND CITY OR TOWN) | 37B. DISTANCE FROM PLACE OF INJURY TO USUAL RESIDENCE, ITEM 19. MILES | 38. WERE LABORATORY TESTS DONE FOR DRUGS OR TOXIC CHEMICALS (SPECIFY YES OR NO) | 39. WERE LABORATORY TESTS DONE FOR ALCOHOL? (SPECIFY YES OR NO)
40. DESCRIBE HOW INJURY OCCURRED (ENTER SEQUENCE OF EVENTS WHICH RESULTED IN INJURY. NATURE OF INJURY SHOULD BE ENTERED IN ITEM 29)

STATE REGISTRAR
A. | B. | C. | D. | E. | F.

VS 11 (9-73)

Figure 4–5 Certificate of death.

cause of your death? When would it occur? How would you have your body disposed of? Where will you be at the moment of death? How will your completed death certificate look? If you could design your death certificate, what would it look life? What kinds of information would it include?

How did each of us develop our fears and attitudes about death? They certainly were not inborn. As a matter of act, Freud claimed that the instinct of death, or what he called thanatos, is present at birth. It could be that this death wish had to have some sort of culturally accepted outlet, and so our responses have been conditioned or learned from society, particularly from our parents. Part of it probably stems from separation anxieties when a parent was not able to minister to our every need. We should consider several relevant questions about the development of our fear of death: How does this aversion start? How is this fear expressed in thought, feelings and behavior? What is the distinction between psychotic, neurotic and normal fear of death, and where would we be on such a hypothetical scale? What individual differences are there in reacting to the various objects of fear? (Who shows what fears?) What do we fear most about death? Finally, and perhaps of most practical importance, what is the role of fear of death in our lives?

In an attempt to overcome the fear of death and oblivion, people resort to many means to achieve immortality. For example, cities and countries are replete with statues and other monuments bearing the names of famous (usually rich or powerful) people. Some monuments are built posthumously, and others by people while they are still living. Many people use money as their monument, occasionally trying, literally, to take it with them by having their jewels and other wealth buried with their bodies in a sarcophagus. Mummifying has been practiced for thousands of years; the modern version is to freeze the body through cryogenics. There are a number of dead bodies "on ice" presently, although it is doubtful that they can ever be brought back to life.

Organ transplants and other means of prolonging physical existence are ways of trying to overcome the fear of death. So is the practice of trying to have male offspring in order to continue the family name. It has been a long-standing value in this male-dominated world, to have a son. Also, the seeking of personal fame is done partially to gain a degree of immortality; this may be achieved through induction into some Hall of Fame or Who's Who. Generally speaking, there are four classifications of how we deal with the death fear in life:

1. Protest—This may take the form of artistic protest or some other statement.

2. A commitment to some cause.

3. Seeking a deeper meaning of life.

4. Developing a mystical belief in the unreality of death (or perhaps it is the reality).

Death as a negative concept is more common in Western than in Eastern societies. Life is depicted as a God-given gift, and death is therefore evil and equated with sin. It is almost as if we had a societal obsession with achieving immortality. The medical profession, in whose hands lie the taking and giving of life, sees death as a failure. A physician's ultimate task is to maintain life, and death is a failure to achieve this task. Obviously, such failure is inevitable in medicine, at least in regard to this one criterion.

In our society, we have turned away from facing and understanding death. The aged, who as a group are closest to death, are often no longer in the family structure. They live isolated from the young, learning population. Children and young adults have very low mortality rates compared with previous decades because of advances in health services and medical care. This all creates the fantasy that life is eternal. In addition, harsh reality of death is masked by elaborate funeral ceremonies, in which a play is staged in funeral homes and is directed by morticians (funeral directors). Religion contributes to this avoidance by focusing on the hereafter rather than on the event.

It is hoped that by studying death and dying, people will learn to participate in the process and work through it rather than to resist and try futilely to overcome it. It is a matter of being ready to face death at all times. By overcoming the fear of death, we can develop the courage and strength necessary to act spontaneously and with freedom. Reconciling ourselves to death will cause us to reach out to life rather than to withdraw, since we are no longer obsessed with constantly protecting ourselves. Behavior will be more decisive, honest and natural, eliminating the hypocrisy that comes with fear of failure. The knowledge that death will eventually come makes us aware that petty things in life are unimportant. Acknowledging death allows us to get to the point of life and to focus on the meaning of living.

Orville Kelly, a former journalist from Burlington, Iowa, started a group called Make Today Count for terminally ill patients and their families. When he learned he had incurable cancer, he felt a need to meet with others in a similar circumstance in order to help overcome isolation and loneliness. This group is now nationwide and has hundreds of chapters. A common phenomenon reported by Kelly and others is that it feels good to have accepted death and not to have to worry about the consequences of one's actions. It is the important and fulfilling task of getting one's affairs in order without having to be devious or dishonest.

In order for you to begin to get in touch with your feelings about death and dying, a list of 20 questions has been provided. Such a list could be much longer, of course, and you could be asked to go into greater depth, but these are basic questions to consider about your feelings and their origin.

Some personal questions about death and dying

1. Who died in your first personal loss due to death?
2. How was death talked about in your family?
3. To what extent do you believe in life after death?
4. What would you like done with your body when you die?
5. How often do you think about death?
6. When would you like to die?
7. When do you think you will die?
8. How do you feel about dying?
9. What do you fear most about dying?
10. To what extent do you think psychological factors influence death?
11. If you died today, how would the world be different?
12. Would you sacrifice your life for anyone?
13. How would you choose to die?
14. How do you feel about nuclear weapons? War? Capital punishment? Mercy killing?
15. Have you ever though about committing suicide?
16. What experiences have you had with death?
17. If married, would you like to outlive your spouse?
18. How much do you think a funeral should cost?

19. If you had a terminal illness, would you want to be told? How would your life change?

20. How do you feel about answering these questions?

Grief

Now that we have covered the salient questions dealing with death of self, we need to delve into what death of others means to us. There are two basic concerns regarding the death of significant others. The first is the projected concern that it could have been, and in fact one day will be, our death. The second concern, which we will focus on now, is handling the loss and separation of someone who has had a meaningful impact on our lives. This is a matter of dealing with the grief that normally accompanies loss.

The first stage that determines the form and intensity of our grief at the death of others occurs before the person has died; it involves all related experiences prior to the actual death. On one level, learning experiences have taught us the cultural mores for grieving. As children, we learned models of behavior by observing how adults mourn the death of others. By not being allowed to observe funerals and grieving, we learned lessons from being excluded, such as that death is a sacred and solemn occasion. On another level, the first stage of learning to handle grief involves preventive intervention. It is the process that people go through when faced with the loss of a particular person. One example of this is the separation anxiety of childhood; we prepare for the deaths of our parents when we are temporarily separated from them early in life. When a person has a terminal illness, however, and there is ample warning time, we go through a period of anticipatory grief. In cases of sudden death there may be no anticipatory grief.

The second stage of dealing with grief involves the act of dying—participating with the other in the dying process. This may simply be allowing that significant other to die as she or he likes, or we may hold, caress, talk with or just be close to the person at the time of death. The optimal situation would be one in which all concerned parties faced death openly and shared their anxieties and fears in order to be able to cope with and overcome them and to function fully in the act of dying and separating.

The last stage in handling grief has been called postvention by the eminent thanatologist Edwin Shneidman. During this period the bereaved person must put his or her life together without the deceased. It involves the immediate intense grief that directly follows death, the prolonged temporary grief that may last from a month to a year or longer and then accepting life without that significant other. There is usually a direct correlation between anticipatory grief and grief after death; the longer the period of anticipatory grief, the less the need for intense mourning.

Whereas bereavement is the separation from some significant other, grief is the pain or suffering accompanying that event, and mourning is the expression of grief. Mourning serves some very functional purposes and helps to emancipate oneself from any bonds the deceased may still hold. Sincere, mournful weeping, for example, helps work out some of the guilt related to the dead person. Guilt feelings may arise from some time during life when we wished, if only figuratively and temporarily, that the other person were gone and dead. There may also be some guilt stemming from the fact that we are still living while another is dead.

Mourning also sets the point of demarcation from which we may start to readjust to a new environment devoid of that significant other. If we are truly grieved, then appropriate mourning will allow us to form new relationships eventually. This may involve restructuring relationships with current acquaintances, friends and relatives and also meeting new people. Another teacher of death education, Dan Leviton, in speaking of the best way to grieve, gives his wife the advice that she should "mourn soon and hard after my death for as long as necessary; donate my body to medical science for organ transplants, the training of novitiate physicians, and cremate the rest keeping costs at a bare minimum; involve yourself in some worthwhile activity or work; and remarry as soon as possible."[7]

People in acute grief usually display a similar syndrome that involves actual bodily disturbances. This commonly takes the form of a tightness in the throat, sighing, loss of appetite, lack of strength and a dry mouth. There may be a preoccupation with a distorted or unrealistic image of the deceased. Just as in the stages of dying, hostility and anger are present. As a matter of fact, any emotions felt will be particularly volatile. There is a loss of social consciousness; dress becomes unimportant, and a general condition of disorganization exists. The customs of visiting the bereaved and providing them with food, friendship and direction are extremely helpful in the period of acute grieving.

Just about every urban community has agencies and services available to give support to grieving or dying people. The Make Today Count group for terminally ill people, their families and others interested has already been mentioned. Dr. Cicely Saunders helped start another community support service for dying patients at St. Christopher's Hospice near London, England. The hospice is a home for dying patients where no heroic life-saving techniques are used and the only medications given are those to prevent pain. The atmosphere is one of happiness and life rather than gloomy depression. As many of the patients as possible live at home, but for those who cannot, their families may stay overnight at the hospice. The first hospice in the United States was established at New Haven, Connecticut, and others are being started all the time.

The fact remains, however, that at present most people die in a hospital, and the last people they see, besides immediate family, are medical personnel. The physician is seen relatively often at first, but less frequently as hope of recovery dwindles. The nurse, of course, sees the patient most often, and as death draws nearer, nurses' aides and orderlies come into more contact with the patient. Even at the time of death, doctors and nurses try to keep the family away from the patient, so people truly do die alone.

EUTHANASIA

The aim of dying, and the phrase that has become exceedingly common, is to "die with dignity." This means to die without pain and anguish and as one chooses. The awareness of dying with dignity has lead to increased interest in the practices of mercy killing and euthanasia. Euthanasia literally means "the good death," but does not involve actually taking someone's life, which is what mercy killing is. Euthanasia is the voluntary choice to discontinue any life-prolonging medical means when existence has become excruciatingly painful or marginal at best. Figure 4–6 shows a living will; it is used by the Euthanasia Society of America to express one's philosophy while in good health and not under the pressures of illness and doctors.

The questions of euthanasia are both ethical and legal. On an ethical basis, we must define the right to die and establish who is to determine who will die. Legally, we are faced with what is the true definition of death, and whether the physician's or nurse's involvement is an act of omission or a direct, purposeful commission. Physicians who choose not to participate in euthanasia generally give fear of liability and legal ramifications as reasons. The ethical arguments take into account religious dictates and ultimate intentional taking of human lives that are deemed unfit. Opinions about euthanasia may seem simple at first glance, but like abortion, it is a complex situation, with many people on either side of the controversy.

HOMICIDE AND SUICIDE

There are other issues and happenings that must be examined in order to form a full view of death. These include war, capital punishment, genocide and the dropping of atomic bombs on Hiroshima and Nagasaki. Rather than go into each of them separately (each does present unique controversial aspects), their common focal point will serve to highlight another consideration—the intentional killing of physically well people. Judgment as to whether killing may ever be justified will not be made in this book; it is something that each of us must reconcile one way or another. From one point of view, if death is seen as a transient condition, perhaps killing undesirable or threatening people will serve the good of the whole. Another extreme holds that it would be better to be killed or enslaved rather than be involved, actively or passively, in killing. In forming and becoming aware of one's attitudes and values, the important thing is first to consider and discuss these phenomena with others; personal judgments can then be made.

Another issue involving killing is the taking of one's own life—suicide. Each of us (up until now, at least) has continued to reaffirm our decision to keep on living. Generally speaking, however, suicide does not have philosophical causes; such suicides are extremely rare. The preponderance of suicides are done out of despair and desperation. They

TO MY FAMILY, MY PHYSICIAN, MY ATTORNEY, MY CLERGYMAN
TO ANY MEDICAL FACILITY IN WHOSE CARE I HAPPEN TO BE
TO ANY INDIVIDUAL WHO MAY BECOME RESPONSIBLE FOR MY
  HEALTH, WELFARE OR AFFAIRS

Death is as much a reality as birth, growth, maturity and old age—it is the one certainty of life. If the time comes when I,_____ can no longer take part in decisions for my own future, let this statement stand as an expression of my wishes, while I am still of sound mind.

If the situation should arise in which there is no reasonable expectation of my recovery from physical or mental disability, I request that I be allowed to die and not be kept alive by artificial means or "heroic measures." I do not fear death itself as much as the indignities of deterioration, dependence, and hopeless pain. I, therefore, ask that medication be mercifully administered to me to alleviate suffering even though this may hasten the moment of death.

This request is made after careful consideration. I hope you who care for me will feel morally bound to follow its mandate. I recognize that this appears to place a heavy responsibility upon you, but it is with the intention of relieving you of such responsibility and of placing it upon myself in accordance with my strong convictions, that this statement is made.

Signed_____

_____   _____
Spouse or Next of Kin   Date

_____   _____
Physician   Witness

_____   _____
Attorney   Witness

_____
Clergyman

Copies of this request have been given to: _____

_____

_____

_____

Figure 4–6   A living will.

result from being unable to cope successfully, and intervention is therefore desirable, provided that follow-up care is available to help bring about successful solutions to problems. Most suicidal people are not fully intent on killing themselves, but they are undecided about living. They usually (about 80 per cent of the time) give warning signs by talking about it or making preliminary feeble and unsuccessful attempts.

Suicide generally follows one of four kinds of crisis: extreme emotional experiences; serious depression, when life seems no longer worth expending energy for; very serious illness; and as an attempt to communicate to or manipulate others. Of course, most people in any of these categories do not resort to suicide, so it is difficult to diagnose someone as being definitely suicidal. We usually see their symptomatic patterns after the fact.

An excellent summary of the pertinent sociological facts of suicide in the United States has been compiled by Lester and Lester:[8]

1. Men tend to complete suicide, while women tend to attempt suicide.

2. For whites, middle and old age are the most common times for suicide, while blacks tend to commit suicide while in their twenties.

3. Cultural factors influence the suicide rate.

4. There is no evidence that any one drug works directly to cause suicide.

5. People who threaten or attempt suicide are more likely than others to subsequently complete suicide.

6. Suicidal people have generally disturbed social relationships.

7. Psychological tests are not good predictors of suicide, but behavioral indicators (like sleep patterns) may be.

8. Suicidal people tend to be rigid in their thinking and tend to think in extremes.

9. Economic depression is followed by an increase in the suicide rate, while war results in a decrease.

10. The weather, the phase of the moon, and activity of sunspots do not affect the suicide rate.

11. Suicide is more common in those who are psychologically disturbed.

THE FUNERAL

The last consideration to be discussed here concerning death is the funeral. Ever since Jessica Mitford wrote her widely read exposé of the funeral industry, *The American Way of Death*, people have become increasingly aware of the difficulties of planning for and carrying out a funeral service within the financial range desired. In other words, it is hard to keep costs down, and it is equally or more difficult to have a memorial service that will please everyone and serve the mourners' real needs.

One factor is that the funeral industry is just that—an industry. As such, mortuaries depend upon showing a financial profit to stay in business. In order to do this, they may sell customers unnecessary extras, such as cement grave linings, the only purpose of which is to keep the lawn from sinking in. Sales people (called funeral directors) try to sell caskets that will bring in the highest profit, and since the family is usually approached at a time of high emotional stress, appropriate sales techniques make it easy to do.

In order for you, as a consumer, to save money, there are a few rules that might be followed.

1. Most important, think ahead or preplan the funeral. Emotionally, this may be difficult to do (have you given this much thought?), but it will save both money and additional grief at the time of death. The easiest way to do this is to join the local Memorial Society (there is usually a small membership fee of about $10) and prearrange the funeral. Cemetary costs

Two common ways of reducing stress.

are not usually included in the Memorial Society fees, but working with this orgnization will save considerable money on funeral service alone.

2. Do not accept an entire professional service package. You might hold a memorial service in a synagogue, a church or another location (beach, mountains, woods and so on) instead of the mortuary chapel. In most states you can decline embalming and cosmetology under most circumstances.

3. Select the simplest and least expensive method of disposing of the body. Cremation does not require purchasing a casket in most states, so it is usually the cheapest way and includes disposal of the ashes. Even less expensive may be donating the body to a medical school. In such cases, many schools will pay all expenses of handling or picking up the body.

The funeral service should be a meaningful experience for the survivors, and therefore should be planned accordingly. More and more people are choosing alternative celebrations for this rite of passage. For example, with families living in various parts of the country, it might be more feasible to wait for summer vacation or Christmas season to gather everyone together for a memorial service. Music need not be confined to funeral dirges, but may include some of the favorites of the deceased.

In addition, funeral directors and others have helped perpetuate taboos of discussing death by using euphemisms. The dead body becomes the remains (or cremains); we do not die, we become deceased or pass on; a coffin is called a casket; and so on. It all comes back to a failure to overcome the fear of death, and consequently hinders optimal functioning.

COPING

To deal with the problems, stresses and other highly emotional situations that face us, we need to develop coping mechanisms. Each person acquires individual sets of coping skills on the basis of what has been tried and has worked in the past. Coping skills allow people to function adequately in the face of adversity, in handling loss, decision making, unexpected disaster, and so on.

Probably the best original source for the enumeration and description of coping mechanisms is Freud. He defined common defenses that form the individual's character traits. These defenses are developed as reactions to events during the stages of growth and development and have been more fully described by Erikson, Murray and other neo-Freudians. Although the developmental phases in which each defense mechanism has its genesis will not be shown here, suffice to say that each originates as a method of coping during a particular stage of growth.

Projection. Handling personal feelings that may lead to guilt or punishment by attributing them to others. This is a method of freeing oneself from potentially harmful impulses or wishes but allowing them to be manifested in another person. This manifestation may not be true but is perceived to be so.

Denial. Failure to perceive reality by denying the existence of threatening objects or events. This has been mentioned previously as the first, simplest response to loss. With this defense awareness is diminished considerably.

Introjection. Taking on the traits of another person either because of the threat of the other person or because of one's own instincts. Hero worship, in which someone takes on the characteristics of an older or more powerful friend or sibling, may be a form of introjection.

Intellectualization. Substituting a societally and personally acceptable reason for one's behavior and wishes for the real, instinctual reasons. This is similar to rationalizing one's action in order to please others and meet their expectations.

Reaction Formation. Focusing on the wishes directly opposite to what one really wants. This defense mechanism is similar to the technique of "paradoxical intention" used by some psychotherapists, in which the person causes to happen exactly what she or he fears. It is as if you were afraid to be obese and therefore became grossly overweight.

Isolation. To separate the connection between cognition and emotions so that we may still be somewhat aware of feelings but not remain threatened. The wishes and desires stay, but we are no longer consciously aware of them.

Undoing. Engaging in certain thoughts or actions in order to cancel out previously threatening thoughts or actions. This may take the form of bargaining (as in that stage of dying), in which a person repents for his or her sins so God will be forgiving and not punishing.

Repression. Remaining unaware of one's instincts in order to avoid anxiety. All threatening cognitive and emotional material is relegated to the unconscious, or forgotten. In psychoanalysis, the technique of dream interpretation is used to bring back repressed matter to a conscious level so that it may be dealt with more directly and satisfactorily.

Sublimation. Instead of following one's instinct, the object (e.g., opposite sexed parent) is substituted for. This involves pursuing socially acceptable sexual partners, and still allows satisfying the libido or sexual drive.

There are many other defense mechanisms, but they have not been identified as originating from a method of coping during any particular developmental stage. For example, we may withdraw from threatening situations, regress to previous infantile behavioral states or compensate for weakness by playing up other strengths.

The pitfall in having these defense mechanisms is that if they are gone we have nothing reliable to help us cope. Therefore, we need to develop strong egos or self-concepts and become as open as possible. Obviously there are limits to openness, and we cannot always follow instinctual behavior. Then defense mechanisms become necessary. It is when we rely on them to the exclusion of direct opening that they become hazardous.

Another way to evaluate coping skills is by the manner in which we go about solving daily problems. The human mind is the computer device we have to serve this function. Halbert Dunn has described eight components of the mind that do our problem solving.[9]

Communication. The more open our communication system is—the more accurate the input, output and integration of information—the more likely we are to have the correct data necessary to solve problems.

Storage. Past experiences, failures and successes, and previously gained knowledge are stored by the brain. As problems arise, we call on this stored material to deal with them. In this regard values that developed when we were young are difficult to change.

Values. Judgments as to which paths to take in our behavior depend in part on the values with which we were reared. This is the cultural part of the psyche, or superego.

Imagination. Although it is commonly thought that creativity and innovation are intangible qualities, they have their genesis in biological phenomena. Imagination provides us with the ability to structure many possible solutions to problems and then decide which is best to try in that situation.

Self-Concept. This equates with ego and allows us to see problems and their solutions in terms of ourselves. To be able to cope well, we need a self-concept that is real or accurate, not one by which we perceive ourselves as more or less than we truly are.

Balance or Integration.   The mechanisms of the mind work constantly to keep us in equilibrium between the inner and outer worlds. The mind is an active participant in the homeostatic process. In fact, it initiates the chain of hormonal action necessary to keep balance.

Maturity in Wholeness.   In order to be effective, all the components of the mind must work together as one. The wholeness of mind, body and spirit must be brought to bear in coping with life's problems.

Purpose.   We do not, or at least should not, live only to maintain equilibrium. Maslow called it self-actualization, and Frankl spoke of the search for meaning. In all of life's situations we need to show a direction so that problem-solving becomes a growing or building process.

Coping does not mean merely "staying afloat." It means actively and creatively using personal skills to grow and develop. The use of coping skills should not be regarded as defensive, but as a positive, constructive mechanism. It is hoped that with such an attitude we can use stress to fulfill life's goals rather than to be overwhelmed by them.

STRESS

The term "stress" has a variety of meanings as used by different people. The average person probably sees stress as an intense situation calling for great amounts of reactive energy. This is not necessarily so. But what can we use for a satisfactory definition?

The person who has done the pioneer work in this area is Hans Selye, a Canadian endocrinologist. He defines stress as "the nonspecific response of the body to any demand made upon it."[10] This definition is based upon the physiological reaction of the body to the presence of a stressor, or stress-producing agent or event. According to Selye,[11] the stress-response action occurs in three stages, which is called the general adaptation syndrome. It should be noted that this triphasic reaction is nonspecific and that the human body is continuously adapting to environmental stressors.

The general adaptation syndrome begins with the introduction of some stressor. In this first stage there is a general alarm reaction that involves the excitation of the hypothalamus portion of the brain by the stressor, which causes the pituitary gland to produce and discharge ACTH (adrenocorticotropic hormone). During this phase, general resistance is lower than normal, and if stress is severe enough, this constitutes the critical period in the disease process. Here, ACTH leads to the secretion of corticoids by the adrenal glands, which in turn elicits specific responses to combat particular stressors.

The second phase is called the stage of resistance. It is here that adaptation to stress takes place. Resistance is significantly higher than normal, and the person is able to think and perform with greater ability than normal.

The third stage, exhaustion, occurs when there is long exposure to the same stressor and the body is no longer able to adjust. Adaptive energy is not strong enough to overcome the stressor. This can be fatal if the signs of the alarm reaction appear again but become irreversible.

Interestingly, the three phases of the general adaptation syndrome have been likened to the three stages of life: childhood, adulthood and aging. During childhood (alarm reaction), resistance is low and response to stress is excessive. Adulthood (stage of resistance) is characterized by increased resistance and enough adaptive energy to cope with most pathogenic stressors. In senility (stage of exhaustion), there is loss of adaptability, high susceptibility to stressors and eventual death.

Stress, as described, is not to be equated with mere nervous tension, although emotional stimuli may activate the general adaptation syndrome. In addition, a stressor may be pleasant or unpleasant. Stress is not something to be avoided, but rather we should be subjected to stress in amounts that we can easily handle.

Imagine if we were to live in a completely stress-free environment. The slightest amount of stress could then be fatal. In the H. G. Wells story "The War of the Worlds," Earth is invaded by aliens from another planet and is nearly conquered by them. Our defeat seems certain until the aliens succumb to the microorganisms in our atmosphere. Having acquired no resistance to these stressors, which they had never before encountered, all the aliens die. Although fictional, this story points out the need to experience various forms of stress in order to strengthen our weaknesses.

It is important to recognize and deal with factors of stress to maintain mental health. We need to learn how to control stress so that we can react appropriately. Just as continued exposure to pathogenic organisms can cause systemic disease, so can we develop ulcers or heart disease, for example, by responding inappropriately to daily psychological and social demands.

RELAXATION TECHNIQUES

There are numerous ways in which we can structure our life styles so that we can cope with undue stress and turn it into a positive, growing experience. The most basic factor is the manner in which we approach life; we must understand how our defense mechanisms work and have realistic perceptions. In addition, there are popular techniques for stress reduction. A few of these will be discussed.

When we lie down or go to sleep, we frequently believe ourselves to be in a state of relaxation, but this may be only partially true. Some muscles of the body may be at ease, but others may be in a very tense or contracted state. This residual tension may manifest itself in the form of irregular breathing, higher pulse rate or blood pressure and slightly observable muscular tension or twitching.

Edmund Jacobson, in *Progressive Relaxation*, described his method of bringing about a more total body relaxation. The aim of progressive relaxation is to learn to relax one group of muscles at a time by intentionally contracting such muscles, then releasing the tension. Ultimately, the most relaxing position will be lying on one's back, with the arms straight at the side, in a quiet place. Starting perhaps with one arm, then the other, the muscles in that arm are tensed, and then the tension is allowed to wane. Actually, the best way to increase tension is to bend or move the arm (or another muscle set) in such a position that some of the muscles will contract. In other words, provide moving tension when possible rather than steady (isometric) tension.

To begin with, the eyes should be gradually closed. Progressive relaxation may then start with the wrist and fingers, for example, moving to the forearm, elbow and upper arm, first on one side and then on the other. The same thing can then be done with the feet and legs, progressing to the trunk, neck and head. Of course, each group of muscles would be relaxed separately. Relaxing the head, for example, would require working on the forehead, brow, eyelids, eyes, visual imagery, cheeks, jaws, lips and then tongue.

Such exercises take time and practice. They would probably be best learned from someone who has had experience with the method. Although this technique is helpful for those who have difficulty relaxing or sleeping, it can benefit anyone. It can also be done while sitting at a desk or in other places, not only in one's bedroom.

The practice of meditation is another method of relaxation that is widely used. Meditation is a passive, receptive exercise aimed at increasing awareness. It is the skill of being quiet and paying attention.

There are quite a variety of techniques used in meditation, some more popular than others, such as transcendental meditation, Zen and Yoga. Generally, however, they all fit into one of two categories: those that restrict awareness, and those that deliberately let stimuli into the consciousness. In either case, the first requirement of meditating is to get into a comfortable position (being able to let go but not fall asleep) in a quiet, calm environment.

Concentrative meditation restricts awareness to one constant object or theme for a period of time. This is called one-pointedness of mind, an example of which is transcendental meditation. Here the object, or mantra, may be a word or phrase that is repeated over again in a melodic rhythm. The focus in a meditative exercise may be the body itself, particularly the center of the body or navel. The meditation may involve concentrating on breathing but does not control the breathing rhythm. Rather, breathing is to be natural, but attention is focused on its in and out rhythm. In the beginning it is difficult to pay continuous close attention to the object, whether it is sound, thought or sight. The undisciplined or "monkey" mind flits from subject to subject as various thoughts and stimuli enter the consciousness. As meditators become more experienced, prolonged, sustained concentration becomes easier.

The other form of meditation involves "letting go" or "going with it" so that we become more sensitive to our environment. To do this one would first get into a comfortable, meditative position, sway back and forth to "settle in," take some deep breaths and start to let go. Sometimes intentional concentration is given to parts of the body for a short time before attending to the chosen technique. Thoughts are not prevented or controlled but flow from one to the other without attempts to manipulate them. Distractions are allowed until attention can be gently brought back to the object of meditation. The objective is to lose ego consciousness and not think in the perspective of "I." The self is forgotten and the outside world of Now opens up. The aim is to experience the sensations of the environment without forming any judgments about it.

Meditation has definite physiological effects upon the body, particularly on respiration and brain activity. Experienced meditators can significantly reduce oxygen consumption and carbon dioxide release by slowing the breathing. Simultaneously, there is a marked change in the electrical activity of the brain. Alpha waves, which are usually predominant when a person is sleeping or otherwise thoroughly relaxed with eyes closed, also dominate during meditation. The resistance of the skin to an electric current has been found to increase during meditation. This greater sensitivity is related to a lowering of anxiety. Finally, as expected, heart beat is lowered while meditating, sometimes to extremely low rates.

When meditation becomes intense, there is a feeling of union with the object of focus. The self becomes lost during the state of contemplation. However, it is not quite the same as nuptial union although it may give the same feeling. It may be closer to what Maslow calls "peak experience," or the feeling of unification and identity at the same time. These are always positive, buoyant states.

The modern, scientific approach to achieving the results of meditation may be seen in biofeedback, the system of learning to control bodily changes (respiration, circulation and so on) through electrically fed back signals. Biofeedback may be used as a deconditioning process whereby a person learns to control responses to threatening stimuli. If someone has anxiety headaches, for example, she or he may be able to read the electrical signals that tell her or him what brain activities are causing headaches to occur. Biofeedback equipment can also record tension in various other parts of the body, and corrective relaxation techniques can then be performed to reduce the specific tension.

Biofeedback research is quite new and is not a reliable tool at present. However, as more research is done, we may be able to pinpoint sources of tension accurately and learn to desensitize the sources of anxiety.

One area of research in which biofeedback is already making discoveries is in the function of the right and left sides of the brain (cerebral cortex). Each of these two sides processes different kinds of information and approaches problem-solving in different ways. It is common knowledge that the right side of the brain controls movement of the left side, and the left side of the brain controls the right side of the body. Hence, a stroke or injury to the left side of the brain will affect movement on the right side of the body.

The left cortical hemisphere, which is connected through the corpus callosum to the right side of the body, tends to be more involved in controlling linear or logical thinking and verbal and mathematical analysis. It processes information sequentially and is the basis of intellect and language. The right side of the brain, on the other hand, appears to be responsible for feeling level activities, aesthetic abilities (art, music and the like) tastes, spatial relations and body image. It is associated with creativity and imagination; but culturally, it is also linked to evil, femininity, the dark side of the I Ching or the Yin of Yin/Yang, sensuousness and so on.

Understanding the anatomy and functions of the split brain allows us to understand more about the duality of the mind. Perhaps it will lead to further knowledge about the physiological basis for Freud's dichotomy of conscious and unconscious mind. The conscious, being accessible to language, may stem from the left side of the brain, whereas the unconscious, not being accessible to verbalization and relying more on body language and voice tone, may stem from the right side of the brain.

The relationship of left and right brain activity to stress reduction may be obvious. If we can comfortably and easily get into predominantly right-sided brain activity, we can accomplish what meditation does. As a matter of fact, that is what probably occurs. By clearing our minds of linear or logical thought processes, we are free to get into holistic right-sided brain experiences.

There are many activities other than meditation that can lead us into right-sided brain activity, and they all seem to involve repetition or some other method of breaking away from patterned thought. For instance, more and more people are becoming running enthusiasts who just cannot do without their daily jog, which usually lasts a minimum of 30 minutes to an hour. The constant rhythm of quickly stepping one foot after another has a hypnotic effect that inhibits left brain thinking. Frequently, people talk about getting off on a "high" from working some sort of crafts activity for long periods of time. It is as if the meditative object were the ceramic being molded or the blanket being crocheted.

William Glasser calls these activities positive addiction, and he describes six criteria to follow in order to become addicted in a beneficial way:[12]

1. It is noncompetitive and requires an hour a day to do.
2. It is easy to do and does not take great mental effort to do well.
3. It can be done alone.
4. It is perceived as having personal value.
5. The addict believes she or he will improve, although achievement need not be objectively measured.
6. It can be done with no self-criticism.

Positive addiction can be risky, however. In addition to being called a nut or a freak, we may get so far into right brain activity that we do not know where we are. For example, the phenomenon of "highway hypnosis" is frequently experienced by motorists who drive long distances on interstate highways or freeways with few environmental distractions; their attention can be diverted so far from the task at hand that they are susceptible to accidents. The same phenomenon may be experienced by runners who run on streets where there is automobile traffic.

CYCLIC RHYTHMS

Just as there is a rhythm to running, and as meditation depends upon the rhythm of breathing and chanting, so too is there a cyclic rhythm to all living things. This rhythm of life is more pervasive in our actions than we can imagine. Certainly the amount of research done on the rhythm of life, although it may seem great, has only begun to scratch the surface of the understanding it influences.

These rhythms, which so deeply but subtly affect us, are brought about by light waves, gravity, electromagnetic forces, atmospheric pressure and sound. We live by the cycles of day and night or light and dark. The moon's phases or revolution and the ebb and flow of the tides affect us. Daily we grow tired and sleep at night and experience restless activity during the day. During an approximately 24-hour period we have constant unnoticeable changes in body temperature (higher in the evening), blood pressure and pulse (lower in the morning), respiration, blood sugar, hemoglobin levels and amino acid levels.

The 24-hour cycle is called a *circadian rhythm*, which literally means "about a day." Our 24-hour clock is actually slightly longer than 24 hours. In experiments performed on people living in caves or compartments away from cultural and other physical time clues, such as light and dark, it was found that the sleep-awake cycle lasted about 25 hours or longer. This situation is termed a "free-running" rhythm. One man who lived in a cavern for 63 days kept a calendar based upon his sleep-awake cycle. When he emerged he thought that he had been there only 38 days. Another man who lives in Philadelphia free-runs in his daily life so that he goes to sleep more than an hour earlier each night, following his body time rather than societal time.

In another experiment in Switzerland, a number of people lived in bunkers, some shielded and others not shielded from magnetic and electrical fields. Although the circadian rhythms of all were longer than 24 hours, those who lived in shielded apartments had a longer period of awakening than those who were not shielded. This suggests that electromagnetic fields might shorten the period of circadian rhythm.

Circadian rhythms can also be observed in plant life, as leaves drop and lift or petals open and close from morning to night. As a matter of fact, Carolus Linnaeus, in the eighteenth century, proposed a flower clock based upon the time of opening and closing of various species. Not all cycles are circadian, however. Rhythms that are shorter than 24 hours are called ultradian, and those that are longer than 24 hours are called infradian. The 90-minute cycles that occur during sleep are examples of ultradian rhythms, whereas monthly menstrual cycles are infradian.

The obvious infradian rhythm of the menstrual cycle has been extensively studied and the symptoms of premenstrual tension have been well described, even to the point where a significant increase in accidents has been noticed during menstruation. Men also undergo monthly changes related to hormonal differences, but they are, of course, not as measurable as the cycles in women. Also of potential importance is the research being done on the effects of light cycles on ovulation. It is believed that light when present at crucial times, may stimulate the release of luteinizing and follicle-stimulating hormones in humans. If this is true, then we could predict and control ovulation as a birth control method.

Circadian rhythms are also helpful in understanding changes in emotions. Emotional rhythms follow both ultradian and infradian patterns. We are in different states in the morning and evening, and fluctuate from week to week (or longer) in moods of depression and elation or tolerance and irritability. One possibility regarding reactions to stress, based upon preliminary animal experimentation, is that trauma experienced in the morning will have far greater effects than if it occurred in the afternoon; this is due to high adrenal hormone concentration in the blood early in the day. Stress during one phase of the cycle may be very damaging, but at other times it may be only slightly annoying.

Biological rhythms also affect a variety of other human conditions, such as birth, death and illness. Most births and deaths take place in the night or early morning. There are seasonal illnesses such as allergies, psychoses and ulcers. Resistance to infection occurs rhythmically. We treat certain ailments, such as epilepsy, by understanding their cyclical nature. Of considerable importance in this jet age is the knowledge of the effects of sudden and drastic changes in time zones. As more people travel great distances by supersonic transports, there is an increase in the "jet lag" phenomenon.

All living creatures follow the circadian pattern of activity and rest or sleep. It is the most observable and predictable rhythmic response. In addition, sleep itself follows an ultradian rhythm of 85 to 110 minutes. We therefore experience three to seven cycles per night. Electroencephalographic (EEG) measurements of brain wave activity have been used to trace sleep cycles.

There are four stages of sleep, ranging from Stage I, light sleep, in which the EEG waves resemble the active pattern of waking, to Stage IV, deep sleep, in which the brain waves are slow, large and even. As we fall asleep, breathing becomes slow and steady, our eyes begin to roll, temperature drops and muscles relax. It takes about 40 minutes to move through to Stage IV deep sleep. During this phase, eye movement is very slow or imperceptible, as opposed to the rapid eye movement (REM) condition of Stage I. At the end of about 90 minutes of sleep, we return to a lighter stage as marked by an REM stage. It is at this point that we experience dreams and other physiological activities.

REM sleep is thought to have a very necessary function. Freudians believe it to be a release of unconscious instinctual material that must be dealt with in order to cope with conscious living. Dreams, in particular, are seen as an ego-preserving mechanism. When Stage I sleep is interrupted and then resumed, an abundance of REM sleep ensues in order to compensate for the loss. A deprivation of REM sleep leads to anxiety and irritability if it is severe enough.

REM sleep occurs more frequently toward morning, whereas Stage IV sleep is more normal early in the night. When a person is severely deprived of Stage IV sleep, depression and lethargy will often occur. If there is no sleep at all for a prolonged period, Stage IV sleep will dominate.

The two prevailing sleep disturbances are insomnia and narcolepsy. Insomnia is marked by a reduction in Stage IV sleep and a lack of normal sleep rhythm, it is a common characteristic of depressed patients. Narcolepsy is characterized by falling asleep during normal waking periods and involves an inordinate amount of REM sleep. As a matter of fact, the sleep pattern resembles that of a newborn infant.

ASSERTIVENESS

One of the most difficult problems to overcome in daily functioning is to act outside one's role, whether it is a sexual, racial, student-teacher, boss-worker or any other role. For the majority of people it is a matter of being able to act against others who represent forces of power and authority. This has recently been brought out in the "women's movement," in which the learning of assertiveness has been stressed. In this regard, women are becoming aware of a history of conciliation and submissiveness and of the need to develop qualities of assertiveness.

Assertiveness, therefore, is a function of showing opposition to a power or force. People representing power are, on the whole, a minority, which does not negate their power, however. An irony about it is that those who are being controlled frequently seize whatever opportunity they have to exercise the little power they might get. A typical example of this is the frustration of encountering a civil service clerk who refuses to allow any deviation from the rules, including such pettinesses as standing in line or filling out forms precisely and neatly. Being assertive in such situations is to stand up for one's rights.

It is important to differentiate between assertiveness and aggression. Aggression is generally described as a response intended to harm or injure another in some way. It can be equated with hostile or antisocial behavior in that it is destructive. It is the satisfaction of one's own needs at the expense of others' needs, and may stem from the fight instinct. Assertiveness, on the other hand, is a constructive behavior based upon strength and understanding. At the other extreme of aggression is submissive behavior, which is defeatist and powerless. In overcoming submissiveness, people sometimes swing all the way to aggressive reactions rather than to the strong assertive position.

Assertiveness is a more direct action that communicates one's steadfastness and confidence. Assertive behavior is authentic or truthful, and therein lies its strength. Women have been as guilty as men of sexism when they used their sex roles to manipulate through apparent submission. It is one of the common role games described by Berne and other transactional analysts.

To be assertive is therefore to have a perception of many choices of action, all of them good. Since assertiveness deals with overt behaviors and openness, there is no need to get bogged down in the chicanery of manipulation and deviousness.

There are a few techniques to becoming assertive and maintaining assertiveness. The first is to build a support system. This is what happens when people undergo assertiveness training in groups. The advantage is that others are around to support assertive behavior. Second, the change to assertiveness needs to be intrinsic or self-motivated. If it does not come from within, it will be only temporary at best. Finally, a change in one's behavior pattern necessitates other changes, both simultaneously and as follow-up actions.

Any change in one's responses brings with it an altered image as perceived both by oneself and by friends and acquaintances. The gain of a new role means the loss of the old role. Becoming assertive is risky, as is any change in character. We must give up some of our previous defenses, although the substitute should be much more adequate. It may lead to the acquisition of new powers and concomitant responsibilities. The primary responsibility is to remain authentic and not use new powers to manipulate or injure others. The changes also lead to questioning of old philosophies and possibly changing of life styles. It is to be hoped that all changes will be handled positively by oneself and by the important others in a person's life.

ENDNOTES

1. Dunn, Halbert: High Level Wellness. 7th ed. Arlington, Va., R. W. Beatty, Ltd., 1972, p. 9.
2. Slater, Philip: The Pursuit of Loneliness. Boston, Beacon Press, 1970, p. 5.
3. Kastenbaum, Robert, and Ruth Aisenberg: The Psychology of Death. New York, Springer Publishing Co., 1972, p. 21.
4. Kübler-Ross, Elisabeth: Death: The Final Stage of Growth. Englewood Cliffs, N. J., Prentice-Hall, 1975.
5. Mothner, Ira: Who's asking life-and-death questions today? Saturday Review/World, September 25, 1973, p. 58.
6. Kastenbaum, Robert: The child's understanding of death: How does it develop? In E. Grollman (Ed.): Explaining Death to Children. Boston, Beacon Press, 1967, pp. 89–110.
7. Leviton, Dan: Death, bereavement, and suicide education. In Donald A. Read (Ed.): New Directions in Health Education. New York, The Macmillan Co., 1971, p. 188.
8. Lester, Gene, and David Lester: Suicide: The Gamble with Death. Englewood Cliffs, N.J., Prentice-Hall, 1971.

9. Dunn, *op. cit.*, pp. 88–89.
10. Selye, Hans: *Stress Without Distress*. Philadelphia, J. B. Lippincott Co., 1974, p. 27.
11. Selye, Hans: *Stress of Life*. New York, McGraw-Hill Book Co., 1956, p. 87.
12. Glasser, William: *Positive Addiction*. New York, Harper & Row, Publishers, 1976, p. 93.

BIBLIOGRAPHY

Aguilera, Donna C., Janice M. Messick, and Marlene S. Farrell: *Crisis Intervention*. St. Louis, The C. V. Mosby Co., 1970.

Arnold, Magda B.: *Emotion and Personality*. Volumes I and II. New York, Columbia University Press, 1960.

Biological Rhythms in Psychiatry and Medicine. Rockville, Maryland, National Institute of Mental Health, 1970.

Camus, Albert: *The Myth of Sisyphus and Other Essays*. New York, Vintage Books, 1955.

Carney, Richard E.: *Risk-Taking Behavior*. Springfield, Ill., Charles C Thomas, Publisher, 1971.

Cofer, Charles N.: *Motivation and Emotion*. Glenview, Ill., Scott, Foresman and Co., 1972.

Dunn, Halbert: *High Level Wellness*, 7th ed. Arlington, Virginia, R. W. Beatty, Ltd., 1972.

Festinger, Leon: *A Theory of Cognitive Dissonance*. Stanford, Stanford University Press, 1957.

Glasser, William: *Positive Addiction*. New York, Harper & Row, Publishers, 1976.

Hochbaum, Godfrey: *Health Behavior*. Belmont, Calif., Wadsworth Publishing Co., 1970.

Jacobson, Edmund: *You Must Relax*. New York, McGraw-Hill Book Co., 1957.

Kastenbaum, Robert, and Ruth Aisenberg: *The Psychology of Death*. New York, Springer Publishing Company, 1972.

Keleman, Stanley: *Living Your Dying*. New York, Random House, 1974.

Kübler-Ross, Elisabeth: *Death: The Final Stage of Growth*. Englewood Cliffs, N.J., Prentice-Hall, 1975.

Kübler-Ross, Elisabeth: *On Death and Dying*. New York, New York, Macmillan Publishing Co., 1969.

Lee, Jung Young: *Death and Beyond in the Eastern Perspective*. New York; Gordon and Breach, Science Publishers, 1974.

Lester, Gene, and David Lester: *Suicide*. Englewood Cliffs, N. J., Prentice-Hall, 1971.

Mannes, Marya: *Last Rights*. New York, William Morrow & Co., 1973.

Mannin, Ethel: *Loneliness*. London, Hutchinson & Co., 1966.

May, Rollo: *Man's Search for Himself*. New York, W. W. Norton & Co., 1953.

Moustakis, Clark: *Loneliness and Love*. Englewood Cliffs, N.J., Prentice-Hall, 1972.

Ornstein, Robert E. (Ed.): *The Nature of Human Consciousness*. San Francisco, W. H. Freeman & Co., 1973.

Ornstein, Robert E.: *The Psychology of Consciousness*. New York, Viking Press, 1972.

Osborn, Susan M., and Gloria G. Harris: *Assertive Training for Women*. Springfield, Ill., Charles C Thomas, Publisher, 1975.

Parad, Howard J. (Ed.): *Crisis Intervention*. New York, Family Service Association of America, 1965.

Powell, John: *Why Am I Afraid to Tell You Who I Am?* Niles, Ill., Argus Communications, 1969.

Selye, Hans: *Stress of Life*. New York, McGraw-Hill Book Co., 1956.

Selye, Hans: *Stress Without Distress*. Philadelphia, J. B. Lippincott Co., 1974.

Shneidman, Edwin S.: *Death: Current Perspectives*. Palo Alto, Calif., Mayfield Publishing Co., 1976.

Slater, Philip: *The Pursuit of Loneliness*. Boston, Beacon Press, 1970.

Tart, Charles F.: *Altered States of Consciousness*. New York, John Wiley & Sons, 1969.

Wood, John: *How Do You Feel?* Englewood Cliffs, N. J., Prentice-Hall, 1974.

CHAPTER 5

GOOD
AND POOR
MENTAL HEALTH

NORMALITY AND DEVIATION

Understanding the concepts of mental health first requires accepting certain basic assumptions. The important concept for our consideration of normality and deviation is behavioral norms. Every common behavioral pattern follows a normal, or bell-shaped, curve when applied to the total population. In other words, when the frequency of a particular behavior is charted for a given population, the resultant graph follows a bell-shaped curve in which the majority of the people (two-thirds) are clustered in the middle and a very small percentage (5 per cent) are at the two extremes. The rest will be evenly distributed in between.

For example, if the average frequency of sexual relations for a couple living together is three times per week, we can expect that many couples will have sex only three times per month and that others will engage in this behavior once a day. The more homogeneous the group, the smaller the range of behavior. Although a normal distribution still occurs, deviant behavior is not so extreme.

Normality, therefore, refers to a range of expected behavior and is not a precise measurement. In mental health, the definition is limited to how most of society acts and how well we conform to role expectations. Our society rewards behavior that is close to the midline, or "normal." Deviates are not easily tolerated and are frequently punished for being different, even though their behavior may not be harmful to others. Examples of this are prejudice against racial minorities and intolerance of individual idiosyncrasies. On the other hand, however, in our culture we expect a certain degree of difference among individuals—as long as it is not too different. It will be left up to you to deal with this paradoxical situation.

The designation of certain behavior patterns as components of mental illness is based partially on culturally accepted norms. It is also a matter of how one integrates and balances the needs of instinct and conscience. In Freudian terms, it is how we externalize id and superego. The ego is also involved, since levels of mental health depend upon our sets of coping mechanisms and the manner in which we display them.

In describing mental illness, it might first be asked whether we are referring to the brain or the mind. Mental illness, as the term is commonly used, encompasses both organic brain disorders and psychological deviations in living patterns. In other words, people have been called mentally ill because their character traits were so different that, in the judgment of professional psychologists and psychiatrists they were unable to function adequately. The underlying cause of the deviant behavior need not have been neurological.

The problem with the term "mental illness" is that it is used to describe a psychosocial condition in a medical context. Mental illness is not infectious in the sense of being transmitted by certain physical, noxious agents. However, as with some diseases, hereditary factors may play a part in its development. Mental illness is more a condition of acting inconsistently within societal norms. When a person is given a series of psychological tests, the level of response is judged to be appropriate or inappropriate, as based on expected, accepted methods of coping. Behavioral norms are set by society, and the standards of mental illness are set by these values or system of ethics. Methods of treatment and diagnosis, however, are medical.

Thomas Szasz, in his book *The Myth of Mental Illness*, has made an excellent, although controversial, case for understanding mental illness as a concept that has been harmed by the necessity of labeling. As Szasz points out, although mental illness may be a myth, the conditions still exist.[1] Rather than dealing with a disease entity, psychiatrists must deal with human beings, understanding their personal needs and motivating forces. Rather than treating patients, the aim should be toward counseling clients how to live their lives best within the framework of society.

R. D. Laing,[2] like Szasz, agrees that many people displaying certain behavioral traits have been assigned labels, such as schizophrenia, that do not help describe a disease state; rather, they are used by some people to designate others who are not like them. Schizophrenia is the general term associated with the inability to distinguish between reality and fantasy. It is not a pathological condition, but a judgment made by one set of people (usually psychiatrists) about another set. The so-called fantasy world of diagnosed "schizophrenics" is thought to be not mature, not rational and not sane.

Socially, as a result of this labeling phenomenon, schizophrenics become Them, and those not diagnosed as having schizophrenia are Us. This turns out to be, according to Laing, a political event[3] as well as a social fact. The diagnosed patient is then put into the role of patient, which is difficult to shake for the rest of his or her life. This is particularly true once that person has been committed to a mental hospital.

It is only recently that psychiatrists, such as Szasz and Laing, have begun to raise questions about the labeling of social deviates as mentally ill. As a result, there appears to be a tendency away from institutionalizing people who act and respond unusually and a tendency toward maximizing outpatient treatment and independent living.

In the context of our definition of normality as a range of behavior, perhaps we should reconsider our attitude toward those who act in a deviant manner. Whatever defense mechanisms are used to cope with the social and ego problems of life should be acceptable as long as they are harmless to others. This does not preclude seeking psychological counseling and therapeutic procedures to cope better when necessary. Consider which is the worse condition — the person who is unable to learn role conformity, or the person who learns it so well as to suffer through boredom and anxieties because of suppressing individuality?

PSYCHOTHERAPY

Normally, there are two aspects of personality. On the one hand is the inner world of experience, and on the other is the outer world of behavior. Experience itself cannot be known except as it is manifested by behavior. We can choose either to conceal or to disclose our inner world. Psychotherapy is the attempt to put together experience and behavior so that they are consistent.

In psychotherapy, various techniques are used to understand the inner world, although this is just the beginning. The ultimate aim is the recovery of the wholeness of being human. The therapist may help a person eliminate the array of defenses, masks and roles that cover up true feelings. In general, the more common methods utilized are free association (verbalizing without inhibiting one's thoughts), interpretation (analysis of dream and behaviors) and transference. *Transference*, as developed by Freud, is the process of expressing one's emotions toward a less threatening substitute, such as the therapist. The therapist, as a nonjudgmental figure, allows the patient to open up the inner world.

The two basic approaches to psychotherapy are *suppressive* and *expressive*. The objective of the suppressive method is to be supportive to the ego in its ability to handle emotionally threatening situations. Stress is reduced, active help is given in dealing with difficulties of living, and ego defenses are supported until the person has developed a certain degree of strength. Expressive (self-expressed) techniques may then be used to uncover emotional conflict that has previously been repressed.

There are three situations that involve psychiatric counseling: crisis intervention, brief psychotherapy and psychoanalysis. *Crisis* intervention serves the purpose of resolving intense, immediate crises so that the individual may again function. The techniques used are short term, and therefore the counselor or therapist is a more active, direct participant. Treatment lasts for only a few sessions. *Brief psychotherapy* may last for a matter of months, perhaps 20 sessions, and is also aimed at alleviating acute, distressful situations. Treatment is still supportive, but the therapist participates less directly and serves more as an observer and guide. *Psychoanalysis*, on the other hand, is a long-term process aimed at restructuring personality patterns. The therapist is nondirective, using uncovering or expressive techniques over an extended period of time.

Laing gives a very interesting and comprehensive progressive description of the voyage from disintegration of the inner and outer worlds to a psychological rebirth. He believes that to overcome psychological distress one must travel through one's condition to the natural depths of alienation or separation and then back to total integration. What is entailed, then, is[4]:

    I. a voyage from outer to inner,
   II. from life to a kind of death,
  III. from going forward to going backward,
  IV. from temporal movement to temporal standstill,
   V. from mundane time to eonic time,
  VI. from the ego to the self,
 VII. from outside (post-birth) back into the womb of all things (pre-birth), and then subsequently a return voyage from
    1. inner to outer,
    2. from death to life,

A voyage through mental distress.

3. from movement back to a movement once more forward,
4. from immortality back to mortality,
5. from eternity back to time,
6. from self to a new ego,
7. from a cosmic fetalization to an existential rebirth.

Regardless of the school of therapy, the progress should be more or less as Laing describes it. Whether it is gestalt therapy, Freudian therapy, direct or nondirect therapy, reality therapy or logotherapy, the patient cannot avoid such a journey through "madness." Deeply repressed inner material must somehow be brought to consciousness so that it can be dealt with. It is this hidden material that directs behavior and personality.

CLASSES OF MENTAL ILLNESS

A system has evolved to describe patterns of psychological behavior, part of which is mental deviation or "illness." While there are built-in pitfalls in labeling people and assigning them to one category or another, it is sometimes necessary to describe these behavioral patterns for the purpose of diagnosis and treatment. Caution must be taken, however, not to stick labels on people as if they were inanimate objects or unchangeable. It is possible that ultimately the drawbacks of labeling exceed the benefits.

NEUROSIS

The least severe form of mental deficiency is *neurosis,* which is an inability to cope with anxiety effectively. It has also been described as a weakness in the functioning ego. In a sense, since all of us suffer from ego weakness or overwhelming anxiety, at least temporarily, we are all neurotic to a degree. When the neurosis persists or is strong enough to interfere seriously with daily living, then professional counseling or short-term therapy is useful and perhaps necessary.

Neurosis may take the form of overindulging in eating, smoking or other such gratifications. It may lead to an inability to control emotional outbursts. Overanxious people frequently suffer from sleep disorders, particularly insomnia. There are many other manifestations of neurosis; usually these are temporary, although some occasionally require professional assistance to be overcome.

PSYCHOSIS

More serious is the group of disorders known as *psychoses,* that is, psychological conditions that are seriously disabling. The psychotic individual may be extremely disoriented or disorganized and is out of touch with reality. Rational communication with others is absent. Psychosis may be organic (pathological) in nature, triggered by some chemically toxic substance, such as alcohol, or it may be functional in that the brain appears physiologically normal. Most schizophrenia, the general classification of a split with reality, is functional. In addition, psychoses may be acute, appearing rapidly and perhaps brought about by a traumatic experience, or they may be chronic, taking years to develop. Although the tendency toward schizophrenia may be inherited, the disorder itself is not passed from generation to generation.

There are four major types of functional psychoses: paranoia, catatonia, hebephrenia and simple psychosis. The *paranoid* individual unrealistically perceives that others are intentionally trying to harm him or her. Because of this, these individuals will attempt to structure life in a way that protects them from others. Paranoia is not uncommon, although for some people there may be a fine line between a normal fear of being hurt by others and a truly imagined, irrational and incapacitating fear.

Catatonia is a totally inactive and mute condition. The catatonic patient is so withdrawn as to shut out all communications with the outside world. *Hebephrenic* patients, on the other hand, exhibit much affect, but in a very inappropriate manner. They will laugh often, but at the wrong times. They appear to be very happy, therefore, in their condition.

In *simple psychosis*, there is very little ego, or it is so weak that there is no real relationship to the outside world. There is no distinction between one's self and what is outside one's self. Differentiation is the major problem, and a person in this state will drift aimlessly through life, literally and figuratively. It is actually a more general term than the other three forms of psychosis.

ANXIETY AND NEUROSES

Another general psychological condition is that of *psychosomatic* disorders, or physiological symptoms brought about by psychological factors. Probably the most widely publicized psychosomatic illness is gastrointestinal ulcers, which is internal bleeding in the stomach or intestine caused by worry and anxiety. In such a case, mental stress causes increased enzyme activity, which is too great for the body to handle adequately. Other common psychosomatic disorders are headaches (most of which are caused by psychological factors), many allergies, some types of diarrhea, and skin problems.

Two forms of anxiety neurosis that are not psychosomatic are hypochondria and hysteria. Hypochondriasis is an imagined physical illness with absolutely no organic abnormality. Nevertheless, the hypochondriac truly believes she or he is physically ill. Hysteria, on the other hand, involves an overreaction of the denial mechanism to such a degree that sensory and other bodily functions cease. In a panic situation, the hysterical person may become blind, be unable to speak or suffer other paralysis.

PERSONALITY DISORDERS

Another pattern of psychological dysfunction is called *personality disorders* (or character disorders), which refers to persons who deviate from the rules of society. Personality disorders involve criminal acts, sexual deviation, drug addiction, alcoholism and other such departures from norms. In regard to treatment, classifying individuals as having personality disorders is not helpful and may only serve the detrimental function of sticking a label on that person. This is not to say that people who break laws and harm others aren't a threat to society, but they don't necessarily need to change in order to function most effectively. Behaviors such as homosexuality and the regular use of marijuana have frequently been misclassified as personality disorders. Obviously, such behaviors are becoming more common and have not been found to be harmful, other than leading to arrest and imprisonment where they have been designated as illegal.

Personality disorders are probably more properly put into the category of neuroses but only when there is a true ego malfunction. For example, someone may be homosexual and have a weak ego as well. The homosexuality need not be tied to his or her ego problems, although it may be. In such a case, then, heterosexuality might be the more appropriate behavior. The same is true of other so-called personality disorders. The antisocial behavior may or may not result directly from a neurotic personality.

THE MENTALLY HEALTHY PERSON

It would be useful to follow a discussion of mental illness with some qualities of mental well-being.

Many professionals in the mental health field have attempted to describe mental wellness. A survey of the clinical staff at the Menninger Foundation Clinic in Topeka, Kansas, showed five characteristics of mentally well people.[6]

1. They have a wide variety of sources of gratification so that if one is not available, another is there to take its place. Children often are heard to complain, "I'm bored, there's nothing to do." In dealing with such situations, they learn how to best fill their time, but if this attitude continues into adulthood, a pattern will be established, and they will not be psychologically gratified.

2. They are flexible under stress and have an array of coping mechanisms to adequately deal with various sources of stress. They are able to easily assume different patterns of response for different situations.

3. They recognize and accept their limitations and assets. In other words, they have a realistic self-concept, or strong ego identity.

4. They treat other people as individuals and have established a

number of fulfilling I-Thou relationships. They are willing to get involved with others.

5. They are active and productive, using their talents and potential. Everyone has a compilation of personal resources, but some people never use many of them.

Combs[7] has identified three important aspects of the adequate personality:

1. A positive view of self, having not only a realistic self-image but also a feeling of being a good, adequate person. A positive self-perception reduces dependency on defenses and leads to a more open and secure individual.

2. The capability to accept oneself and others. Everyone has both strengths and weaknesses, and we must learn to accept them.

3. A high degree of identification with other people. The part of the social self doesn't necessitate an extroverted personality or party goer but the comfortable feeling that others are trustworthy and safe.

In studying self-actualized people, Abraham Maslow[8] identified a number of characteristics common to these psychologically healthy people. The subjects in his study were contemporary, historical and public figures who had achieved greatness in a positive way. Included were such people as Thomas Jefferson, Albert Einstein, Eleanor Roosevelt, Albert Schweitzer and Aldous Huxley. He described the following criteria of psychological health:

1. A greater perception of reality and less fear of the unknown.

2. A great degree of acceptance of self, others and nature.

3. Acting with spontaneity and behaving simply and naturally, not in a strained manner.

4. Problem-centered rather than ego-centered. Problems are not of a personal nature themselves so much as they involve a mission or purpose in life.

5. A need for solitude and privacy; to detach from certain situations and perceive things objectively.

6. Autonomy and independence from physical and social environment, being propelled by growth motivation (positive) rather than deficiency motivation (negative).

7. Continued freshness of appreciation and new, rich, authentic emotional reactions.

8. Frequent peak or mystic experiences which flow from strong emotions.

9. An identification with all humankind — what Alfred Adler called Gemeinschaftsgefühl or Fromm's brotherly love.

10. Deep and profound interpersonal relationships.

11. A deeply democratic character structure, judging and accepting others on the basis of suitable character rather than class distinctions such as race, religion, education.

12. Accurate discrimination between means and ends, good and evil, right and wrong.

13. A sense of humor, which is more philosophical and not hostile toward others.

14. Creativeness; originality, or inventiveness.

15. Resistance to enculturation, transcending any particular culture. In this sense, they are not well adjusted to their culture, although they do accept all cultures.

16. A solidly based value system, but the ability to change certain values.

This portrait of a psychologically healthy individual is helpful in the sense that it gives us an ideal to work toward. It is not based upon traditional, statistically sound research methods, but it does identify important characteristics of adequate personality and behavior.

Whatever one's definition of the mentally healthy individual, it is not simply the absence of mental illness or the opposite of mental disease. Nor can we think of it as functioning within the range of normality.

Marie Jahoda, after examining a number of approaches to defining mental health, came up with six criteria for positive mental health.[9]

1. Attitudes of an individual toward his/her self. This includes how much of the self is consciously known, how accurate self-concept is, ego strength and how good the person feels about who he/she is.

2. The degree of growth, development or self-actualization. This concept encompasses such psychological thinking as Erikson's developmental stages and Maslow's self-actualization or motivational theory.

3. Integration of all processes and attributes of the individual. This refers to a balance of one's psychic forces, a unifying philosophy of life and the ability to handle stress.

4. Autonomy from social influences or the relationship between the individual and the environment as he/she makes decisions. Such autonomy refers to deciding which environmental factors to accept (those personally important) and which to reject.

5. A perception of reality that is free from distortion but sensitive to social conditions.

6. The ability to master one's environment including being able to love, work and play adequately, have successful interpersonal relations, effectively meet situational requirements, adjust or adapt when necessary, and possess problem-solving skills.

It should be obvious that current writings defining positive mental wellness overlap and move in similar directions. Nevertheless, intellectual awareness of what constitutes good mental health is only a first step in achieving it. Transferring the knowledge into behavior is the hard part.

ENDNOTES

1. Szasz, Thomas: *Ideology and Insanity*. Garden City, N.Y., Doubleday & Co., 1970, p. 21.
2. Laing, R. D.: *The Politics of Experience*. New York, Ballantine Books, 1967, p. 103.
3. *Ibid.* p. 121.
4. *Ibid.*, pp. 128–129.
5. Martin, Leolon E.: *Mental Health/Mental Illness*. New York, McGraw-Hill Book Co., 1970, p. 25.
6. Levinson, Harry: How good is your mental health? *In* Jones, Herbert L., Margaret B. Schutt, and Ann L. Shelton:*Science and Theory of Health*. Dubuque, Iowa, Wm. C. Brown Co., Publishers, 1966, p. 34.
7. Combs, Arthur W.: Personality theory and its implications for curriculum development. *In: Learning More About Learning*. Washington, D.C., Association for Supervision and Curriculum Development, 1959, pp. 5–20.
8. Maslow, Abraham: *Motivation and Personality*. New York, Harper & Row, Publishers, 1970, pp. 149–180.
9. Jahoda, Marie: *Current Concepts of Positive Mental Health*. New York, Basic Books, 1958, p. 23.

BIBLIOGRAPHY

Boyers, Robert: *R. D. Laing and Anti-Psychiatry*. New York, Harper & Row, Publishers, 1971.
Glasser, William: *Mental Health or Mental Illness?* New York, Harper & Row, Publishers, 1960.
Jahoda, Marie: *Current Concepts of Positive Mental Health*. New York, Basic Books, 1958.
Laing, R. D.: *The Divided Self*. New York, Random House, 1960.
Laing, R. D.: *The Politics of Experience*. New York, Ballantine Books, 1967.
Maslow, Abraham: *Motivation and Personality*. New York, Harper & Row, Publishers, 1970.
Szasz, Thomas: *The Myth of Mental Illness*. New York, Delta Publishing Co., 1961.
Szasz, Thomas: *Ideology and Insanity*. Garden City, N.Y., Doubleday & Co., 1970.

SECTION THREE
HUMAN SEXUALITY AND THE SEXUAL YOU

Sexuality—what is it? This question is being asked more and more often in today's rapidly changing, mobile society. Perhaps no other aspect of life in modern America is so filled with paradox, confusion and misunderstanding. This problem has followed us throughout the ages, and even in our so-called free, open and liberated life style of today, we continue to be plagued by what Rollo May calls a schizoid attitude toward sex and sexuality.

Although sex and sexuality have much in common, sex is only one of the many components of one's sexuality. Thus, it is important that we first grasp these differences and develop an understanding, in a definitive sense, of what "sexuality" means. The often used, and virtually as often misunderstood, term *sexuality* deals with much more than biological functions. As many writers have pointed out, Sex is what you are born with, sexuality is what you are. Sexuality, then, could be viewed as an expression of self in an integrated, individual, unique manner.

We see examples of sexuality every day. It is displayed by a small child who clings to his mother for reassurance, by two 11-year-old boys who taunt and tease their female classmates, in the face of a father who views his newborn daughter for the first time, and in the touching and fondling of two lovers.

What does all this really mean from the point of view of the individual? Let's approach the answer to that question by using a simple example. Although I am a man in a biological sense (i.e., I have a penis and XY chromosomes), my sexuality, or sexual identity, operates on a broad continuum. Sexuality may be generally based on biological information, but that is only one kind of determination, and one must also

How do we display sexuality?

consider social and psychological factors as well as experience within a family setting when examining a so-called "sexual style." As a male, I may be socially aggressive or reticent. I may prefer males or females as lovers, friends, or other associates. I may exhibit "feminine," "masculine" or "androgynous" (both feminine and masculine) behaviors as defined in a traditional sex role sense. And all these characteristics may change with circumstances or environment. The important point, however, is that I am a total person who has examined himself thoroughly and can now identify my self as a sexual being in a complete sense.

In order to fully understand one's own sexuality, it is essential that each individual reflect on his or her personal experiences and values and utilize the decision-making process discussed earlier (Chap. 1). In order to learn about human sexuality in general and one's own sexuality specifically, the individual must not only deal with personal experience, values and knowledge but also test them against a variety of experiences, attitudes, insights and values. Only through this process can one have adequate data upon which to make logical rational decisions in regard to self and the relation of self to others.

To begin the search regarding ourselves as sexual beings, let's first look at sex and sexual differences in a biological, social and psychological frame of reference.

CHAPTER 6

SEX AND SEXUAL DIFFERENCES

BIOLOGICAL VARIATION

As noted above, a part of one's sexuality—and perhaps the part most written and talked about over the years—is the genital structure that determines whether an individual is an anatomical male or female. Thus, anatomy and physiology play an important role in sexuality, for it is through the study of the structure and function of the sexual organs that we gain insight into some of the reasons for variations in sexuality.

It is a well-known fact that for most people in our society sexual intercourse serves two important functions: reproduction and pleasure. However, if we are to understand these functions, a major prerequisite is a basic understanding of the functional parts that allow both procreation and sexual pleasure. The following is merely a cursory overview of the genital systems.

THE FEMALE REPRODUCTIVE SYSTEM

It is well known that females have both external and internal genitalia, although greater consideration is usually given to the internal structures, since they are essential for reproduction and the penis is placed internally during sexual intercourse. In our discussion of the female reproductive system, we will first consider the deep internal structures and then progress to the external structures.

Ovaries. These paired structures, which are located deep within the pelvic cavity, serve two important interrelated functions: they form the mature egg (ovum), which is essential for conception, and produce the ovarian hormones estrogen and progesterone (to be discussed later).

Fallopian Tubes (Oviducts). These short, approximately 4-inch (9.6-cm) tubes extend from the uterus toward (but do not attach to) the ovaries. The fimbriated end of the fallopian tube "captures" the egg after it has been expelled from the ovary and passes it into the main body of the tube where it is then carried toward the uterus via the action of the cilia

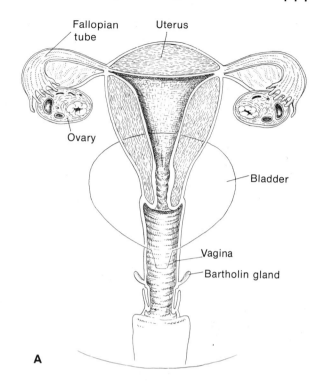

Fallopian tube

Uterus

Ovary

Bladder

Vagina

Bartholin gland

Figure 6-1 The female reproductive system. *A,* Front view. *B,* Side view.

A

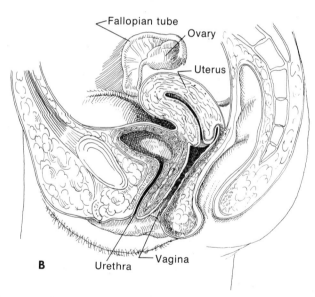

Fallopian tube

Ovary

Uterus

Vagina

B Urethra

(hairlike structures) that line the tube. This transport system is aided by contractions of the fallopian tube walls. It is important to note that, since the egg has no means of self-locomotion, both ciliary action and contraction of the tube are necessary for the egg to be passed along the tube and into the uterus.

It is in the fallopian tube that, under normal circumstances, fertilization will occur. This is due to the fact it takes approximately three to four days to transport the egg from the ovary to the uterus, but the egg itself has a viable period of only about 24 hours before it begins to degenerate.

Uterus (Womb).   Located in the pelvis behind and above the bladder, the uterus is a 3-inch long by 2-inch wide pear-shaped structure that serves as the organ for the nourishment and development of the embryo and fetus. The upper, wider, portion of the uterus is the *fundus;* the lower, narrow part is the *cervix.* The uterus is suspended by several ligaments and generally tilts slightly forward. Certain factors, such as disease, childbirth or congenital disorders, may cause the uterus to be displaced from its normal position so that there may be difficulties in conception or carrying a fetus to full term.

The uterus is composed of three separate and distinct layers, each of which serves a unique function. The outer layer, or *pericardium*, is a thin, fibrous covering that tends to protect and maintain the shape of the uterus. The middle layer, or *myometrium*, is a thick, muscular layer which expands during pregnancy so that the uterus stretches from its normal length of about 3 inches to about 10 to 12 inches and contracts during labor and delivery to push the fetus out of the uterus. The *endometrium*, or inner layer, is essential for both implantation of the fertilized egg (zygote) and the development of the embryo. This layer is replete with glands and blood vessels needed for normal gestation.

Vagina.   This structure is an elastic muscular canal that extends from the cervix of the uterus to the external genitalia, a distance of about 3 to 4 inches. The function of the vagina is threefold in that it not only serves as the organ of sexual intercourse but also is the passage for uterine menstrual discharge and the birth canal. The vagina can expand to accommodate a full-term infant at birth or contract to less than $1/2$ inch in width. It is lined with mucous membrane, which produces a secretion that keeps the vagina moist. This mucous secretion increases during sexual arousal; but it does not correspond to ejaculation, which occurs during the male orgasmic response.

External Genitalia.   The female external genitalia (Fig. 6–2) have little to do with the procreative function of sexual intercourse, but four structures that may play a significant role in the pleasure function are the (1) mons veneris, (2) labia, (3) clitoris, and (4) hymen.

The *mons veneris,* or mount of Venus, is a cushion of adipose (fatty) tissue located over the lower abdominal area and above the creases and folds of skin (labia) surrounding the opening, or vestibule, of the vagina. The mons is quite prominent in children but is not as easily identified in adults due to the fact that is becomes covered, at puberty, with the pubic hair.

The *labia* consist of two pairs of skin folds, or lips, which protect the vaginal opening. The labia majora (outer lips) may be covered with hair and are larger than the labia minora (inner lips). During sexual arousal the labia become engorged with blood and expand, allowing greater accessibility to the vagina.

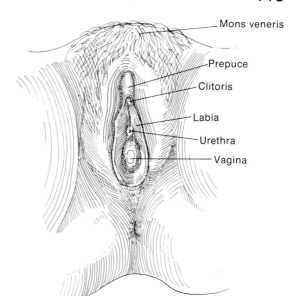

Mons veneris

Prepuce

Clitoris

Labia

Urethra

Vagina

Figure 6-2   The female external genitalia.

Located where the upper, or forward, ends of the labia minora are joined is a small, sensitive structure known as the *clitoris*. It is generally less than ½ inch in length but serves as a major center of sexual excitation in most females. The clitoris has an extremely large number of nerve endings over its surface and becomes erect during sexual arousal. In this sense, the clitoris is homologous to the penis; however, it should be noted that the two structures are not similar in every way. The clitoris does *not* contain a urethra for urination, and it is *not* the organ for sexual intercourse. In fact, it is fully possible for a woman without a clitoris to participate in sexual activity.

Perhaps the most talked about and yet misunderstood (by the public) female genital structure is the *hymen*. There are many myths and fallacies about this structure, which itself is really quite simple. The hymen is simply a membrane (which varies in size and thickness, depending upon the individual) that *partially* closes the opening of the vagina. The mystery of the hymen centers around the belief that if it is broken, the female has had sexual relations. The truth of the matter is that rupture of the membrane is not necessarily related to sexual activity. Perforation may be the result of a medical examination, the use of tampons, physical exercise, or some other general activity. The hymen may even be absent at birth. Fortunately, the public is gradually becoming educated to realize that there is not a definite relationship between loss of virginity and a ruptured hymen. (That is, assuming virginity is important in one's attitude; this will be discussed later in dealing with sexual attitudes.)

Menstruation.   One of the most significant signs of physical maturation as well as biological sexuality is menstruation, the somewhat regular discharge of blood, tissue and cellular fragments from the uterine lining (endometrium). Menstruation is one of four phases in the menstrual cycle.

An understanding of these four phases enables a better understanding of sexual response as well as birth control and contraception. If we begin with the menstrual flow and follow the cycle through the normal pattern of events, the phases would occur in the following order: (1) menstrual or destructive phase, (2) proliferative or follicular phase, (3) ovulation, and (4) secretory or luteal phase. It is important to keep in mind that these phases may overlap and that the time for each may vary considerably among women and even within the same woman.

The menstrual phase is triggered by low levels of ovarian hormones in the blood, resulting in a discharge. Generally, the total amount of this discharge ranges from 1 to 6 ounces (about 30 to 180 ml); about two-thirds is blood, the remainder being mucus and endometrial tissue. This initial phase, which overlaps the proliferative phase, lasts 3 to 7 days.

In the proliferative (follicular) phase, which begins during menstruation, the endometrium grows (proliferates). This proliferation, stimulated by an increase in the ovarian hormone estrogen, prepares the uterus for pregnancy. The phase lasts about 14 days but may vary from 9 to 17 days.

Occurring near the end of the proliferative phase is phase three, known as ovulation. At this point the egg (ovum) is fully mature and capable of being fertilized and is discharged from the ovary. Although ovulation generally occurs on about the fourteenth day of the cycle, there is a wide variation among women.

During phase four—the secretory, or luteal, phase—the ovary not only supplies the endometrium with estrogen but also stimulates the production of progesterone by the ruptured follicle, or corpus luteum. Under the influence of these two hormones, the endometrium becomes even more dense and begins to secrete nutrients to prepare itself for implantation of the fertilized egg. This phase averages about 13 days and ends with the onset of menstruation.

THE MALE REPRODUCTIVE SYSTEM

Like the female, the male has both external and internal reproductive organs. The major difference lies in the functional aspects; the anatomical structures involved in the act of sexual intercourse are located externally in the male but internally in the female. The major anatomical reproductive parts in the male are the testes, scrotum, epididymides, vasa deferentia, seminal vesicles, prostate gland, Cowper's glands, and penis (Fig. 6–3).

Testes and Scrotum. The testes are almond-shaped, paired structures that serve two distinct functions. They produce the sperm needed for reproduction as well as the androgenic hormone testosterone. This hormone is responsible for the development of the secondary sex characteristics of the male.

The testes are suspended from the body cavity within the pouch-like structure known as the scrotum. The scrotum protects the testes from

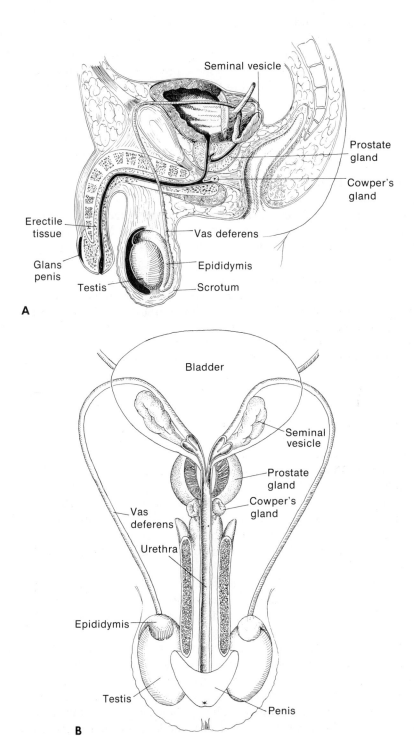

Figure 6–3   The male reproductive system. *A*, Side view. *B*, Front view.

mechanical injury and keeps them at a rather constant temperature. This thermostatic role is essential to the reproductive function, since sperm cannot be produced at normal body temperature. In order to maintain the testes at optimal temperature for sperm production the scrotal sac will contract during cold to bring the testes closer to the body and relax in heat.

Sperm production, which begins at puberty and continues at varied rates throughout the male's life, takes place in the cells of the seminiferous tubules. These highly coiled tubules are located within the interior chambers of each testis.

Epididymis and Vas Deferens.   The sperm-producing seminiferous tubules empty directly into the epididymis, a coiled tube lying on the upper portion of each testis. Here the sperm are stored for a period which allows them to mature and enhance their viability. Movement of sperm out of the epididymis generally takes from 2 to 4 weeks but is dependent upon the frequency of ejaculations. If the sperm are not ejaculated from the body, they will disintegrate and be resorbed.

Each epididymis drains into a duct about 18 inches (43 cm) long known as the vas deferens. The vasa deferentia then join the ducts from the seminal vesicles to form the ejaculatory duct, which leads to the urethra. The vasa deferentia serve as channels for passing sperm from the epididymides to the urethra by spasmodic contractions during ejaculation as well as storage areas for sperm.

Seminal Vesicles.   The seminal vesicles, which form the ejaculatory duct with the vasa deferentia, are paired glandular structures located at the base of the bladder. These structures secrete seminal fluid composed of water, fructose, fibrinogen, ascorbic acid and citric acid, which supply energy and mobility for the sperm.

Prostate Gland.   As shown in Figure 6–3, the prostate is a large gland located below the bladder. The contraction of the prostate during ejaculation causes it to secrete a slightly alkaline fluid, which aids in sperm transport. The prostatic fluid contains water, buffers, enzymes and prostaglandins, which neutralize the normal acidity (which would kill the sperm) of the male urethra and help to counteract the acid medium of the vagina.

Cowper's Glands.   These paired glands, which are located at either side of the urethra, secrete an alkaline fluid and mucus prior to ejaculation to remove urine from the urethra as well as lubricate the tube.

Penis.   This structure, serving as the organ for both urination and reproduction, is composed of erectile tissue covered with epidermal tissue. As with most anatomical parts, the physical dimensions of the penis vary greatly, the average erect penis being about 6 inches in length and 1½ to 2 inches in diameter. The penis is generally viewed as having two areas: (1) the shaft, composed of three layers or columns of erectile tissue, and (2) the glans, located at the tip of the penis, containing a large number of nerve endings making it quite sensitive to stimulation.

HEALTH PROBLEMS OF THE REPRODUCTIVE SYSTEM

MALE

Cryptorchidism. The testes of the male fetus lie inside the abdominal cavity close to the kidneys, but, under the influence of male sex hormones, they descend into the scrotum at about the seventh month of fetal life. Failure of the testes to descend, a situation occurring in about 1 to 7 per cent of males, is known as cryptorchidism. In such cases, if descent does not occur spontaneously, surgery or hormone therapy may be necessary. This problem, if not treated, may result in sterility.

Gynecomastia. Gynecomastia is characterized by enlargement of the breasts. The condition has been noted in males who have undergone estrogen treatment and has been associated with the use of marijuana. The swelling is generally not great enough to cause severe distress and will usually disappear within 6 to 36 months.

Penis Size. One of the greatest and yet unwarranted fears of the American male is that of the small penis. As noted earlier, normal penises vary greatly in size, ranging from 2 to 10 inches in the relaxed state. The size of erection, however, is inversely related to the flaccid size so that the increase in size of a small penis is proportionally greater than that for a large one. As a result, penises are closer in size when erect than when relaxed. It is important to note, however, that the size of the penis is not a significant factor in sexual satisfaction or conception.

The penis generally matures during puberty. The failure of this development results in microphallus, which is corrected by hormone therapy.

These are just a few of the general physiological and anatomical problems that could cause sex dysfunction in the male if not cared for and treated in their early stages. Other problems which generally call for medical attention are characterized by a discharge or bleeding from the penis, painful intercourse, impotence, burning or difficulty during urination, genital sores or blisters or pain in the genital area. If any of these symptoms occur, it is advisable to see a doctor.

FEMALE

Dysmenorrhea. This rather common problem, characterized by menstrual pain or cramps, may be caused by physiological phenomena (e.g., low blood calcium or changes in hormone level) in the reproductive system. However, psychological problems, such as those related to tension or self-concept, appear to be the more prevalent cause.

Vaginitis. This condition results in vaginal soreness, burning, itching or discharge and is rather common, occurring in perhaps 75 per cent of the female population. It is caused by a variety of factors—most often by strong chemicals, foreign objects, drugs or infectious agents—and may require treatment with an antibiotic or fungicide, depending on the causative agent.

Cystitis. Cystitis is an infection of the bladder. Symptoms include frequent and burning urination, lower abdominal pain and painful intercourse. Although microorganisms may be the cause, cystitis may be psychological in origin or may be initiated by frequent intercourse. Treatment depends upon the cause and may involve use of antibiotics, decreasing frequency of intercourse, use of lubricating jelly, or psychotherapy.

As with the male, many problems of the female reproductive system warrant a visit to a physician. Some symptoms of these problems are bleeding or vaginal discharge between menstrual periods, painful intercourse, painful menstruation, absence of menstruation, genital sores or pain and burning or painful urination.

CONTRACEPTION AND BIRTH CONTROL

When a couple chooses to engage in sexual activity they should be willing to either accept all the possible consequences of their behavior or to decide on some method of preventing the most serious consequence — pregnancy. This section will deal with a number of alternative means of contraception. The discussion is based on the assumption that the individuals involved in the coital act have given much thought to their actions and have reached this decision using the decision-making model suggested in Chapter 1.

As you will learn from the following information, most of the contraceptive techniques and devices are to be used by the female. This has placed a significant decision-making burden on women today and may be one of the reasons the gentleman on the next page appears as he does. The decision of whether or not to use contraception and which method to choose is not a simple one, and since both participants derive pleasure from sexual intercourse, it seems only reasonable for the male to share the responsibility in making decisions regarding birth control.

It is important to understand that no specific birth control technique is perfect for everyone. We must realize that every method has advantages and disadvantages, a certain degree of success and failure. Each will intrude in some manner, physiologically and psychologically, on one's being.

Virtually any contraceptive technique will work reasonably well if it is followed faithfully. For example, the condom, in theory, is an effective contraceptive; however, human behavior does not always bear out the theory, even though we human beings seem to have the innate ability to set virtually everything aside for the period of sexual intercourse. Thus, many methods may be very efficient in the controlled environment of a laboratory but are either not utilized or utilized improperly or haphazardly when practiced out of those confines. Any couple or individual contemplating using any contraceptive must therefore keep in mind the

degree to which that particular technique or device interferes with their personal life.

If a contraceptive is to be acceptable to a large number of people, it must meet several criteria. One of those criteria is that it must be effective. Effectiveness is generally determined by calculating the number of pregnancies per year for every 100 women using that method and comparing that rate with the rate of 80 per cent, which is the pregnancy rate under normal conditions when no contraceptive is used. Other criteria for widespread acceptance are ease of use and, particularly among young people, reversibility. No method that requires a great deal of time to administer or has significant side effects that threaten the body image will be judiciously selected and used. Keeping these criteria in mind, let us now examine the various alternatives to fertility control.

Abstinence. Trainer has noted, somewhat tongue in cheek, that the practice of restraint from sexual intercourse is 100 per cent effective and 0 per cent utilized. While this 0 per cent figure is certainly not true, it would be rather naïve to believe that this impractical method would become very popular.

Coitus Interruptus (Withdrawal). Much research indicates that this method of contraception is used by a significant number of college students today. Withdrawal is perhaps one of the oldest techniques known (it is even mentioned in the Old Testament), and yet it is one of the most ineffective, having a pregnancy rate of about 18 per cent.

Perhaps the reason that withdrawal is so popular is the alleged ease of administration. It simply requires that the penis be withdrawn from the vagina prior to ejaculation. However, in practice it is not always so simple. One reason is that the secretion from Cowper's gland that appears at the tip of the penis prior to ejaculation contains viable sperm. A second problem is the timing of withdrawal before the ejaculate enters the vagina or is deposited near the vaginal opening.

The third and perhaps overriding reason for the failure of this method is simply that although the couple may have every intention of using it, one or both of them may be so lost in their passion that withdrawal is either forgotten or is not allowed to occur. Consequently, the method cannot be effective if it isn't really used.

Oral-Genital Substitution. Oral stimulation of the genitals is practiced more or less regularly by about 60 per cent of couples having sexual relations. This method, which is illegal even today in many states, is 100 per cent effective.

Rhythm. The supposed effectiveness of this method (which actually has pregnancy rate of 27 per cent) is based on the knowledge that (1) the female generally produces one mature egg per month, (2) the egg is viable for only about 24 hours, and (3) sperm can remain alive inside the female's body after intercourse for only 24 to 72 hours. To prevent conception, the couple need only refrain from intercourse for a six-day period during each menstrual cycle (about 28 days). The problem arises in attempting to determine the days on which conception might occur and abstention is advisable.

This would be an easy problem to solve if each woman ovulated (expelled an egg from the ovary) at the same time. Unfortunately, this is not true, and even though research shows that most women ovulate around the middle (day 14) of the cycle, not all women have 28-day cycles, nor are their cycles always regular. Some cycles are as short as 21 days, while others may be 38 days. A woman may vary as much as eight or nine days between her longest and shortest cycles.

In order to increase the effectiveness of the rhythm method, one must take into account these irregularities in determining the "safe days" for intercourse. To do this, the woman should note the exact length of each cycle for a 12-month period. She then subtracts 18 from the shortest cycle and thereby determines her first fertile day. She subtracts 11 from the longest cycle and determines the last fertile day. Abstinence during this "unsafe" period should provide effective birth control.

Let us now use an example to see how the method works. Betty religiously notes the length of each cycle for 12 consecutive cycles. Her records show that her longest cycle was 29 days and her shortest was 21 days. She subtracts 11 from 29 and determines that day 18 is her last fertile day. By subtracting 18 from 21 she notes day 3 as her first fertile day. Therefore, she abstains from intercourse between days 3 and 18. Since this is the greater part of a month, in all likelihood this couple will not use this method.

One way of increasing the effectiveness of the rhythm method is to chart the female's daily basal body temperature (BBT), since ovulation is known to cause a rise in temperature that persists until menstruation and is due to a high level of progesterone. To determine when ovulation occurs, a woman uses a basal thermometer, which shows gradations of one-tenth degree to show small changes in temperature, to take her temperature upon awakening and before getting out of bed. She records this temperature each day. During the first part of the menstrual cycle the temperature remains relatively constant, but somewhere around the middle of the cycle it rises several tenths of a degree. This rise occurs on the day following ovulation. It should be noted that such factors as illness, depression or physical activity may also increase the BBT and may be misinterpreted as indicating ovulation.

Condom. The condom, perhaps the contraceptive having the widest variety of names (e.g., prophylactic, "rubber"), is simply a thin sheath, generally made of synthetic rubber, worn over the penis during intercourse. This device has two unique qualities in that it is the only contraceptive that also may be used to prevent venereal disease and it is one of the few devices used by the man.

The relative ineffectiveness (pregnancy rate about 15 to 18 per cent) of the condom relates to both mechanical and psychological matters. If defective, they may be broken easily or have a hole in them. Also, they may be removed too close to the vagina, or the penis may be reinserted after ejaculation without wiping off the semen. Efficiency can be increased by (1) wearing the condom throughout intercourse and being sure it is on the penis properly before insertion into the vagina; (2) leaving a reservoir in the tip for pooling of ejaculate; (3) using a lubricant (not petroleum jelly) to prevent tearing; (4) holding the condom on when withdrawing the penis from the vagina; and (5) removing the condom and cleansing the penis away from the vagina.

Many couples have claimed that the greatest drawback to use of the condom is the interruption of foreplay while the condom is placed on the penis. Significantly most individuals feel that the condom may decrease sensation. However, is not an ounce of prevention worth 8 pounds of cure?

It should be noted that the effectiveness of the condom increases significantly when it is used in conjunction with either a diaphragm or spermicidal chemical.

Diaphragm.   This rubber cap is designed as a mechanical barrier to block the progress of the sperm from the vagina into the uterus. Within the dome is a flexible metal spring that holds it in place over the cervix. Because of the variation in size and shape of the female genitalia, careful fitting by a physician is necessary if the device is to be effective.

The effectiveness of the diaphragm (pregnancy rate of 12 to 20 per cent) depends upon a number of variables. Perhaps as important as the fit is the use of some type of spermicide. This combination provides both a mechanical and a chemical barrier. Still another factor is proper insertion and retention of the diaphragm for a minimum of six hours after intercourse.

When the device is properly positioned over the cervix its presence is not felt by either partner and should not hinder the coital act. When used in conjunction with a spermicide as well as a condom, the diaphragm can be extremely effective.

Intrauterine Devices (IUD).   Thus far, the techniques and devices discussed have, by either physical or mechanical means, prevented the sperm and egg from joining and thereby causing conception. The IUD, however, is a birth control device, rather than a contraceptive, inasmuch as it does not prevent conception but merely prevents the product of the conception—a fertilized egg—from becoming implanted in the uterus.

The devices, which vary in size, shape and material, are generally composed of either polyethylene plastic in the shape of a spiral, loop or bow (Fig. 6–5) or copper in the shape of a T. In order to be effective (effectiveness varies with the type of device but averages about 5 per cent), it must be inserted into the uterus by a physician. As long as the device is properly in place, it should provide fertility protection. If conception is desired, the device may be removed by a physician, and fertility will be restored.

Side effects that may affect one's decision to use the IUD include (1)

  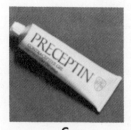

A   B   C

Figure 6–4   Three common birth control devices. *A*, Condom. *B*, Diaphragm. *C*, Spermicidal cream. (From *Life and Health*, published by CRM Books, Del Mar, Calif., 1972, pp. 256 and 257.)

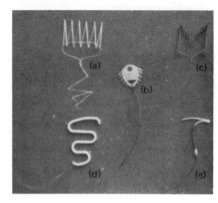

Figure 6-5 Five types of IUD's. *a*, Majzlin spring device. *b*, Dalkon shield. *c*, "M" device. *d*, Lippes loop. *e*, "Seven" device. (From Clausen, J. P., et al.: *Maternity Nursing Today.* New York, McGraw-Hill Book Co., 1973, p. 275.)

expulsion from the uterus, (2) perforation of the uterus, (3) increased menstrual flow, (4) vaginal discharge, (5) low back pain, (6) bleeding, and (7) cramps. Most of these side effects appear to be short-term problems and seem to occur more frequently in women who have not borne children. The effectiveness of the IUD is lower in women who have not borne children and therefore may not be the method of choice for young people.

Spermicidal Chemicals. There are many preparations presently available which are capable of killing human sperm. These spermicidal products, which are sold as foams, gels, creams, foaming tablets, and suppositories, have a functional pregnancy rate of 20 to 30 per cent when used alone. However, when used in conjunction with other techniques, such as the condom or diaphragm, the effectiveness is greatly increased.

Most of the spermicides are inserted into the vagina several minutes before intercourse with an applicator that deposits the preparation high in the vaginal canal near the cervix. The user must keep in mind that an application is effective for only one ejaculation and must be repeated for each intercourse.

The major drawbacks to the use of spermicidal products, other than their rather low rate of effectiveness, seem to be the need for preparation and thereby loss of some spontaneity as well as some seepage from the vaginal tract which some find rather unesthetic.

Douche. One of the great myths about contraception is that one can prevent conception simply by washing away the sperm after intercourse. The evidence of this myth can be easily seen by noting the pregnancy rate from douching is between 30 and 40 per cent.

The principal reason for this low rate of effectiveness, regardless of the douching solution used, is that sperm are generally deposited high in the vagina and move quite rapidly into the uterus. A douche is effective for washing out the vagina but, unfortunately, does not remove sperm from the uterus.

Oral Contraceptives (the Pill). The main function of oral contraceptives is to prevent ovulation or expulsion of the mature egg from the ovary. This is accomplished by taking a pill containing the ovarian

Figure 6-6   One of the many types of oral contraceptives. (From *Life and Health,* published by CRM Books, Del Mar, Calif., 1972, p. 256.)

hormones estrogen and progesterone. The presence of these hormones (even though they are synthetic) in the body inhibits the production of the follicle-stimulating hormone (FSH) by the pituitary gland to cause maturation of an egg. Since FSH is not produced, the egg does not mature and ovulation does not occur.

Although many brands are available, they are all one of two types: combined or sequential. The sequential pills follow the normal sequence of hormonal events in the body. Pills containing estrogen are taken for the first two weeks, and those containing progesterone are taken during the third week. The combined pills, on the other hand, contain both hormones, with progesterone as the major component. Many of the sequential pills have been removed from the market because of their greater side effects as well as lower effectiveness rates. The effectiveness of the oral contraceptive is extremely high, with a pregnancy rate of about 0.1 to 1 per cent.

The major problem with oral contraceptives seems to be the high number of side effects encountered by about 10 per cent of the users. A survey of the medical literature in this area indicates that the increased risk of thromboembolism is somewhat equivalent to the risk during pregnancy. Oral contraceptives have also been associated with a higher incidence of cancer; venereal disease; disorders of carbohydrate metabolism; liver, thyroid and adrenal dysfunction; headaches; skin disorders; and coronary artery disease; however, no direct causal relationship has yet been proved. It must be clearly understood that the pill changes, to some extent, the body chemistry and therefore is an "unnatural" substance. The question is, Are these side effects more or less dangerous than pregnancy?

Sterilization.   The preceding methods have all been reversible; sterility is the only irreversible method of contraception.

Sterilization of the male is accomplished by a *vasectomy.* This procedure consists of cutting and tying the vasa deferentia, which join the testes to the ejaculatory duct. The sex organs and glands are not affected; the male continues to produce semen and is able to ejaculate upon orgasm, but the ejaculate contains no sperm. A vasectomy requires only two small incisions in the scrotum and may be done in the physician's office in about one hour.

Female sterilization is accomplished by removal or disruption of the function of some part of the reproductive system. This may involve the ovaries, fallopian tubes, or uterus. Generally, removal of the uterus (hysterectomy) or the ovaries (ovariectomy) are high-risk procedures that are not performed for sterilization purposes only.

The technique generally used for female sterilization is tubal ligation, which involves severing the fallopian tubes and is accomplished by either laparoscopy or culdoscopy. In *laparoscopy,* a small incision is made in the lower abdominal wall and an electrode is used to cauterize a small portion of each tube. The tube is then cut at the point of cauterization. In *culdoscopy,* tubal ligation is accomplished through the vagina rather than the abdominal wall. Both procedures require relatively short periods of time to perform and only brief hospitalization.

BIBLIOGRAPHY

Bibliographic references for Chapter 6 can be found at the end of Section Three, on p. 144.

CHAPTER 7

SEXUALITY AND
SEX ROLES

There are an infinite number of ways to express one's individual concept of oneself as a sexual being. A problem arises only when the chosen behavior differs from that which is deemed acceptable. For a brief moment examine the following pictures and write down your immediate feelings.

126

Is it okay for this *man* to assume the role of chef or should *women* be the master cooks? How do we deal with girls wanting to play on sandlot baseball teams traditionally reserved for boys?

Much recent research shows that the differences between what have been termed masculine behavior and feminine behavior are no longer so great but that some basic characteristics are still used to describe certain gender tasks. When asked to list traditional masculine traits, persons almost invariably include concern for objects and being essentially active and task-oriented, while a list of feminine traits characteristically include concern for interpersonal relationships and affection. It is important to note that each person does not exhibit only certain kinds of traits but each trait is present in varying degrees so that some persons demonstrate an even mixture while in others the masculine or feminine traits are emphasized. At the end of this chapter is an exercise to help you find out how you display or at least internalize your own masculinity-femininity.

Even though a case is presently being made for the removal of sex roles, it remains important to examine what, if any, differences exist between the sexes.

DEVELOPMENT OF SEX DIFFERENCES

From biology, physiology and other areas of study we know it is believed that the first living organisms on earth were unicellular and asexual. Over a period of time, more complex organisms that were capable of sexual reproduction appeared, and it was at that point that we can note variation in offspring, which were no longer exact duplicates of the parents.

Thus began the process that led to the first differentiation between males and females. If sexual reproduction were to take place, it was necessary for there to be a division of the reproductive labor. One type of reproductive cell needed to be mobile and energetic, while the other type needed to be somewhat sedentary and to serve as a source of nourishment for the development to continue. These roles were filled by the sperm and the egg, respectively. And so we find the first example of sex roles in the union of the sperm (produced by the millions, with many being expendable) and the egg (produced one at a time from the limited number of primary oocytes present at birth) to produce the offspring that will carry on the species.

Out of this competition among sperm to be the one to cause fertilization may have come the rather rampant competition among males to win the favor of a select female. Indeed, anthropologists tell us that the initial social differences between human males and females grew from this competition. The biologists and anthropologists have examined the process of natural selection, in which certain traits and characteristics that are superior will thrive, survive and be reproduced.

If we apply natural selection and our theory of competition to human beings, we can see that the female traditionally was in the position of being able to select the male who best met her needs. The preferred males were those who could best provide food, shelter and protection. These males also were more likely to produce children who survived. The male children modeled their father's behavior, while the surviving females, who were the best nurturers in the rigorous environment, reproduced females with similar capabilities. And so the sex roles of male-as-provider and female-as-nurturer were established.

But as the world progressed, the needs of society changed. It was no longer necessary for the male to hunt and build and provide protection in the same physical manner. Survival in the modern world could now be measured by brain power rather then muscle power. The female need not devote tedious hours and many years providing a nurturing environment and was able to spend more time out of the home.

The result, of course, is that the gross psychosocial differences between the sexes were significantly narrowed toward androgyny. In fact, some writers believe there are no longer traits which are only male or female but that some males have more traditional female traits and vice versa. This, then, would allow greater differences within male and female behaviors than between the two.

PSYCHOLOGICAL DIFFERENCES

Many writers have noted what appear to be psychological differences between the genders. Some of these differences, such as a greater sensitivity to temperature and touch in females, have been noted in infants. Other studies have found that infant males cry more, are more demanding of attention and sleep less than females.

Still others have shown that when given personality tests females tend to show greater sensitivity and are more verbal, while males are more experimental. Erikson has noted that boys appeared to be "outward" oriented while girls are "inward" oriented. This is somewhat validated by the observation of job choices where men choose to deal with objects and women deal with people.

It is difficult, however, to separate how much of these factors and behaviors are innate and how much is due to socialization. The role of socialization as the primary influence on role identity is strongly supported by many writers who feel that the only true differences that exist between the genders are only those related to the genitals. All else is learned. Boys are given toys such as trucks, balls, soldiers, and guns and are reinforced for using them. Girls, on the other hand, are encouraged to play with dolls and to wear pretty dresses.

Another view, one expounded upon by Freud, states that one's biological make-up predetermines one's psychological orientation. Credence is given to this argument by experiments that have shown that male behavior is exhibited by a female monkey if the female fetus is injected with male hormones. And so we have the ongoing controversy.

PHYSICAL DIFFERENCES

It is obvious that there are some distinct, nongenital differences between males and females. Men have larger and heavier bones and bulkier muscles, while women have smaller lungs and get by on less air, a smaller larynx (giving a higher pitched voice), more sensitive skin and a more highly developed sense of smell. Men have more muscle, while women have more fat tissue. Most of these characteristics were much more important in a primitive environment than they are today.

We also find that males have a shorter life span, contract more illness and die from more causes. It is thought that the male hormones may make the male more vulnerable to various diseases.

SEX ROLES

NEED FOR SEX ROLES

If masculine and feminine behaviors are becoming so intertwined, why is it so important that we have sex roles or that the individual assume a sex role? Sex role orientation may be important for some because it helps them arrive at an identity. It gives them something to hold on to and a goal to work toward. To be sure, not all cultures have the same sex roles, but each culture seems to have its own set of roles assigned to each gender.

A second function of sex roles lies in the idea that all societies must, in order to survive, have some guides or norms for social and personal behavior. It is easier to rely on "normal" or "expected" behaviors when in new social settings and to remove the norm only when the inter- and intrapersonal relationship has progressed.

Still another reason for understanding masculinity-femininity as it relates to society is that much that occurs to us as individuals, as a couple or even within a group is affected and to some extent controlled by the dynamics of the situation. Thus, in order to make decisions regarding ourselves as sexual beings, we must understand the role we play in society and the effect of that role on self and others.

THE LEARNING OF SEX ROLES

If we are to understand the concept of sex role and how it functions in our lives, it is imperative that we examine how we learn the role we choose and understand whether we have chosen a role or whether it has been laid upon us.

A great deal of research dealing with roles and the learning of roles indicates that such variables as social class, race, education, familial expectations and close relationships, as well as religion, have a profound effect on the expression of one's sexuality. Much of this same research has pointed out that the male appears to learn more regarding sex role from society, while the female's chief means of role education is the mother, and that both genders identify more closely with the female parent than with the male parent. This would indicate perhaps that males have significantly greater anxiety about role behavior than females, and this is borne out by the literature in this area. Perhaps we can explain the behavior of our friend in the picture below as having to show that he has lived up to the role as he sees it defined as well as a rather low-level means of relieving anxiety.

I'm tougher than any of you guys!

Or perhaps the "little man" (you see, we always identify by role) is merely demonstrating another factor that is important in learning—the need for models. The extent to which the parent becomes involved in child-rearing appears to be in direct proportion to the degree in which the child models the parent. This point is brought home quite vividly in the literature dealing with boys from homes in which the father was absent. Such boys tend to exhibit the so-called masculine traits of independence and aggression very strongly and may attempt to overcompensate for this

Do you think it's okay to dress him in pink?

sex role confusion by overreacting in a masculine manner. (Could this be our "little man"?)

Not only do we learn sex roles from our family, but society in all its "wisdom" becomes a teacher for everyone. The couple pictured above has already begun to instill the idea of sex role in their baby. As this child

I thought you said you'd get the broads.

learns from his environment, he will undoubtedly find out very early in life (rightly or wrongly) that there are basic differences between boys and girls and that boys can do certain things but not others because they are not masculine. Just as the "boys" on the corner can be men of the world and assume their role so can the couple assume their role of concern, caring and affection.

As the world changes, the opportunity for differences in role identification will become greater and more varied. The key to dealing with your sexuality is to view yourself in a positive light and make the best choice(s) for you as an individual sexual being in a society of sexual beings.

SEXUAL DRIVE

There is some question as to the extent of the sex drive (libido) in both the male and the female and even more question as to what a "normal" sex drive is. One thing is certain—the "normal" sex drive varies with age, peaking at 18 to 20 years of age in the male and around 40 years of age in the female, and of course, is different for each individual.

Many factors play a significant role in the motivation of a given individual toward sexual activity. Stress of all kinds can either increase or decrease a person's need for sex. The same is true for the general environment. Factors such as atmosphere, social setting, temperature, food, drink and state of health affect not only one's sexual response but also the motivation for sex.

A significant factor in the sex drive is prior sexual and social experience. Human beings, like all other animals, tend to do things they find pleasurable and avoid things they find painful. If pleasure was derived from a previous experience, the individual is likely to repeat that activity. The converse is true, of course, for unpleasant experiences.

Cultural influences also play a role in sexual motivation. Sexual activity may be discouraged by one's religion or certain types of legislation or may be encouraged through literature and mass media. It is said by some that sexual needs may be inherited and that genotype is responsible for an invididual's particular level of excitability.

There is strong evidence which indicates that androgenic (male) hormone levels play a strong role in the sex drive and arousal levels of both men and women. Other factors such as age, the five senses, nervous stimulation and the time elapsed since the last orgasm tend to affect not only the level of excitability but also the sex drive. However, it is important to keep in mind that there is no norm and that each individual has his or her own needs.

The motivation toward sex is different in men and women, but once more we face the socialization vs. biology question. Some feel that the need for sex is acquired and can be learned through experience. Others state that sex is a basic drive and that only the manner of dealing with it is learned.

SEXUAL RESPONSE

Just as there are a variety of components to one's overall sexuality, so are there both biological and psychosocial components to human sexual response patterns. With this in mind, let's look at the physiological and psychological responses of both males and females and examine the roles they play in the procreative and pleasurable aspects of sexual behavior.

Physiological Responses. In recent years many writers have begun to examine the physiology of sexual response in both the male and female in an attempt to ascertain optimal sexual function. Perhaps the most well known of these investigators have been Masters and Johnson, who published the first comprehensive report on the topic in 1966. In their work Masters and Johnson noted that two significant changes in physiology occurred in both male and female during response to sexual stimulation: (1) vasocongestion, or an accumulation of blood in certain blood vessels, and (2) myotonia, or increased muscular tension. Masters and Johnson noted that in both men and women the sexual response pattern can be divided into basically four phases: (1) excitement, (2) plateau, (3) orgasm, and (4) resolution. As we trace the changes occurring during each of the phases, it is not difficult to see that the pattern of response does not vary greatly between the genders and that it involves not merely the genitals but the entire body.

In the *excitement phase* the male, through central nervous system impulses, achieves an erection due to vasocongestion in the erectile tissue of the penis. There is a concomitant elevation of the scrotum and testes as well as a thickening of the skin of the scrotum and enlargement of the testes.

In the female, vaginal lubrication begins and the inner two-thirds of the vagina expand. Vasocongestion causes the labia minora to enlarge, and the labia majora are spread open.

Others organs also become involved, resulting in increased heart rate and blood pressure, nipple erection in females and some males, involuntary muscle tensing and the so-called "sex flush" or rash on the skin.

During the second phase, or *plateau*, the labia majora and minora become engorged with blood, and secretion from Bartholin's glands near the opening of the vagina give added lubrication. The clitoris retracts under the clitoral prepuce, and the outer third of the vagina becomes engorged with venous blood.

In the male, the testes increase in size by about 50 per cent. The penis increases in circumference and becomes dark red. At this point the mucous secretion from Cowper's glands may appear at the opening of the urethra.

The nongenital changes during this phase include sex flush over the entire body, tension in both voluntary and involuntary muscles, increase in breast size, hyperventilation and greater increase in blood pressure and heart rate.

The *orgasmic phase* is identified in the male by the contractions of the urethra and ejaculation. This follows contraction of the epididymides, vasa deferentia, seminal vesicles and prostate and the closing of the sphincter leading from the bladder.

The female orgasmic response is seen as contractions of the uterus and the orgasmic platform, which comprises the congested outer third of the vagina and the labia minora.

Extragenital orgasmic responses include the sex flush, rectal sphincter contraction, involuntary muscle contractions, increased respiratory rate, increased heart rate and increased blood pressure.

During the final phase, *resolution*, vasocongestion decreases and there is a gradual loss of myotonia, with a concomitant decrease in rate of respiration, pulse, and blood pressure. In the female there is a relaxation of the vaginal walls, the labia and clitoris return to their normal size and position, breast size decreases, and the sex flush fades. In the males the penis becomes flaccid, and the scrotum and testes return to their normal size and configuration.

Psychosocial Needs.   We may read all that is available regarding the biology of sexual response, or may study "marriage manuals," which describe various sexual techniques in great detail, and still we may have the same problems as the couple pictured on pg. 135. So let us now look beyond the physical aspects and consider some psychological factors.

It has been said that because the male can ejaculate, he has no, or at the most very limited, psychosocial pressures that limit his orgasmic experience. Traditionally, his sexual behavior is much more acceptable, and any fears about performance are based on achieving erection rather than ejaculation. The presumption is, of course, that with the proper excitement orgasm will occur. In other words, so long as the male gets

Don't tell me you've got *another* headache!

through the first phase of the pattern he is sure to reach the third phase.

In regard to the female, however, it has been assumed that the orgasmic response is far more difficult to achieve and requires a specific type of stimulation. In addition, the environment had to be psychologically conducive. Recent evidence, however, has attempted to dispel this myth, since it has been found that *both* male and female responses to sexual stimuli can be greatly increased or decreased by the psychological setting. Perhaps the most important factor in the female sexual response pattern is her attitude toward her partner. (Perhaps our male friend pictured above should take note and reexamine himself.)

Another factor which may play an important role in female sexual response is that of learning. Not only heredity but social and psychological influences as well may not have allowed the female to be a complete sexual person. With greater awareness, the female may achieve a fuller sexual reponse.

OTHER SEXUAL PROBLEMS

MALE

Premature Ejaculation. Premature ejaculation is characterized by expulsion of semen prior to or immediately following insertion of the penis into the vagina. It may occur if foreplay has been extensive, with much fondling and petting, or if there has been a long interval between sexual experiences. If the problem becomes chronic, a physician or psychologist trained in this area of sexual dysfunction should be consulted.

Dyspareunia. Dyspareunia (painful sexual intercourse) may be due to penile inflammation or infection, or previous gonorrheal infection. As noted earlier, if pain occurs during intercourse, a physician should be consulted.

Paraphimosis. This problem is characterized by discomfort on the penis caused by a tight foreskin. Treatment consists of circumcision.

Impotence. The inability to maintain an erection may have a psychological or physiological basis.

Physical causes include poor health, fever, diabetes, and hypothyroidism. Handling or manipulating the penis, as in masturbation, seems to bear no relationship to impotence.

Psychological causes may originate in early childhood if the child was taught that a penis was bad and that sex was dirty and evil. Impotence may also be due to unpleasant sexual experiences or a feeling of inadequacy.

At one time or another most males experience impotence. The key to resolving the problem is to not develop great anxieties. If the problem becomes chronic, a physician should be consulted.

FEMALE

Vaginismus. This concern is characterized by involuntary tightening or closing of the vaginal opening and represents an unconscious attempt to avoid penile penetration. The cause is generally considered to be psychological, and the assistance of a therapist may be required.

Dyspareunia. Painful intercourse may be caused by an inflammation of the vagina, inadequate lubrication or menopause. In the case of menopause, little can be done, although hormone treatment is sometimes effective. Lubrication may be provided by the use of a water-soluble gel.

DECISION MAKING ABOUT SEXUAL BEHAVIOR

Now that we have discussed the motivations for sexual activity and the response to sexual arousal, the next question to consider is whether or not to engage in the physical and psychological act of intercourse. Using the decision-making model in Chapter 1, each person must develop standards and criteria of sexual morality for himself or herself.

Sexual Value Systems. In order to determine our motives for behavior and make decisions it is important to examine our values and use these values as a source of data in decision making. Since no one value system is acceptable to everyone, let's examine the prominent standards in our society as described by Ira Reiss. For many people, the first step in deciding about premarital sexual activities is to explore the spectrum of sexual value systems and find their place in it. Ira Reiss has described four viewpoints in this spectrum:

1. *Abstinence*—Sexual intercourse before marriage is wrong for both males and females; it should be reserved for marriage.

2. *The Double Standard*—Sexual intercourse before marriage is fine for males, but taboo for females; female virginity is prized.

3. *Permissiveness with Affection*—Sexual relations between unmarrieds is permissible as long as there is a deep mutual affection and a shared stable relationship beyond sex.

4. *Permissiveness without Affection*—Intercourse between mutually consenting unmarrieds is permissible; physical attraction and desire are emphasized rather than love.

Which of these value systems best fits the manner in which you choose to display your physical sexuality? Perhaps none fits totally or at all. The fact is that none of these specify such sexual behaviors as fondling, petting to orgasm, and oral-genital stimulation.

EFFECTS OF NONMARITAL SEX

A second consideration centers around the effect that this act may have on the participants. If sex is not a moral issue, it must be a physical, social or emotional issue and must be examined and evaluated in that context.

Physical Factors. The obvious physical considerations are pregnancy and venereal disease. Through proper planning (as discussed earlier), the probability of encountering these hazards may be decreased. However, a third physical hazard must also be dealt with. Studies indicate that intercourse in early adolescence and with multiple partners increases the incidence of herpes viral infection and cervical cancer.

To make a rational decision regarding sexual behavior, the individual who feels sexual intercourse is acceptable would first be sure the partner is not infected with venereal disease and then use some type of birth control unless conception is desired.

Psychological Considerations. It is virtually impossible to state conclusively that nonmarital sexual intercourse is always positive or always negative on the development of one's personality.

Participation in sexual activities in an attempt to win love and affection or acceptance or to cover up various problems suggests that such behavior has negative connotations and may contribute to personality distortions. On the other hand, a caring, loving, nonexploitative sexual relationship may be of no harm.

The key word here is nonexploitative. In the decision-making process, it is essential that one's attitudes toward and concern for others' values be included as a source of information. With this in mind, it is imperative that the desire to exploit another and the effect it will have on oneself be weighed and possible alternatives examined.

Consideration of Others. The effect of this decision on others is also a consideration in the decision-making process. In this case, others may include a future husband or wife and how they might feel toward you or your present partner. Still another factor would be the possibility of conception and a concern for the unborn. Parents and their attitudes and values are certainly significant considerations as well.

Future Considerations. Studies on the effect of premarital intercourse on subsequent marriages have shown that individuals who have had a variety of partners before marriage have a greater probability of being divorced or unhappily married. Others have found that a positive relationship exists between virginity prior to marriage and marital happiness. Although some investigators noted that sexually experienced women have a significantly easier adjustment on the honeymoon than do inexperienced females, no difference existed after about two weeks.

All in all, a decision about any aspect of sexual behavior, like any other decision, requires much input and answers to such questions as the following:

1. How does this behavior fit our values?
2. How does this behavior fit the values of society?
3. What are the possible consequences of this act?
4. Are we willing to accept the consequences?
5. How can we avoid or decrease the probability of the consequences?
6. What are our *real* reasons for doing this?
7. What are the possible alternatives?
8. How will others such as parents, friends and partner be affected?

These are only a few of the questions to be examined. Note that all questions are phrased in the plural. Since the sex act requires more than one person, the decision-making process includes more than one person.

EXERCISES FOR THOUGHT

Now that we have a general understanding of sexuality and its physical, social and psychological dimensions, let's look at some activities that will point out values and attitudes that are held and are essential for decision making.

ACTIVITY 1

One of the concerns to deal with in deciding whether or not to engage in sexual activity is the effect on self and on others. Below is a list and explanation of value systems in sexuality developed by Isadore Rubin. Read each and decide which one best represents your values and write it down. Then have your parents, closest friend, and boyfriend or girlfriend read the list and write down their values. How do they compare and what are the implications of this for your decision?

Value Systems in Sexuality

1. Traditional Repressive Asceticism. This system, which is still embodied in most of our official codes and laws, proscribes any kind of sexual activity outside of the marriage relationship and accepts sex in marriage grudgingly, insisting that the major purpose of sex is procreation. This value system is intolerant of all deviations from restrictive patterns of heterosexual behavior; it conceives of sex morality solely in absolute terms of "though shalt" and "thou shalt not."

2. Enlightened Asceticism. As exemplified in the views of such spokesmen as David Mace, this begins with a basic acceptance of the ascetic point of view. Mace sees asceticism as a safeguard against the "softness" to which we so easily fall prey in an age when opportunities for self-indulgence are so abundant. He sees youth as the time when invaluable lessons of self-control and discipline must be learned, with sex as one of the supreme areas in which self-mastery may be demonstrated, and he opposes any slackening of the sexual code. However, he takes neither a negative nor a dogmatic attitude toward sex and has been an ardent exponent of the "open forum" in which issues can be stated and weighed.

3. Humanistic Liberalism. Humanistic liberalism is best exemplified by the views of Lester Kirkendall and Mary Calderone. Kirkendall opposes inflexible absolutes and makes his prime concern the concept of interpersonal relationship. He sees the criterion of morality as not the commission or omission of a particular act, but the consequence of the act upon the interrelationships of people, not only the immediate people concerned but broader relationships. Kirkendall thus is searching for a value system which will help supply internalized controls for the individual in a period when older social and religious controls are collapsing.

4. Humanistic Radicalism.   This is exemplified best by the views of Walter Stokes. He accepts the humanistic position of Kirkendall and goes further in proposing that society should make it possible for young people to have relatively complete sexual freedom. He makes it clear, however, that society must create certain preconditions before this goal may be achieved. He envisions a cultural engineering project which may take generations to complete.

5. Fun Morality.   This philosophy has as its most consistent spokesmen Albert Ellis and Hugh Hefner. Without compromise, they uphold the belief that sex is fun and that the more sexual enjoyment a human being has, the better and more psychologically sound he or she is likely to be. They believe that despite the risk of pregnancy, premarital intercourse should be freely permitted, and at times encouraged, for well-informed and reasonably well adjusted persons.

6. Sexual Anarchy.   Sexual anarchy has as its philosopher the late French jurist Rena Guyon. Guyon attacks chastity, virginity, and monogamy and calls for the elimination of all sexual taboos and all notions of sexual immorality and shame. The only restriction that would apply in the general social principle is that no one may injure or do violence to another.

ACTIVITY 2

Much has been said about male and female roles and what it is to be masculine or feminine. The following series of questions will help you examine your position and attitudes in relation to sex roles. In an attempt to bring out these values, respond to each of the statements on a 7-point continuum, giving *1* to those statements with which you *strongly disagree, 7* to those with which you *strongly agree* and *4* to those on which you are neutral. The scoring sheet (don't look at it now) at the end of the questionnaire will allow you to relate your values to your behaviors and to examine what this means to you and your concept of sexuality.

n.m.   1. A career for a married woman is most appropriate after her children are grown.

n.m.   2. A woman may be employed, but should not compete with her husband for professional success.

o.f.   3. A woman can best achieve full self-development by ignoring men and the system that men have built.

n.m.   4. Women are better suited to work for men than men are suited to work for women — in making things run smoothly and efficiently with quiet assistance.

o.f.   5. The world can be run much more efficiently by women than by men.

n.f.   6. Alimony should be abolished.

n.m.   7. It is a good idea for a woman to marry someone in the same field of work in order to be a helpmate.

o.f.   8. If a woman marries, it is a good idea to marry someone in her field in order to work as a team, as colleagues, or as competitors.

n.f.   9. The husband should be willing to move if the wife's job demands it.

n.f. 10. A father in a two-career family is likely to be closer to his children than one who is the sole breadwinner.

o.f. 11. Men, because they are more subject to heart attacks and ulcers, and because they feel a need always to be in an authoritative position, are less equipped to handle difficult responsibilities than women are.

n.f. 12. Women should be able to have abortions on demand.

n.m. 13. Women are inherently more intuitive and empathetic than men.

n.m. 14. Women have special talents unique to their sex that should be better utilized.

n.m. 15. A woman should be free to pursue whatever interest or vocation she pleases, provided that it does not inconvenience her husband.

o.m. 16. Women's natural work is in the home, but men should now and then assist them with their work.

o.f. 17. It is not society or the "system," but men who oppress women.

o.m. 18. Women are instinctively maternal and nurturing.

o.m. 19. Women should be educated but should not strive to become powerful or influential in public activity.

n.m. 20. Women's most useful work in the world is to do the idealistic, community-minded things often neglected by men.

n.m. 21. Women should be free to pursue many avenues of endeavor because modern men need women who are interesting, flexible and capable.

n.f. 22. Sex roles are obsolete, and we should move toward desegregation of the sexes so that eventually there will be no "female" or "male" roles.

o.f. 23. Women can and should try to be like men.

o.f. 24. The enemy of women is men.

o.m. 25. Girls should be raised in such a way that they will be proud to say that their sole vocation is wife and mother.

o.f. 26. Women should "wear the pants."

o.m. 27. A woman's best job cannot be salaried — keeping a man happy.

n.f.   28.   Women as well as men should be included in the draft.

n.f.   29.   Girls should be free to ask boys for a date and to initiate sexual relationships.

o.m.   30.   Much as women would like to be good scientists, first and foremost they want and need to be mothers and companions to men.

o.f.   31.   A woman would necessarily make a better President than a man.

o.m.   32.   A woman cannot physically, emotionally, or psychologically do the work men do.

o.f.   33.   It is better to be single than to be subordinate to a man.

o.f.   34.   Women are superior to men in every way.

o.m.   35.   The trend toward desexualization in clothes, jobs, recreation and education is dangerous.

o.m.   36.   Men have a greater inherent ability to think logically than do women.

n.f.   37.   Men have the advantage in our society because they have power and esteem.

o.f.   38.   A woman can best achieve full self-development by getting the best education and training possible.

o.m.   39.   Most women do not want to be indepentent but want a man to take care of them.

n.m.   40.   Man's inherent strengths are different from woman's and those strengths complement one another.

n.m.   41.   Women are naturally more expressive emotionally than men and any moves toward liberation should enhance this quality.

n.f.   42.   Child care should be provided by the state for all who want it.

o.m.   43.   Generally speaking, men do not have the emotional make-up to stay home and assume the domestic role.

n.f.   44.   Most men are afraid of strong and competent women.

n.f.   45.   Men and women can best overcome discrimination through the revolutionary overthrow of the present system.

o.m.   46.   Women have the advantage in our society because they have protection, leisure and freedom from the pressures to achieve.

o.m.   47.   A man can best achieve full self-development by being a good husband and provider.

n.m.   48.   Women can best overcome discrimination by working individually to prove their abilities.

o.f.   49.   Men treat women as toys.

n.f.   50.   Men and women have the same biological (genetic) range of emotional and intellectual capacities. The differences present in our society are all learned.

n.f. 51. Women can best overcome discrimination by working in exclusively female groups.

o.f. 52. Men neglect issues of health and welfare, and therefore women are appropriate political leaders of our country.

n.f. 53. Almost all men are sexists—either consciously or unconsciously.

n.m. 54. Women are really the "stronger sex"—they provide emotional support for the man so he can achieve. . . . behind every great man there is a woman.

o.m. 55. The husband should have the final decision on important matters.

n.m. 56. A woman can best achieve full self-development by taking a job that utilizes her unique skills and qualities.

Add up the points for each attitude—o.m., n.m., o.f., n.f.—and enter the total in the appropriate column. A high score represents an identification with that attitude.

Score Sheet

Attitude	Scores for Each	Total
o.m. (old masculinist)		
n.m. (new masculinist)		
o.f. (old feminist)		
n.f. (new feminist)		

Attitudes:

Old masculinist: Biology is destiny.
New masculinist: Vive la difference, but down with discrimination.
Old feminist: Anything men can do, women can do better.
New feminist: Sex-linked roles are obsolete.

ACTIVITY 3

We have seen that sexuality deals with more than the genitals and in fact is composed of all the differences as well as likenesses between men and women. With this in mind, apply the decision-making model to the following situation: You are married and have just had a baby boy. You have read much and are extremely concerned about sex roles for this child. Decide how you will rear this child and what roles it will play in twentieth century America.

BIBLIOGRAPHY

Avers, C. J.: *Biology of Sex.* New York, John Wiley, 1974.

Barbach, L. G.: *For Yourself—The Fulfillment of Female Sexuality.* Doubleday and Company, New York, 1975.

Brenton, M.: *The American Male.* New York, Coward-McCann, 1966.

Broverman, I. K. et al.: Sex role stereotypes: A current appraisal. *Journal of Social Issues,* 28(2):59–78, 1972.

DeMartino, O. F. (Ed.): *Sexual Behavior and Personality Characteristics.* New York, Grove Press, 1963.

Erikson, Eric,: Sex differences in the play configuration of preadolescents. *American Journal of Orthopsychiatry,* 21:667–692, 1951.

Eysenck, N. J.: Masculinity-femininity, personality and sexual attitudes. *Journal of Sex Research,* 7:83–88, May, 1971.

Gardner, S., and R. Gelinas (Eds.): *Birth Control Handbook.* Box 1000, Station G, Montreal 130, Quebec.

Kogan, B. A.: *Human Sexual Expression.* New York, Harcourt Brace Jovanovich, 1970.

Masters, W. H., and V. E. Johnson: *Human Sexual Response.* Boston, Little, Brown and Company, 1966.

Masters, W. H., and V. E. Johnson: *The Pleasure Bond.* Boston, Little, Brown and Company, 1975.

Osofsky, J. D., and H. J. Osofsky: Androgyny as a life style. *Family Coordinator,* October, 1972.

Reiss, I. L.: *Premarital Sexual Standards in America,* New York, The Free Press, 1960.

Rubin, I.: Transition in sex values—Implications for the education of adolescents. *The Journal of Marriage and the Family,* 27:2, May 1965.

Taylor, D. L. (Ed.): *Human Sexual Development,* Philadelphia, F. A. Davis Co., 1970.

Trainer, J. B.: *Physiologic Foundations for Marriage Counseling,* St. Louis, The C. V. Mosby Co., 1965.

ASSIMILATED SUBSTANCES AND OUR CULTURE

CHAPTER 8

CLASSIFICATION OF DRUGS AND THEIR CHEMICAL ACTIONS

The use of chemical substances to alter man's consciousness is not a twentieth century phenomenon. Historians have found evidence that drugs such as marijuana were in use prior to 2000 B.C. It has been documented that such chemical substances were initially used as a means of dispelling evil spirits or sickness. From such beliefs of magic potions came the search for the fountain of youth or a magical substance that would preserve youth. Man today is no different from primitive man with regard to seeking the magical cure for what ails him. This search has brought about longevity and the belief that there are miracle drugs. The twentieth century individual may well be using drugs, such as ephedrine, reserpine and marijuana, that were first discovered by earlier civilizations.

History tells us that various substances that were consumed actually showed the individual no physiological benefit, but they provided a psychological benefit in that the individual believed they would cure him. This is still true today in cases in which an individual consumes a substance that has no positive or negative physiological effect on the symptoms or disease but feels better because he expects the remedy to alleviate the symptom or pain. Physicians comment that patients may not feel they are getting their "money's worth" unless they are given a prescription or expensive therapy. Patients are often unable to cope with simple advice, such as, "all you need is a day of rest" or "go home and go to bed and let it run its course." Researchers have found that antibiotics are being ranked as the second most prescribed drugs in the nation. Is this not doing the people an injustice? Is this an overworked miracle? Could not the overuse cause bacterial mutations that might later cause massive epidemics?

From the earliest times human beings have sought a substance that would virtually cure any sickness or ailment. We, as a nation, seem to be striving to orient our lives around chemical substances rather than assuming the responsibility for preventive measures.

147

Today, both legal and illegal substances are available in virtually every community in the United States. The use of chemical substances for other than physical illness is common. We cannot turn on the television or radio without being bombarded with a means to solving some immediate problem through the use of a substance that will enable us to relax, sleep, or stay awake, or even cure our indigestion. The television has replaced the traveling huckster of yesterday. Instead of being subjected to high-pressure selling techniques, the public is subtly persuaded that they need a particular substance in order to function with the rest of society or to enjoy themselves. Headaches have been given numbers, new diseases have been created, and comparisons are made to sell the public a substance for every conceivable problem.

Is the public aware of this chemical indoctrination? Perhaps we are but wish to shield ourselves from reality. Most individuals, however, are ignorant of their orientation into a drug-taking society. There has been no valid attempt, either by the public or by various professions, to educate the individuals utilizing chemical substances either for curative powers or for euphoric purposes. It is a matter of record that the modern wonder drugs have been forced on the public by the very professions who claim the right to dispense these chemical solutions. We are not speaking of the prescription abuser but the over-the-counter, self-curing individual. These people structure their day around an assortment of drugstore purchases but do not hesitate to condemn an individual with a drinking problem or to criticize pot-smoking youth of today. This is not to say that those who take illicit drugs or who are addicted to alcohol are acting appropriately in doing their own thing or in condemning the "establishment."

It might be noted at this point that until recently, alcohol and tobacco were not construed as drugs, since both substances were socially acceptable. Nonetheless, nicotine, ethyl alcohol and caffeine are mood-altering chemicals that have definite physiological effects as well. If the general public does not accept these substances as drugs, then how is a drug defined? It has been suggested that a drug is any substance that by its chemical nature alters structure or function in the living organism. Such a definition would include the food preservatives we eat daily, the vitamins that are religiously taken every morning, birth control pills, and a host of other substances heretofore unclassified as drugs.

It might be more practical to accept the definition put forth by the American School Health Association, which states that drugs are "substances intended for use in the diagnosis, cure, treatment, or prevention of disease, or in the relief of pain or discomfort." The medical profession aligns itself with this orientation to drug taking, as is evident from the extensive use of chemotherapy for virtually every disease known to man. This method of treatment is not limited to the viral and bacterial infections but is also applied to chronic diseases, genetic disorders and mental illness. Without prescription drugs, available only through a physician's order, and over-the-counter drugs, the American public would undoubtedly have been unable to live as long or as comfortably or be relieved of such a multitude of ailments. The medical profession indicates that drugs should be used correctly and not experimentally on patients. However, it is usually the patient who does the experimenting, such as using leftover prescriptions or taking drugs prescribed for others, instead of seeking medical help for an ailment. Is this drug abuse? Since there is no such thing as a good drug or a bad drug, what causes the effects of drugs? People?

In this century, there have been significant advances in the development of drugs, including antitoxins, antibiotics, and mood modifiers. Other substances have been developed to cope with chronic conditions such as arthritis or epileptic convulsions, but the major advances have been made in the area of pain relief. These substances range from over-the-counter aspirin to heroin. The increasing tensions of the modern world have prompted the development of numerous drugs for anxiety relief. Such brand-name tranquilizers as Valium and Librium are among the top four prescribed drugs in the nation. Various natural and synthetic substances have been made available for such purposes as relieving the body of excess fluids (diuretics) and suppressing allergic reactions (antihistamines).

Has the total effect of these substances being introduced on the market today increased our life expectancy, or has it been detrimental? Scientists and gerontologists have stated that, through *proper* use of prescribed substances, an individual can expect to increase his longevity five decades over that of individuals of corresponding age who lived during the early 1900's. Gerontologists indicate the positive role that modern medicine and drugs have played in the over-65 population, now numbering close to 6 million. Without chemical substances to cure previous illness, this population would be only in the thousands. An indication of how dramatically life has changed is the statistic that close to 96 per cent of the prescribed drugs were not available, in their present form, a quarter of a century ago. It is safe to estimate that close to 1000 drugs are being prescribed and used daily throughout the nation. Have we not indeed become a drug-taking society? Were not our forefathers drug-oriented? History will tell our role in the perpetuation of a drug- or chemical-oriented society, but we do know that societies that preceded ours were users of chemical substances and that some even worshiped plants from which a substance was obtained.

PHARMACOLOGICAL ACTION OF DRUGS

It is important to recognize that not all artificially produced chemicals are foreign substances to the human body. Our bodies produce various hormones (male and female), enzymes and insulin. There are six pharmacological principles that govern virtually every chemical action in man:

1. Drug effect is algebraically additive with physiological state and with the effect of other drugs.
2. No true pharmacological antagonism exists among drugs taken by human beings.
3. Depressant drugs in low concentration have a slight excitatory effect on the body.
4. Stimulant drugs in low concentration have a slight depressant effect on the body.
5. Active, excessive stimulation of the cerebrospinal axis is normally followed by depression.
6. Chronic drug-induced depression is followed by prolonged hyperexcitability upon withdrawal of medication.

The proper application of these principles will enhance one's ability to recognize the possible effects of a chemical substance on the human body. The introduction of foreign substances into the natural sequence of chemical phenomenon of the body can result in unanticipated results or reactions, often referred to as side effects. The severity of these side effects cannot be predicted for all individuals; thus, although the use of a substance uncommon to the body could be detrimental, the magnitude of the effect is an unknown entity. This does not preclude possible side effects from prescribed substances. Physicians are usually aware of the possible reactions an individual may have to a certain drug and may compensate for this with a lower dosage. However, since each person's body is different and thus has a unique chemistry, reactions to a particular drug vary among individuals.

DRUGS AND THE HUMAN BODY

Assimilated substances have been classified legally, chemically, physiologically, psychologically, medicinally, and by origin. For the lay person, there may be only two classifications: legal and illegal, or prescription and nonprescription. There seems to be no clear-cut manner in which the classifications are used. The distinction could be based on whether substances are used for medicinal versus recreational purposes. Prescription, or medicinal, drugs are often designated as purely ethical drugs — substances that cannot be obtained without a prescription — when in fact, prescribed drugs tend to be a major source of recreational drug use. It must be realized that the same drug not only may act differently on an individual at a different time but also may have a harmful effect on another individual for whom it was not prescribed. The dosage of a prescribed drug is based on the individual's age, weight, and general physical condition. With this in mind, under what circumstances would you justify the use of another person's prescription? If this justification were warranted, why would such a situation arise? An individual who knowingly gives a prescribed drug to another person could be sued for illegally practicing medicine, for that privilege is reserved for physicians, dentists, and osteopaths only. Even a pharmacist may not prescribe a drug, despite tales of the reliability of the local apothecary "doctor."

Table 8–1 lists legal and illegal substances used in social situations or for recreation. It is system-oriented in that the drugs all affect the central nervous system. Substances that enhance or decrease the functioning of a specific organ (e.g., digitalis, anticoagulants, insulin) have not been included. If the drugs were classified as to source (organic and inorganic substances), such a broad classification could be confusing and might present problems in dealing with the assimilation of various substances.

The classification of legal and illegal chemical substances in terms of misuse and abuse for the purpose of legal prosecution has been greatly confused and is in need of revision. Currently the legal schedules and restrictions in Table 8–2 are used by the federal and state governments for the prosecution of individuals either using or selling the listed substances. However, some states do have different laws with regard to the use and distribution of drugs. Examine Table 8–2 and see what discrepancies exist with your state. Have you seen a gradual change in these standards? Should this be restructured? If so, how?

TABLE 8-1   EFFECTS OF DRUGS USED FOR SOCIAL OR RECREATIONAL PURPOSES

Drug	Physiological and Psychological Effects	Physical Dependence	Psychological Dependence	Increased Tolerance with Use	Major Dangerous Side Effects
1. Narcotics Opium Morphine Heroin Codeine Paregoric	Constricted pupils, watery eyes, running nose, chills, sweating, loss of appetite and weight, mental and physical dullness, drowsiness, sleepiness, stupor	Yes	Yes	Yes	General physical deterioration, antisocial (and sometimes criminal) behavior, interference of pain threshold; painful withdrawal symptoms; death from overdose
2. Barbiturates (sleeping pills) Tuinals (rainbows) Luminal Nembutal (yellow jackets) Amytal (blue angels) Seconal (red devils)	Constricted pupils, drunken appearance, slurred speech, incoherency, depression, drowsiness, dullness, unconsciousness	Yes	Yes	Yes	Brain damage, liver damage, possibly kidney damage; painful withdrawal symptoms (more severe than from narcotics); pneumonia, convulsions, death from overdose
3. Amphetamines (pep pills) Benzedrine Dexedrine Methedrine (speed)	Dilated pupils, dry mouth and mucous membranes, bad breath, rapid speech, euphoria, extreme fatigue, confused thinking, excitability, sleeplessness, nervousness	Possible	Yes	Slight	Malnutrition, exhaustion, pneumonia, delusions and delirium, high blood pressure, heart attack, damage to circulatory system; potential for brain damage; severe depression after discontinuation
4. Cocaine	Dilated pupils, loss of appetite and weight, euphoria, feeling of well-being, excitability, restlessness, trembling of hands	Possible	Yes	Slight	Mental confusion, dizziness, depression, paranoia, convulsions; death from overdose
5. Psychedelics LSD Mescaline (peyote button) Psilocybin DMT (dimethyltryptamine) STP (dimethoxy-methylamphetamine) MMDA Morning glory seeds	Dilated pupils, cold hands and feet, goose pimples, nausea and vomiting, chills, trembling, delusions, hallucinations, inappropriate or uncontrollable laughing or crying, incoherent speech	No	Yes	Slight	Mental confusion and dizziness, depression, paranoia; convulsions; death from overdose

6. *Cannabis sativa* Marijuana Hashish	Reddening of eyes, dry mouth and throat, coughing spells, euphoria, exaggerated sensory perceptions, talkativeness, laughing, drunken behavior, increase in appetite, general relaxation	No	Yes	No	May hinder physical and mental functions; distortions in sense perceptions, especially in time; can facilitate contact with persons using more dangerous drugs; interferes with pain threshold
7. *Tranquilizers* Major tranquilizers Phenothiazines* (chlorpromazine) Minor tranquilizers Meprobromate (Equanil, Miltown) Valium Librium	Sweating, skin rash, increased or decreased libido, nausea and vomiting, depression, mental sluggishness, urinary retention, constipation, anxiety, tension, agitation, excitability, slurred speech, apparent apathy	Minor possible	Yes	Slight	Visual disturbances, dizziness, hyperexcitability, hazardous irrational behavior; perceptual misjudgment, drowsiness; interferes with pain threshold
8. *Volatile substances* Airplane glue Plastic cement Toluene Paint thinners Gasoline Freon	Dilatation of pupils, double vision; excessive oral secretions; irritation around nose and mouth, sneezing, coughing, chest pain; hearing difficulties, drunk appearance, angry or irritable mood; drowsiness, unconsciousness	No	Yes	No	Bizarre mental effects, antisocial acts, dangerous acts due to sense of invulnerability; long and heavy use has potential for serious damage to brain, heart, lung, liver, kidney, blood-forming and other organs; death may result from choking or suffocation, indirectly from plastic bags used to concentrate the fumes, and directly from paralysis of respiratory system
9. *Ethyl alcohol*	Heartburn, gastritis, nausea, vomiting, increased urinary flow, malnutrition, lowered resistance to disease, altered mood, aggressive behavior, anger-anxiety, tension-fear, belligerent	Yes	Yes	Yes	Antisocial behavior, depression that may lead to suicide; interference with pain threshold; irreversible damage to brain and other organs; coma, shock, circulatory and respiratory failure, resulting in death

*Major tranquilizers are those with antipsychotic activity and essentially include that group of psychoactive substances known as the phenothiazines. They are primarily indicated when confusion, hyperactivity, and agitation are the prominent symptoms, but are sometimes used for depressive states. Although seemingly paradoxical, these drugs occasionally have been effective in treating depression because they help to suppress the accompanying anxiety.

TABLE 8-2   SCHEDULES OF CONTROLLED SUBSTANCES

Schedule	Representative Drugs
Schedule I—These drugs legally have *no* accepted medical use in the United States.	Heroin, marijuana, LSD, peyote, mescaline, psilocybin, synthetic tetrahydrocannabinols, benzylmorphine, dihydromorphine, morphine methylsulfonate, nicocodeine, nicomorphine
Schedule II—The drugs in this category include those previously referred to as "Class A Narcotics," in addition to amphetamines and methamphetamines.	Opium, morphine, codeine, Percodan, Pantopon, cocaine, Percobarb, Edrisal with Codeine, Dilaudid, Dolophine, Demerol, Benzedrine, Dexedrine, Dexamyl, D.A.S., Dex-sule, Desbutal, Leritine, Merpergan, Levo-Dromoran, Eskatrol, Am Plus, AmBar, Dexobarb, Amvicel, methedrine, Alvodine, Eskabarb, Obocell, Biphetamine, Syndrox, Desoxyn, Obedrin, D.O.E.
Schedule III—These drugs include those previously known as "Class B Narcotics."	Empirin with Codeine, A.S.A. with Codeine, Codempiral #2, Tylenol with Codeine, Hycodan, Tussionex, Phenaphen with Codeine, Hycomine, Soma Compound with Codeine, Donnagesic #1, Noludar, Chlorhexadol, Alurate, Doriden, Preludin, Ritalin, Carbrital, Amytal, Tuinal, Nembutal, Butisol, Fiorinal, Paregoric
Schedule IV—Drugs that previously had been exempted from the schedules have now been placed in this category.	Librium, Valium, Barbital, Phenobarbital, Valmid, Paraldehyde, Beta-Chlor, Equanil, Kesso-Bamate, Noctec, Felsules, Kessodrate, Somnos, Methohexital, Methylphenobarbital, Placidyl, Miltown, Petrichloral
Schedule V—These drugs include those formerly known as "exempt narcotics," such as the cough syrups containing codeine.	Robitussin A-C, Terpin Hydrate with Codeine, Cheracol with Codeine, Cosadein

Retail Dispensing Restrictions for Controlled Substances

Schedule V controlled substances and any non-prescription drugs in Schedules II, III, and IV may be dispensed without a prescription at retail but only by a pharmacist or pharmacist intern and not by any other employee, even under the direct supervision of a pharmacist. However, after the pharmacist has fulfilled his professional and moral responsibilities, the actual payment, credit transaction or delivery may be carried out by other employees.

Controlled prescription drugs in these schedules must be written by a physician licensed in the state where the drug is prescribed. The term prescription refers to a medication that is dispensed to or for an ultimate user but does not include an order which is dispensed for immediate administration of the medication to the ultimate user; e.g., an order to dispense for immediate administration of a drug to a bed patient in a hospital is *not* a prescription.

A discussion of drugs can become even more complicated, depending upon the language used, ranging from street language to pharmacological or medical terminology. Unfortunately, this has caused a great deal of misinformation to be disseminated. A central nervous system depressant in one category may be any drug that induces sleep, whereas in another classification it may include tranquilizers, which do not induce sleep but merely allow an individual to relax.

No matter how the drug is taken into the body, it will have the intended effect. However, the degree to which it will function is totally dependent on the route of administration and the psyche of the individual taking the drug.

ROUTE OF ADMINISTRATION

Drugs are introduced into the human body in a variety of ways. Some specific action drugs can be taken orally (ingested). Other drugs must not be exposed to the digestive tract and therefore must be injected into the system. Although drugs enter the body through various means, the distribution is always via the blood stream. Drugs enter the cellular structure, for which they were meant, through intercellular membranes. The molecular structure of a majority of drugs is identical to that of the cell.

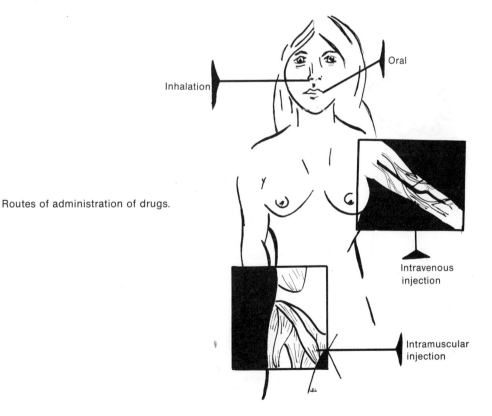

Routes of administration of drugs.

EFFECTS OF DRUGS

Drugs affect some system of the body, usually the central nervous system. These substances are classified generally as stimulants or depressants, but what is being stimulated or depressed? Basically, a stimulant causes the rapid release of neurotransmitters, thus allowing an impulse to travel much more rapidly through the neurons. Conversely, depressants work by inhibiting the release of neurotransmitters and slowing the impulse. This may become a bit clearer if we follow the release of neurotransmitter through monoamine oxidase in the synaptic cleft (Fig. 8–1).

Once the drug enters the body, it may not produce an effect until it has been distributed by the blood stream to the various organs, tissues, and cells with which it will react. The effect of the drug may occur on the surface of the cells, within the cells or in the fluid surrounding the cells. Primarily, the action takes place within the cellular walls and results in an effect on the central nervous system. How does a drug enter the cell from the blood stream? And if the entrance does occur, what takes place

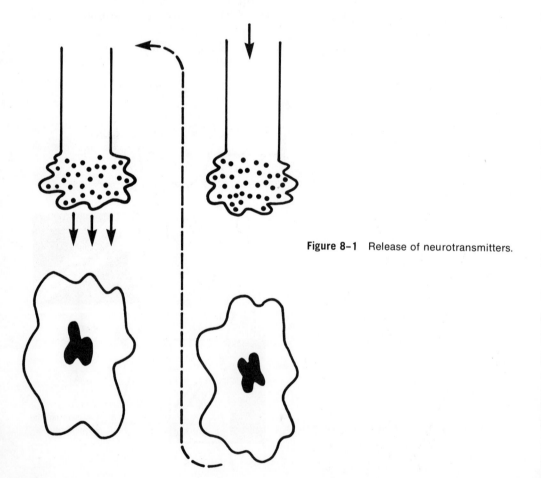

Figure 8-1   Release of neurotransmitters.

with regard to cellular destruction? Drugs enter body cells in the same manner (through a semipermeable membrane) as other substances taken into the body. Drugs that resemble chemicals already present in the body are assimilated in the normal growth of the cell and its chemical function. Conversely, a foreign substance introduced into the system may cause cellular dysfunction and uncontrollable consequences in the central nervous system. In the case of prescribed drugs and illegal substances, the drug may cause the cellular process to be abnormal. If this is the desired result, the drug is said to have a therapeutic effect; if this is not the desired effect, adverse reactions within various systems of the body may be severe.

When examining the major actions and effects of assimilated substances, it is desirable to determine whether a substance is directed toward local action or systemic actions, perhaps with a cumulative effect. The chemical action of a given drug in the body is designated as the *action of the drug.* This factor, however, must be considered in relation to the drug's interaction within the user's body; that is, the chemical mixes with other chemicals that one has ingested or secreted, and then the final effects of a drug can be specified. In order to understand the effect of a drug, one must analyze the drug, the user, the environment in which the drug was taken, and the intended purpose for the drug. Factors that influence the effect of any given chemical substance within the category of the drug itself are the type of drug, the amount or dosage of the drug, the manner in which it was administered, and the mode of action. Factors that must be considered in regard to the drug user are the user's personality, psychological state of mind, physiological state (disease state vs. well-being), and basal metabolic rate. Factors within the domain of the environment include the time of administration, the place, the social setting, and the general environment (e.g., at a party vs. in isolation).

In addition to the preceding considerations, one must be aware of the antagonistic effect of one drug on another. Depending on the type of drug, this effect is defined as synergism or interaction. *Drug interaction* is defined as the action of a drug upon the effectiveness or toxicity of another drug taken into the body simultaneously, earlier, or even later. *Synergism* is defined as the multiplication effect of depressants on each other to cause incalculable effect. An example of synergism is the ingestion of alcohol and barbiturates, which are both depressants that will multiply the effects of one another. In addition, an individual's hypersensitivity to a drug, or the effect of a drug on an individual who has an adverse reaction, is called a *contraindication.*

TERMINOLOGY

Most of the drugs introduced in our society over the past two centuries have been developed for legitimate and useful purposes. The "use" and "abuse" of these substances has brought about a sense of misconception in the terminology involving these drugs. These terms have varying definitions. Those most applicable seem to be:

1. *Drug use:* The use of any chemical substance that affects behavior or physiological function.

2. *Drug abuse:* The use of a drug or other substance in a manner which is not medically indicated or socially acceptable. *Comment:* For drugs that cause stimulation or depression of the central nervous system (brain and spinal cord complex), abuse can lead to certain changes, such as increased tolerance, physical dependence, and psychological dependence.

3. *Tolerance:* A phenomenon characterized by an increase in the body's ability to metabolize a drug, and by the need for larger and larger doses to achieve the same effect as obtained from the first, smaller dose. Drugs showing tolerance are amphetamines, narcotics, alcohol, barbiturates, nonbarbiturate sedative-hypnotics, and minor tranquilizers.

4. *Psychological dependence:* The mental craving for a drug, independent of physical dependence, which compulsively drives the abuser to seek a drug continually.

5. *Physical dependence:* That biochemical change in one's body, induced by a drug, which requires intake of that drug for normal function of the body. If the drug is denied, withdrawal symptoms will result. Drugs which yield physical dependence are narcotics, alcohol, barbiturates, minor tranquilizers, and nonbarbiturate sedative-hypnotics.

EXERCISE FOR THOUGHT

The terms habituating and addicting have been overused, and with no clear definitions being set forth, it seems appropriate to establish some at this point. Culturally, definitions may vary, but essentially the above definitions are generally accepted. Notably, drug usage may or may not be a high-risk factor. The risk-taking behaviors of drug users may be akin to those behaviors of everyday life. Complete the following risk-taking inventory quickly. Then review your responses. Do your patterns of everyday life and drug use contradict each other?

Below are 25 behaviors that involve a degree of risk. On the five-point scale at the right, circle the average degree of risk you believe an individual runs when he engages in each activity.

	1	2	3	4	5
1. Use of amphetamines	1	2	3	4	5
2. Legal abortion	1	2	3	4	5
3. High blood pressure	1	2	3	4	5
4. Working in a polluted environment	1	2	3	4	5
5. Auto racing	1	2	3	4	5
6. Smoking cigars	1	2	3	4	5
7. Self-medication or treatment	1	2	3	4	5
8. Drinking alcoholic beverages	1	2	3	4	5
9. Unmarried sexual intercourse	1	2	3	4	5
10. Participating in a protest demonstration	1	2	3	4	5
11. Use of marijuana	1	2	3	4	5
12. Unwed motherhood	1	2	3	4	5
13. Smoking cigarettes	1	2	3	4	5
14. Cheating on college exams	1	2	3	4	5
15. Use of tranquilizers	1	2	3	4	5
16. Smoking during pregnancy	1	2	3	4	5
17. Use of LSD	1	2	3	4	5
18. A 30-year history of smoking	1	2	3	4	5
19. Divorce	1	2	3	4	5
20. Marriage	1	2	3	4	5
21. Venereal disease	1	2	3	4	5
22. Drinking and driving	1	2	3	4	5
23. Use of contraceptives	1	2	3	4	5
24. Irregular physical examinations	1	2	3	4	5
25. Playing contact football	1	2	3	4	5

CHAPTER 9

EFFECTS OF DRUGS AND DRUG ABUSE

For a better understanding of drugs and their potential, this chapter presents an abbreviated listing of recreational substances to further explain how such drugs may relate to the habituation and addiction controversy.

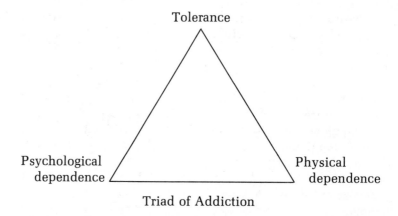

Triad of Addiction

Drugs not consistently used for recreational euphoria have not been listed. The changing mood regarding the use of such substances and new chemicals may mark the beginning of a new chemical euphoria. The classification of substances with regard to the central nervous system provides the reader with major categories by which drug effects may be determined.

THE DEPRESSANTS

The depressants are a broad group of drugs and chemical compounds that depress the activity of the central and peripheral nervous system. The stages of CNS depression are classified as sedation, hypnosis, anesthesia, coma, and ultimately death.

I. THE VOLATILE SOLVENTS

A. *Pharmacological category:* CNS depressants
B. *Mode of action:* The solvents are extremely soluble in the mucous membranes of the respiratory tract and quickly depress the central nervous system and motor activity because they reach high concentrations in the blood shortly after inhalation.
C. *Examples*
    1. Glue
    2. Fingernail polish and remover
    3. Paint thinners
    4. Freon and other aerosol propellents
    5. Gasoline
D. *Source:* Most of the solvents listed above may be found in the home.
E. *Route of administration:* Inhalation, often with the aid of a paper or plastic bag, which concentrates the vapors of the solvent.
F. *Medicinal uses:* NONE. It should be noted, however, that these solvents are similar in action to general anesthetics used during surgery.
G. *Short-term effects*
    1. Feeling of drunkenness
    2. Slurring of speech
    3. Dizziness
    4. Impaired sensory perception
    5. Disorganized and uncoordinated muscular activity
    6. Unconsciousness, which can even lead to death
H. *Long-term effects*
    1. Damage to the heart, lungs, kidneys, and liver
    2. Impaired perception, coordination, and judgment
I. *Unique problems:* Cardiac arrhythmias due to sensitization of the myocardium by the solvents have caused documented deaths. This phenomenon has been referred to as "sudden sniffing death."
J. *Tolerance potential:* Unknown
K. *Psychological dependence potential:* Yes
L. *Physical dependence potential:* No

II. ALCOHOL (ETHYL ALCOHOL)

A. *Pharmacological category:* CNS depressant
B. *Mode of action:* Depression of the central nervous system and motor function through depression of the cortical inhibitory centers. Alcohol is metabolized in the liver (at the rate of 10 to 30 ml per hour) to acetaldehyde.
C. *Source:* Alcoholic beverages produced by fermentation of grains, fruits and vegetables
D. *Route of administration:* Primarily oral

E. *Medical uses*
   1. Tranquilizer
   2. Antiseptic
   3. Antibacterial agent
   4. Vasodilator
F. *Short-term effects*
   1. Decreased mental acuity
   2. Reduced motor coordination
   3. Blurring of vision
   4. Slurring of speech
   5. Loss of balance
   6. Respiratory depression
   7. Increased diuresis
G. *Long-term effects*
   1. Occasional blackouts
   2. Loss of weight
   3. Vitamin deficiency and malnutrition
   4. Nervous system damage
   5. Liver damage
   6. Cardiovascular disorders
   7. Brain damage
H. *Unique problems*
   1. Alcohol is the most widely abused drug in this country
   2. Alcoholism, the complete physical and psychological dependence on alcohol
      a. It is estimated that there are 10 to 11 million alcoholics in the United States.
      b. Fewer than 3 per cent of alcoholics are on skid row.
      c. In this country the ratio of male to female alcoholics is 5:3.
I. *Tolerance potential:* Yes
J. *Psychological dependence potential:* Yes
K. *Physical dependence potential:* Yes, with the following symptoms
   1. Shakes
   2. Chills
   3. Muscle weakness
   4. Cramps
   5. Delirium tremens
L. *Legality:*
   1. Federal Trade Commission governs the sale of alcoholic beverages.
   2. States govern the legal age for drinking.

III. BARBITURATES

A. *Pharmacological category:* CNS depressants which act as sedatives and hypnotics

B. *Mode of action:* Barbiturates interfere with the transmission of impulses to the cortex of the brain.
C. *Examples*
1. Long-acting barbiturates (long-term use is generally safe if controlled by a physician) — Phenobarbital
2. Intermediate- to short-acting barbiturates (*most often abused*)
a. Amobarbital (blue heavens, blue birds, blue devils)
b. Pentobarbital (yellow jackets, nembies)
c. Secobarbital (reds, pinks, red devils, red birds)
d. Amobarbital and Secobarbital (Tuinal) (rainbows, Christmas trees)
D. *Source:* Manufactured by the drug industry
E. *Dosage forms*
1. Capsules
2. Tablets
F. *Routes of administration*
1. Oral
2. Parenteral
G. *Medical indications*
1. Preoperative sedation
2. Insomnia
3. Epilepsy (Phenobarbital)
4. Anxiety, tension
H. *Short-term effects*
1. Low dosage (30 mg)
a. Depression of sensory function
b. Sedation without analgesia
c. Drowsiness
d. Anticonvulsant activity
2. High dosage (100 mg)
a. Depression of motor function
b. Depression of medulla (circulation, respiration)
c. Sleep
d. Anesthesia
I. *Long-term effects with overdose*
1. Mental confusion
2. Nervous system damage
3. Dermatitis
4. Liver damage
J. *Unique problems*
1. Death due to overdosage is common because the fatal dose for an individual does not increase with tolerance to the psychoactive effects of the drug. There is also a narrower range between toxic and therapeutic levels than with other depressants.
2. Withdrawal effects from barbiturates are more severe than those from heroin.
K. *Tolerance potential:* Yes
L. *Psychological dependence potential:* Yes

M. *Physical dependence potential:* Yes, with withdrawal symptoms
   1. Weakness
   2. Increased blood pressure, anxiety, apprehension, agitation
   3. Dehydration
   4. Weight loss
   5. Psychosis (similar to delirium tremens)
   6. Convulsions are possible and may be fatal up to fifth day of withdrawal
N. *Legality:* Controlled Substances Act of 1970

IV. MINOR TRANQUILIZERS

A. *Pharmacological category:* CNS depressants
B. *Mode of action:* Tranquilizers generally act at a subcortical level by CNS depression.
C. *Examples*
   1. Meprobamate (Equanil, Miltown)
   2. Chlordiazepoxide (Librium)
   3. Diazepam (Valium)
D. *Sources:* The drug industry manufactures tranquilizers from natural or synthetic products.
E. *Dosage forms abused*
   1. Capsules
   2. Tablets
F. *Route of administration:* Generally, oral
G. *Medical uses* (with a prescription)
   1. Muscle relaxants
   2. Anticonvulsants
   3. Relief of anxiety and mild tension
   4. To decrease vomiting center activity
H. *Short-term effects*
   1. Reduction in motor activity
   2. Mild drowsiness
   3. Block of conditioned reflexes
   4. Reduction of anxiety
   5. Dermatitis
I. *Long-term effects*
   1. Obstructive hepatitis
   2. Bone marrow depression
   3. Induced nervous disorders (e.g., parkinsonism)
K. *Tolerance potential:* Yes
L. *Physical dependence potential:* Possible
M. *Psychological dependence potential:* Yes
N. *Legality:* Controlled Substances Act of 1970

V. THE NARCOTIC OPIATES AND THEIR DERIVATIVES

A. *Pharmacological category:* CNS depressants which act as analgesics, sedatives, and cough suppressants.

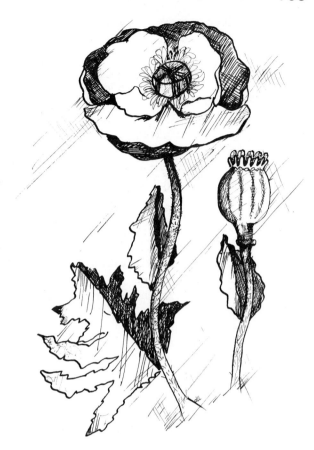

B. *Mode of action:* Narcotics depress the following CNS centers
   1. Pain perception center
   2. Respiratory center
   3. Smooth muscle stimulating center
   4. Vasomotor center
C. *Examples*
   1. Opium derivatives
      a. Morphine
      b. Codeine
      c. Paregoric (camphorated tincture of opium)
      d. Heroin (semisynthetic)
   2. Synthetic forms
      a. Hydromorphone (Dilaudid)
      b. Meperidine (Demerol)
      c. Oxymorphone (Numorphan)
      d. Methadone (Dolophine)
D. *Sources*
   1. Opium poppy (source of crude opium, grown in Turkey)
   2. Synthesized by drug industry

E. *Dosage forms abused*
   1. Capsules
   2. Tablets
   3. Powder for injection
   4. Cough preparations
F. *Routes of administration*
   1. Oral
   2. Nasal (sniffing)
   3. Parenteral
      a. Intradermal ("skin popping")
      b. Intravenous ("mainlining")
G. *Medical uses* (with a prescription)
   1. Morphine and morphine derivatives are used for severe pain
   2. Codeine is used to depress coughing and relieve pain
   3. Paregoric is used to control diarrhea and to relieve pain of teething
H. *Short-term effects*
   1. Reduction in sensitivity to pain (elevation of pain threshold)
   2. Drowsiness
   3. Induced sleep
   4. Reduction in physical activity
   5. Constipation
   6. Constriction of pupils
   7. Respiratory depression
I. *Long-term effects*
   1. Physical dependence
   2. Tolerance
   3. Psychological dependence
J. *Unique problems:* Heroin is the *most addicting drug* known to man and causes both medical and social problems.
   1. Medical problems
      a. Hepatitis due to septic administration
      b. Death from overdosage
      c. Skin infections due to septic administration
   2. Social problems
      a. Heroin eventually will most likely be injected ("mainlined"), and the addict may resort to crude instruments for administration.
      b. The craving for heroin leads most addicts to commit crimes in order to obtain $15 to $150 per day to support the habit.
      c. Heroin is diluted, or "cut," by the dealers, who add lactose, quinine, or other material until the concentration of heroin is only about 3 to 10 per cent.
      d. Therapy for the addict is often unsuccessful because of the strong psychological dependence.
         (1) Natural withdrawal from the drug with supportive therapy (cold turkey)
         (2) Methadone therapy (substitution of methadone, a similar drug, for the heroin and then tapering off this drug)

(3) Newer drug therapy (e.g., naloxone, cyclazine CO_2)
K. *Tolerance potential:* Yes
L. *Legality:* Controlled Substances Act of 1970

THE STIMULANTS

I. AMPHETAMINES

A. *Pharmacological category:* CNS stimulants
B. *Mode of action:* Amphetamines increase the release of norepine-
   phrine from nerve endings and neurosynaptic junction in the CNS
   and sympathetic nervous system, yielding a generalized increase
   in nerve activity.
C. *Examples*
   1. Dextroamphetamine
   2. Amphetamine
   3. Methamphetamine
   4. Phenmetrazine (Preludin)
   5. Methylphenidate (Ritalin)
D. *Source:* Synthesized primarily by the drug industry
E. *Dosage forms abused*
   1. Capsules (time-released)
   2. Tablets
   3. Crystalline powder to be injected in solution
F. *Routes of administration*
   1. Oral
   2. Intravenous injection
G. Slang terminology
   1. Speed
   2. Hearts
   3. Bennys
   4. Footballs
   5. Crystal
   6. Uppers
   7. Meth
   8. Copilots
H. *Medical uses* (with a prescription)
   1. For narcolepsy (overwhelming episodes of sleep)
   2. To reduce mental depression
   3. To control appetite and obesity (*effectiveness doubtful*)
   4. Paradoxically, for hyperactive children (increases the child's
      attention span)
I. *Short-term effects*
   1. Transient sense of alertness, wakefulness, well-being, and men-
      tal clarity
   2. Hunger is diminished (decreases with tolerance)
   3. Increased heart rate
   4. Increased blood pressure

     5. Dilatation of pupils

     6. Dryness in mouth and throat

     7. Sweating

J. *Long-term effects* (characteristic of mainlining methamphetamine)

     1. Damage to heart and brain

     2. General exhaustion

     3. Nutritional deficiencies due to poor eating habits

     4. Psychotic episodes—paranoia, hallucinations

     5. Infections caused by the unsanitary injections

K. *Unique problems*

     1. Amphetamine abuse causes overexertion of normal body function, yielding such symptoms as nausea, exhaustion, and cramps, compositely referred to as "crashing."

     2. Depressants (alcohol, heroin, tranquilizers, and barbiturates) are often taken to relieve these symptoms.

L. *Tolerance potential:* Yes
M. *Psychological dependence potential:* Yes
N. *Physical dependence potential:* Questionable
O. *Legality:* Controlled Substances Act of 1970

II. COCAINE

A. *Pharmacological category:* Stimulant and local anesthetic
B. *Mode of action:* Cocaine elevates the threshold of inhibitory nerve excitability and thus enhances normal stimulation of the CNS
C. *Slang terminology*
   1. Coke
   2. Snow
   3. Stardust
   4. Flake
   5. Speedball (combination with heroin)
D. *Source:* Cocaine is an odorless, white, fluffy powder derived from the coca tree, grown in Bolivia, Peru, and Chile.
E. *Routes of administration*
   1. Through nasal mucous membranes, by "snorting"
   2. Intravenous injection
F. *Medical uses:* None; has been used as a local (topical) anesthetic.
G. *Short-term effects*
   1. Euphoria
   2. Energetic sensations
   3. Possible hallucinations and delusions
   4. Dilated pupils
   5. Loss of appetite
H. *Long-term effects*
   1. Digestive disorders
   2. Loss of weight
   3. Insomnia
   4. Occasional convulsions
   5. Possible perforation of the septum of the nose
I. *Tolerance potential:* None
J. *Psychological dependence potential:* Yes, very strong
K. *Physical dependence potential:* No
L. *Legality:* Controlled Substances Act of 1970

HALLUCINOGENS

The hallucinogens represent a broad group of drugs, both natural and synthetic, which have the ability to induce hallucinations and illusions through alterations of sensory perception.

I. LSD (LYSERGIC ACID DIETHYLAMIDE)

A. *Mode of action:* LSD may alter the levels of certain natural chemicals in the brain, including serotonin, which could produce changes in the brain's electrical activity. This mechanism has not yet been proved.

B. *Source:* LSD is a modified form of lysergic acid, a chemical obtained from a fungus that grows on rye and wheat. In 1943, Dr. Albert Hoffman, a Swiss chemist, accidentally discovered LSD's psychoactive activity by ingesting a small amount of the drug.

C. *Routes of administration*
   1. Oral
   2. Injection (rare)

D. *Common dosage forms:* LSD in pure form is a white powder that is easily dissolved and may be incorporated into numerous substances for oral administration.
   1. Sugar cubes
   2. Cookies
   3. Tablets
   4. Capsules
   5. Paper
   6. Beverages
   7. Glycerin wafers ("window panes")

E. *Medical uses:* LSD has no medical uses today in this country. Researchers at the National Institute of Mental Health are solely in charge of the studies on LSD. They have studied possible applications in treatment of
   1. Alcoholism
   2. Emotional disorders
   3. Terminal illnesses

F. *Short-term physical effects* (lasting 8 to 10 hours)
   1. Slight increase in heart rate
   2. Slight increase in blood pressure
   3. Slight increase in temperature
   4. Dilated pupils
   5. Shaking of hands and feet
   6. Cold, sweaty palms
   7. Loss of appetite with nausea
   8. Irregular breathing

G. *Short-term psychological effects*
   1. Sudden changes in sensory perception
   2. Synesthesia (scrambling of sensory input)
   3. Feeling of detachment from reality
   4. Alterations of mood
   5. Altered perception of time and space
   6. Alteration of thinking, feelings, and perception (unpredictable)
   7. Depersonalization, loss of identity

H. *Long-term effects:* Severe mental illness is the only documented long-term effect of LSD. To date, no conclusive or direct link has yet been found between LSD and chromosomal breakage; however, LSD may be associated with teratological effects on fetuses.

  I. *Unique problems*
1. Dose (1 ounce of pure LSD is sufficient for 300,000 doses)
2. Severe panic may accompany many LSD trips
3. Paranoia may persist up to 72 hours (or longer) after the drug has worn off
4. Accidental deaths
5. The drug state may recur days, weeks, or even months after using LSD, without repeating use of drug ("flashback")

  J. *Legality:* Controlled Substances Act of 1970

  K. *Tolerance potential:* Possible

  L. *Psychological dependence potential:* Possible

  M. *Physical dependence potential:* No

II. OTHER HALLUCINOGENS

These drugs have short-term activity similar to that of LSD, but even less is known about their long-term effects.

  A. *STP* (DOM; dimethoxy-methyl amphetamine)
1. One-tenth as potent as LSD
2. Synthetic
3. Taken orally in tablet or capsule form

B. *Mescaline*
  1. 1/2000 as potent as LSD
  2. Active ingredient of the peyote cactus button
  3. Taken orally
C. *Phencyclidine*
  1. Taken by injection or orally, or may be smoked in tobacco, marijuana, or spices
  2. Once used as a general anesthetic (sensory blocking agent) in medicine but removed because of side reactions. Now available only for veterinary use.
  3. Used to counterfeit drugs (e.g., mescaline, THC, psilocybin)
D. *DMT* (dimethyltryptamine)
  1. Short-acting
  2. Taken by injection, smoked in tobacco or other plant material (sniffed?)
  3. Causes more pronounced rise in blood pressure

MARIJUANA AND ITS DERIVATIVES

A. *Pharmacological category*
  1. Marijuana—intoxicant

2. Hashish—intoxicant to hallucinogenic
3. THC—intoxicant to hallucinogenic

B. *Mode of action:* The active ingredient in marijuana is 9-THC (tetra-hydrocannabinol), and its mode of action is unknown. Research has shown that it affects the brain and nervous system.

C. *Source:* Both drug forms come from the *Cannabis sativa* plant (Indian hemp), which grows throughout the world.
   1. Marijuana—from flowering tops of female plant
   2. Hashish—from the resinous exudate of this plant

D. *Slang terminology*
   1. Pot
   2. Tea
   3. Grass
   4. Mary jane
   5. Weed

E. *Abused dosage forms:* Crude plant material, hashish (resin), "oil concentrates" (extracts)

F. *Routes of administration*
   1. Smoked—rolled in paper, as cigarettes (weed, joint) or in a pipe
   2. Added to food and taken orally

G. *Medical uses:* None

H. *Short-term physical effects* (lasting 2 to 4 hours)
   1. Enters blood stream quickly
   2. Increased heart rate
   3. Reddening of the eyes
   4. Increased hunger
   5. Irritation of the mucous membranes of the nose and bronchioles from smoke

I. *Short-term psychological effects*
   1. Alteration of moods and thinking processes; tranquilizing effect
   2. Alteration of spatial sense
   3. Alteration of time perception
   4. Uncontrollable hilarity
   5. Illusions (in high doses)
   6. Possible paranoia

J. *Long-term effects* (in human beings)
   1. Bronchitis
   2. Alienation from society

K. *Tolerance potential:* Mild to none

L. *Psychological dependence potential:* Yes

M. *Physical dependence potential:* No

N. *Legality:* Controlled Substances Act of 1970

CHAPTER 10

PHYSIOLOGICAL, SOCIAL AND LEGAL DRUG PROBLEMS

Human beings, like all living organisms, have dependencies. We depend on our environment for food and shelter, and we depend on each other for love and understanding. When normal dependencies are not satisfied, particularly when interpersonal exchanges are not gratifying, people often develop abnormal dependencies in an attempt to achieve satisfaction. In our society, excesses of food and/or drugs are frequently used as a means of alleviating frustration in life. Almost invariably, abnormal dependencies are self-defeating. Dependence on consciousness-altering drugs in lieu of a successful social role results in mental incapacitation and an inability to perform socially accepted functions.

ALCOHOL

In our society, alcohol is the most abused drug. It is accepted as a means to relieve tension and uneasiness in normal social exchanges. Because of this, people can fall into patterns of overindulgence. Those who feel excessively ill at ease with their roles in life depend more on alcohol's numbing effect. As alcohol further incapacitates them, they use it in even greater amounts. The problem is compounded by the physical addictiveness of alcohol. The body comes to crave it to avoid the physiological pains of withdrawal—delirium tremens.

There are many varieties of alcohol. Methyl (wood) alcohol, or methanol, is used as antifreeze and fuel. Isopropyl alcohol is commonly known as "rubbing alcohol." Ethyl (grain) alcohol, or ethanol, is the only kind of alcohol that can be consumed. Alcohol refers to a group of beverages, including distilled spirits, wine, and beer, that contain ethanol (CH_3CH_2OH). Alcohol is classified as a food because of its caloric content, but it is more accurately described as a fuel, since pure alcohol has no nutritional value. Pharmacologically, alcohol is classified as a CNS depressant.

174

Our bodies absorb alcohol into the blood stream through the lining of the stomach and small intestines. Eighty to 90 per cent of the alcohol is rapidly broken down by the liver and other organs. The remaining 10 to 20 per cent is carried by the blood throughout the body. The alcohol and its by-products carried to the brain cause intoxication. Alcohol is metabolized in the body at a fairly constant rate of 1 ounce per hour. As a person drinks at a rate faster than alcohol can be metabolized, the drug accumulates, resulting in higher and higher concentrations in the body.

A 12-ounce can of domestic beer is equivalent to 1 ounce of 90-proof whiskey. Consuming 2 ounces of whiskey creates a blood alcohol concentration of 0.05 per cent. That amount of alcohol dulls the top layers of the cerebral cortex as well as the reticular formation. These parts of the brain normally act as psychological and physical inhibitors. The drinker abandons minor conventions and courtesies, feels free and relaxed, experiences euphoria, and demonstrates fewer social constraints.

Effects of Alcohol

1. Alcohol is a sedative and depressant that slows down the action of the brain. Most of the effects associated with moderate drinking are due to alcohol's influence on the brain rather than to its direct effects on other body organs.

2. Alcohol affects sensory perception. Sight is impaired, hearing is affected (to a lesser extent than sight), and senses of equilibrium, taste, smell, and touch are impaired.

3. At all blood alcohol levels, muscle control is impaired, resulting in loss of coordination and lengthened reaction time.

4. Judgment and self-control are altered. Since alcohol produces temporary euphoria, the desire to achieve euphoria is one of the main reasons that people drink. The euphoria results in a carelessness that precludes good judgment and self-control at rather low blood alcohol levels.

5. Alcohol interferes with both the storage and retrieval of information.

6. For moderate drinkers there may be a slight improvement in the digestion, but in heavy drinkers alcohol may damage the gastrointestinal tract. In addition, since alcohol is eliminated from the body through the liver, liver ailments are especially common among alcoholics.

7. The abuse of alcohol places a great burden on society in terms of economics, loss of creativity and productivity, deaths from driving accidents, juvenile delinquency, and broken homes. Some police departments estimate that as much as 75 per cent of their time is spent in dealing with people who have been drinking excessively, but perhaps the greatest price of alcohol abuse is that paid by members of the problem drinker's family.

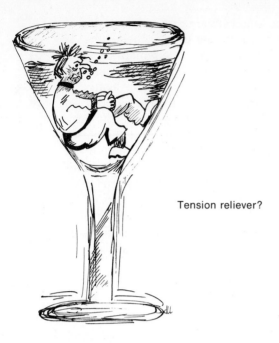

Tension reliever?

ALCOHOLISM

Because so much research has been done and so much reliable data has been gathered, one can look at alcoholism with more reliability than any other of the addictions. With alcoholism the dependency state is characterized by a person's reliance on a substance in increasing doses to achieve a desired effect. This is *acquired tolerance*. Most addictions are characterized by withdrawal symptoms when the substance of the dependence is no longer ingested. Since many are similar in their effects on the human body and psyche, alcohol may be a guide for understanding other kinds of addictions.

A single bout of excessive drinking does not indicate alcoholism, although it can begin with occasional drinking for relief of tension. As relief drinking becomes a behavioral pattern, tolerance increases, and it takes more alcohol to achieve the desired effect. The drinker's memory occasionally blacks out and progressively worsens. Drinking is done surreptitiously. The drinker begins to rely on alcohol and he urgently looks forward to the first drink of the day. This leads to guilt. The drinker feels unable to discuss the problem with anyone even though he or she cannot control it. The drinker can't stop drinking when friends do, makes excuses that become more and more grandiose, becomes more aggressive, and is in a constant stage of remorse, relieved only by further drinking.

The alcoholic's promises to stop drinking are meaningless — the drinker runs. Nothing helps. Family and friends are avoided. The drinker's work suffers and he becomes resentful. Appetite disappears along with any will power. The drinker now shakes upon wakening. The solution is a drink. Alcohol tolerance level increases. The alcoholic is

"Booze? No, that's not a drug!"

drunk for extended periods of time. Thinking is impaired, and he or she is alive with fears. The drinker is now obsessed with drinking and has no more alibis. The alcoholic finally admits to complete defeat and powerlessness over alcohol.

Alcoholism is a chronic behavioral disease that might stem from many different causes: unfulfilled dependencies in early childhood, genetic influences, or learned behavior. It represents a true chemical addiction as well as a psychological dependence. Because so much research has been done and so much reliable data gathered, we can look at alcoholism with more certainty than we can at any other addictions. It has

"Alcohol? It just makes me enjoy people—in fact, it tends to improve my sex life!"

been estimated that 1 in every 20 adults in the United States is an alcoholic.

Recent studies of our population strongly support a genetic cause of alcoholism, as well as several other abnormal dependencies. In a significant number of cases, children of alcoholic parents, although reared by nonalcoholic foster parents, developed high rates of alcoholism as adults. Psychoanalysts, on the other hand, see alcoholism developing after birth. Psychoanalytic theory traces alcoholism to unfulfilled primitive oral needs in infancy. The resulting exaggerated or pathological dependency state may manifest itself in the adult as compulsive overeating or smoking or as alcoholism.

Social learning theory represents the alcoholic as someone who, through a series of circumstances that involve drinking, becomes publicly labeled as an alcoholic and begins to behave accordingly. Alcoholism is seen as a form of social role-playing. Personality theorists propose that drug-dependent people, including alcoholics, possess essential personality traits that predispose them to extreme dependency states. Behaviorists view dependency on alcohol as a learned response to a stimulus. The recurring stimulus may be anxiety, fear, or frustration. Cultural theory finds the key to alcohol addiction in the drinker's repeated attempts to escape or alleviate the tensions and stresses that society imposes on the individual in the process of perpetuating its institutions.

Although the psychological and social reasons for addiction remain unclear, we are somewhat more certain of the physiological phenomenon of addiction. When alcohol is consumed, it undergoes a series of chemical reactions through which it is converted to acetaldehyde. This acetaldehyde, in turn, alters other substances, diverting the pathway from the body into a normally untraveled route. The by-product of this alternate pathway is a morphine-like substance. It is theorized, based on substantial biochemical evidence, that the alcoholic can be addicted at the cellular level to a morphine-like substance rather than to alcohol.

Some believe that we should try to replace pathological dependencies on such substances as alcohol, heroin, cigarettes, and food with normal dependencies on meaningful interpersonal relationships and fulfilling, socially acceptable life patterns.

Since alcoholism is partially socially acceptable while other drug addictions are not, it is conceivable that the potential for alcoholism in this country has not been realized. Thus, alcoholism is actually the number one health problem in the United States. The most important factor in the treatment of this problem is the recognition of the syndrome as an illness, both mental and physical. Presently, wide variation of treatment facilities has not allowed either state or federal guidelines to be set forth.

Social allowances for releasing the stigma have yet to be realized to full potential. Although acceptable, we as Americans accept only a portion of guilt for alcoholism and ignore other aspects of this state of drug dependency.

Alcoholism: Summary

1. Alcoholism is a chronic behavioral disorder manifested by excessive drinking that interferes with a useful life.

2. The causes of alcoholism are still not definitely known. Most authorities feel that alcoholism is caused by a personality disorder, but others prefer to relate alcoholism to some physical factor, such as the presence or absence of some enzyme in the body.

3. The first sign of alcoholism consists of drinking specifically for the effects of alcohol on the body.

4. The alcoholic blackout is a period of temporary amnesia during which the individual remains conscious and seems fully aware of what he is doing; however, he will have no recollection of what took place during the blackout.

5. The most important symptom of alcoholism is the alcoholic's inability to stop drinking until he is drunk or sick.

6. The person with a tendency toward alcoholism spends much of his time thinking about drinking or wanting a drink. The alcoholic often "belts" or gulps his drinks.

7. The problem drinker often develops a sense of guilt about the amount he is drinking, and as a result he may drink secretly or rationalize his drinking behavior.

8. Alcoholics are usually very unhappy and often suffer from feelings of persecution. To feel better, the alcoholic relives past glories.

9. Until the alcoholic realizes that drinking is the cause of his problems, the problems continue to increase.

10. Alcoholics usually have problems finding employment and keeping a job; if employed, the alcoholic is likely to have serious financial troubles because of his expensive habit.

11. Commonly, marital problems are due to financial difficulties and the alcoholic's loss of sexual drive, which often leads to jealousy, the alcoholic accusing the spouse of having extramarital love affairs. The alcoholic's family tends to become socially isolated.

12. A sign of true alcohol addiction is regular morning drinking. The fully addicted alcoholic will manifest all symptoms of withdrawal if deprived of alcohol.

13. Many alcoholics eventually suffer a drastic disintegration of personality. The alcoholic's thought processes become completely disrupted, and all functions of the nervous system are impaired. The alcoholic who reaches this stage will either die or spend the rest of his life in an institution.

14. Initial medical treatment may involve hospitalization and drug therapy during detoxification.

15. Psychotherapy for alcoholism involves the use of drugs that cause nausea and vomiting if the patient drinks alcohol. The approach depends upon the nature of the alcoholic and the experience of the therapist, but to be successful, the person must want to stop drinking.

16. Alcoholics Anonymous is one of the most successful approaches

TABLE 10–1

Drug	Possible Effect with Alcohol
Antabuse	Severe nausea and vomiting
Aspirin	Stomach upset; intestinal bleeding may occur in persons with a history of ulcers.
Benadryl	Increased sedative effect
Caffeine (coffee)	Will reduce CNS depression but will not improve judgment or ability to perform tasks such as driving
Chloral hydrate	Chloral hydrate inhibits the ability of the body to destroy alcohol, thus prolonging and increasing alcohol's effects: also increases CNS depression
Codeine (Empirin Compound 3)	Pain-relieving property of codeine increased; depression caused by alcohol is also increased
Compazine	Increased CNS depression
Coumadin	Activity of Coumadin may be increased or decreased, depending on the individual; therefore, alcohol intake should be limited
Dalmane	Increased CNS depression
Darvon	Pain-relieving properties of Darvon may be increased; CNS depression also increased; Darvon Compound also contains aspirin (see aspirin)
Demerol	Pain-relieving properties of Demerol increased; CNS depression increased
Dilantin	Effectiveness of Dilantin reduced
Doriden	CNS depression increased
Elavil	This combination causes extreme sedation, which adversely affects skills such as driving, especially during the first few days of therapy
Insulin	Unusually low blood sugar levels

to treatment of alcoholism to date. However, the person must have a desire to stop drinking, for AA is not a cure but a method of control.

ALCOHOL REACTIONS AND INTERACTIONS

An interesting quality associated with alcohol is its ability to act as an aphrodisiac. However, as Shakespeare pointed out in *Macbeth*, alcohol provokes "...nose painting, sleep, and urine. Lechery, sir, it provokes and unprovokes; it provokes the desire but unprovokes the performance. . . ."

The response to alcohol varies greatly, depending not only on the amount ingested but also on the individual. Such things as age, weight,

TABLE 10-1 *Continued*

Drug	Possible Effect with Alcohol
Iron	Probability of stomach upset is increased
Librium	CNS depressant effects increased; anti-anxiety properties of Librium enhanced; individual tolerance to alcohol decreased
Mellaril	CNS depressant effects increased
Miltown	Increases alcohol's ability to impair coordination and judgment
Morphine	Morphine's pain-relieving qualities, as well as CNS depressant action, increased
Nembutal	Both act to depress the CNS; reaction time is decreased and judgment is impaired, while confidence in judgments is increased
Orinase	Causes destruction of Orinase by the body and increases the blood sugar levels; may also produce nausea and vomiting
Phenobarbital	Both act to depress the CNS
Quaalude	Both act to depress the CNS
Reserpine	Sedative effects of alcohol increased; action of reserpine increased
Seconal	Both act to depress the CNS; reaction time is decreased and judgment is impaired, while confidence in judgments is increased
Tetracycline	Action of tetracycline increased
Thorazine	CNS depressant action of Thorazine increased; mental and/or physical abilities may be impaired
Tuinal	Both act to depress the CNS; reaction time is decreased and judgment is impaired while confidence in judgments is increased
Valium	Sedative effects of alcohol increased; decreased tolerance to alcohol; Valium's tension-relieving qualities increased
Vitamin B_{12}	Absorption of vitamin B_{12} reduced

sex, and overall physical health can drastically change the action of even small amounts of alcohol, but perhaps one of the most important variables associated with alcohol is other drugs. A list of commonly used medications and the possible effect of this combination with alcohol is provided on Table 10–1; it is designed as a guideline to reduce the incidence of undesirable drug reactions.

TOBACCO SMOKE AND ITS EFFECTS

In 1773 Samuel Johnson wrote, "Smoking has gone out," but if it ever did, it was well rekindled, for the Department of Agriculture reported that in 1976 the consumption of cigarettes totaled approximately 5000 per adult in the United States and that total expenditures for cigarettes amounted to $8.5 billion.

Tobacco seems to have been one of the New World's contributions to civilization. The mound builder smoked his pipe, and the cliff dwellers of Arizona and New Mexico smoked cigarettes rolled in corn husks. The early explorers learned its use from the Indians and called it tobacco because of the Y-shaped pipes, called tobaccos, in which it was smoked, one fork of the pipe being inserted in each nostril. Later the Portuguese named it nicotiana because Johannes I. Nicot, French Ambassador to Portugal, introduced the plant into that country.

Tobacco contains the drug nicotine, a colorless, oily compound which in concentrated form is one of the most powerful poisons known. The death of a man of average weight in a few minutes can be caused by 70 mg, or about one drop. Nicotine acts on the heart, blood vessels, digestive tract, kidneys, and nervous system. In large doses, nicotine first stimulates and then paralyzes the sympathetic nerve endings. This depressant effect on the sympathetic and the central nervous systems, as well as on the endings of the motor nerves that activate the voluntary muscles, lasts far longer than the initial stimulation. Smoking produces a rise in the level of sugar in the blood. The temporary stimulating effect may be due to the increased amount of sugar in the blood, caused by the release of glucose. Habitual users of tobacco actually can take only a small amount of this poison into their mouth and lungs at one time. Nicotine is not an addicting drug because the smoker develops no tolerance to the physiological effects of smoking; however, it is habitual.

The amount of nicotine absorbed varies with method of use. In powdered tobacco, used as snuff, the proportion of nicotine absorbed is higher than that in either chewing or smoking. Chewing, in turn, results in more absorption than smoking.

Other chemicals and carcinogens are tars, carbon monoxide, and hydrocarbons produced by the burning of tobacco. Carbon monoxide reduces the oxygen-carrying capacity of the red blood cells. The poisonous effect of carbon monoxide is due to the fact that it forms a compound with hemoglobin, which is from 100 to 200 times as stable as oxyhemoglobin. Therefore, levels sufficient to sustain life are prevented from reaching the tissues when the carbon monoxide "steals" sufficient hemoglobin.

Tobacco tar, which can cause brownish stains of fingers and teeth, is a sticky mixture of a number of chemicals, several of which produce an irregular growth of cells if applied to the skin or bronchi of laboratory animals: these are carcinogenic. Other carcinogens increase the activation of substances to irritate membranes lining the nose, trachea, larynx, bronchi, and lungs.

Physiological effects of tobacco on the body vary from those too slight to be measured to acute poisoning. The delayed reactions are accompanied by symptoms of dizziness, faintness, cold clammy skin, rapid pulse, weakness and sometimes vomiting, nausea, and diarrhea. These symp-

Smoking section please!

toms often occur in persons not used to smoking tobacco, but similar effects may be experienced by habitual smokers. The effects are of short duration and usually have little influence on the general health.

The greater importance lies in the effect of the use of tobacco over long periods of time. Evidence from other countries has indicated that habitual tobacco chewing or the use of snuff produces constriction of the smaller arteries, and that chewing tobacco and snuff are major causes of cancer of the mouth, tongue, and nasopharynx. Smoking sometimes seems to soothe the nerves and calm the spirits, particularly of heavy smokers, but usually its effects are irritating, deleterious and occasionally fatal.

Rapid smoking tends to concentrate the nicotine in the smoke, but slow smoking permits more of the nicotine to escape into the air. Consequently, the fast chain-smoker takes more nicotine into his body than does the person who smokes slowly. Since the overall effects of smoking vary considerably with the individual smoker's tolerance and smoking habits, it is difficult to classify people as "heavy" or "light" smokers, but the American Cancer Society is using the following categories for rating cigarette smokers:

    1. Light smokers smoke less than half a pack a day.
    2. Moderate smokers smoke a pack or less a day.

3. Heavy smokers consume between one and two packs a day.

4. Very heavy smokers use more than two packs a day.

Smoking causes a distinct rise in the blood pressure of the average smoker, and this effect tends to persist for 30 to 45 minutes after smoking. The higher the pressure, the more work the heart must perform, for it must pump the blood against greater resistance.

Most people with "normal" blood pressure probably suffer no ill effects from the slight rise resulting from moderate smoking. Since the longevity of heavy and moderate smokers is lower than that of light smokers and nonsmokers, there seems to be a correlation between increased work load on the heart over a long period of time and regular, long-term smoking. For persons who have severe high blood pressure or a defective heart, smoking is definitely a serious risk.

Nicotine has an effect on the sympathetic nervous system, causing it to constrict the blood vessels. This constriction results in an inadequate blood supply to all parts of the body and an increase in both blood pressure and pulse rate.

Through the constricting action on the blood vessels, smoking thus causes the temperature of the skin in the hands and feet to decrease from 1 to 9 degrees Fahrenheit or more, and this change continues for 30 or more minutes. The lessened blood flow accounts for the cold, clammy hands of many smokers. Also, the danger of serious illness or death from such infectious lung diseases as influenza, pneumonia, and tuberculosis is increased if the lungs have been damaged by smoke.

Scientific studies in this country and abroad report the following effects on the cardiovascular system:

1. Compared to nonsmokers, death rates from coronary heart disease are 2.8 times as high for men and 2 times as high for women who smoke a package or more of cigarettes a day.

2. Death rates increase with the number of cigarettes smoked per day, with the degree of inhalation, and with the age at which smoking was begun, being one-third higher for those who started to smoke before 15 than for those who started to smoke after 25 years of age.

3. The greatest excess of deaths among smokers as compared to nonsmokers is in the 40- to 49-year-old age group, with less difference in each succeeding decade.

4. Coronary death rates are a little higher for pipe or cigar smokers than for nonsmokers.

5. Death rates decrease with the cessation of smoking.

6. Microscopic examinations of the heart show that there is definitely more atherosclerosis of the coronary arteries among smokers than among nonsmokers. A study of Harvard graduates showed that those who smoked more than 10 cigarettes a day had twice as many strokes as those who smoked fewer cigarettes or none at all.

No one would be surprised to find out that the smoke in the proverbial smoke-filled room is hazardous to your health. The dimensions of the irritation and hazard from cigarettes — to smokers and nonsmokers — have never been hypothesized.

1. Carbon monoxide level exceeds clean air standards for outdoors.

2. Formaldehyde, a gas with a suffocating odor, also quickly exceeds air quality standards.

3. Acrolein, another chemical with a stifling odor that is used rather widely in industry, exceeds clean air standards.

The effect in a smoke-filled room is really most dramatic on eyes, rather than on breathing, as one might assume. Studies indicate that acrolein, since it is so far in excess of normal minimum levels, probably produces the bulk of the irritation. In the average room, the reasonable limit is between 5 and 10 cigarettes. After that, something has to be done about ventilation. (A normally ventilated room would be twice as efficient in removing cigarette smoke.)

With such a vast wealth of knowledge, why do more young people begin smoking each year? Are the numbers of smokers increasing? Recent problems in college eating areas have brought about smoking and nonsmoking areas. Is this violating the rights of the smoker? What do you suggest?

A discussion of tobacco products would not be complete without mention of the practice of chewing tobacco. Common in some areas of the United States, it has been thought to be less hazardous to the user since the tobacco was not being burned. Although carcinogens are not inhaled, the deposit of tars on teeth and gums has been known to create oral abnormalities, e.g., cancer.

MARIJUANA, COCAINE, AND PCP

Of the psychoactive drugs most "popular" for recreational use (excluding alcohol, the nation's drug of choice), several are rising in prominence. Marijuana, cocaine, and PCP (phencyclidine) are the most frequently used illegal substances. Although the media protray heroin as the major problem, the number of users is small in comparison to the number of persons using marijuana, cocaine and PCP.

MARIJUANA

During the past decade the use of marijuana has changed in character. Previously, marijuana was thought to be popular among the young and counterculture-oriented individuals. Today marijuana users fit no stereotype, and they are very likely to use alcohol simultaneously. Sociologists state that marijuana (because of its legal status and widespread cultural acceptance) use is not displacing the more prevalent, traditional use of alcohol.

Popular use may be attributed to the lack of hard evidence that marijuana has a detrimental effect on the human body. The effects of marijuana are divided into two categories: (1) acute effects and (2) long-range effects due to regular use. Obviously, it would be easier to obtain information on the first rather than the second. Lay persons have reported an increase in heart rate and reddening of the eyes as the most common physiological effects of "grass." Although the 1975 "Marijuana and Health: In Perspective," issued by the secretary of HEW, indicates isolated research in these areas, definitive data does not seem available. The report does suggest some special chronic use "potential" problems, including hormonal imbalance and the reduction of the body's immune response to various diseases. However, no adequate clinical findings are available to predict any correlation between marijuana use and chronic conditions. The absence of documented clinical findings does not necessarily mean that there are no adverse effects. As the numbers of Americans using marijuana increases, large-scale studies may indicate some chronic, even degenerative effects.

Marijuana is seemingly unsuitable for medical purposes, other than as a tranquilizer. However, it has a low biological toxicity — in other words, it is extremely hard to overdose with marijuana. Its usefulness as a medication for chronic disorders is being explored, but it may prove to be greatly limited.

Few responsible scientists, however, would question the statement that marijuana can be harmful, especially when taken in great quantities over an extended period of time. This is true of almost any drug, licit and illicit, with alcohol and tobacco ranking at the top of the list of potential health hazards. But in pursuing a policy of discouraging use of alcohol and tobacco, especially at harmful levels, we have not framed our laws to make criminals of users.[1]

An article by Robert Carr in the May 1976 issue of *Human Behavior*, states that

Marijuana is here to stay. No conceivable law enforcement program can curb its availability. The evidence to date should convince all but the most obstinate that the criminal law is not the answer and has failed to deter or decrease marijuana use. The attitudes those laws embody have gone up in smoke. A substantial number of Americans have voted with their lungs for their repeal.

The relative youth of today's marijuana users, their wide geographic spread and their heavy representation in the ranks from which the power structure of the future will be drawn makes the decriminalization of their drug of recreation inevitable. The major remaining question is the final cost of maintaining the archaic legal code that is bound to collapse sooner or later.[2]

COCAINE—THE "COKE" GENERATION

Cocaine of late has become the drug of choice of various subcultures. Expensive, but readily available, this stimulant is nonaddictive, with few physiological problems. The following historical background offers a conceptual approach to the drug.

Pre-Columbian Civilization

According to the Inca legend, cocaine was used by the Incas as early as 500 BC. (Artifacts of faces during this period revealed bulging cheeks.) The children of the sun were presented with the coca bush (*Erythroxylon coca*) on the occasion of the formation of the Inca Empire. This gift was said to satisfy the hungry, provide the weary and fainting with new vigor, and cause the unhappy to forget their miseries.

At first, cocaine was the privilege of the Inca royalty—the drug of political and religious rulers. The Inca priesthood gave the plant a divine status, placing the coca leaf on the royal emblem. (It is known that the first Inca queen was named Mama Cuca.) The highest form of noble largesse was to bestow a small quantity of coca leaves upon a trusted lieutenant or aide.

The use of cocaine gradually filtered down to the common laborers, messengers and soldiers. It was used by the masses to increase strength and to alleviate symptoms of fatigue. Cocaine also served as an appetite depressant to anesthetize the lining of the stomach and combat the sensation of hunger during strenuous labor. The highland messengers used cocaine when they traveled for long distances at high altitudes.

The Incas prepared "cocada," which was a ball of coca leaves mixed with an alkali (lime) obtained from bricks of pressed ashes, usually from "guinoa," a local pigweed, with cornstarch added for adhesion or wrapped around bird droppings (guano). Cocaine anesthetized the mouth lining to counteract the bitter taste. The effects of chewing the cocada lasted for about 40 minutes, and it was chewed three or four times a day. The importance attached to "cocada" in the everyday lives of the Incas is reflected in their naming a unit of time (40 minutes) and a linear measure (the distance a man could run under the effects of coca leaves—between 2 and 3 kilometers) after the cocada.

European Conquest (Pizzaro)

Religious authorities who followed Pizzaro tried to eradicate the use of coca unsuccessfully. Instead, European and other political rulers used coca to exploit indigenous labor. Workers in mines were paid with coca leaves, a currency which stimulated them to greater production and which helped them bear up under inadequate diets and unhygienic working and living conditions. By the sixteenth century the use of cocaine spread to the common man.

Late Nineteenth Century

In 1859 the Austrian explorer Karl Von Scherzer brought coca leaves to Europe to study. Subsequently, Niemann isolated cocaine from coca leaves and give it the name "cocaine." Cocaine remained an exotic curiosity in the medical profession 30 years after its discovery. In 1884 Sigmund Freud tested its potential to wean morphine addicts from their habits. Carol Koller, Freud's colleague, discovered cocaine's important local anesthetic action by accidentally dropping a few drops in his eye and noticing a temporary loss of sensation on the surface of the eye.

For a time, cocaine was used as a spinal anesthetic, but it was stopped when symptoms terminated in several convulsive seizures resulting in heart and respiratory failure. Like morphine and other major drugs of the late nineteenth century, cocaine became a prime ingredient of patent medicines and home remedies: French "wine of coca" was believed to be the ideal tonic; "Vin Coca Mariana," in which leaves were fused into wine, appeared on drug and grocery shelves across the nation. Coca Cola contained cocaine until 1906.

The coca plant became cultivated in South America, Java, Ceylon, and sparingly in southern Florida and California commercially.

Sir Arthur Conan Doyle portrayed his famous Sherlock Holmes as taking the drug to stimulate his brain and increase endurance.

Twentieth Century

In 1902 Richard Willstatter in Germany synthesized the drug. That year the Crothers Survey revealed that 3 to 8 per cent of the total amount of cocaine sold in five major U.S. cities went to medicine, dentistry, and veterinary medicine. Cocaine appeared in soft drinks (Coca Cola) until the Pure Food and Drug Laws of 1906. The Harrison Act of 1914 classified cocaine as a narcotic, driving its recreational use underground, where its use decreased gradually over the next 30 to 40 years.

Medically, cocaine has been used as a local anesthetic. A dilution of 1:5000 paralyzes nerve endings without stimulating or injuring surrounding tissues. It was used primarily as a mucous membrane anesthetic on the eye, nose, pharynx, larynx, esophagus, stomach, urethra, bladder, vagina and rectum. Procaine, a safer synthetic drug, which produces Novocain, has largely replaced cocaine as a local anesthetic.

Many have tried cocaine (snorting the powder) only once because it is difficult to obtain and is very expensive. Those who inject cocaine mix it with a longer lasting euphoriant (heroin) because the cocaine high lasts for only about one-half hour.

Eight million people in the moutain areas of northwestern Argentina, Bolivia, Colombia, Peru and the adjacent lowlands of the Amazon Valley continue to chew coca leaves routinely, much like Americans use tobacco.

THE NEW KID ON THE BLOCK—PCP

Numerous myths have been put forth concerning phencyclidine (PCP). The problems associated with any street drug are also found with PCP. Only 50 per cent of the samples analyzed to date have been correctly labeled as containing PCP. The remaining 50 per cent were erroneous; either no drug was found in the sample supposed to contain PCP or the sample had been submitted as THC, embalming fluid, DMT, or unknown and was found to contain PCP. In any event, nearly half of the drugs sampled as involving PCP were not PCP. With this background, it is necessary to investigate the chemistry and pharmacology of PCP and its effects on human beings.

Phencyclidine (Sernylan, Parke, Davis & Co.; Sernyl, Bio-Ceutic Laboratories) is classified as a nonvolatile general anesthetic. It is chemically and pharmacologically related to ketamine and tiletamine. Phencyclidine is commonly referred to as PCP. The origin of this abbreviation comes from its chemical name, 1-(1-phenylcyclohexyl)piperidine. It has also been referred to as the peace pill, hog, angel dust, mist, and monkey tranquilizer.

Presently, PCP is used legally as an animal tranquilizer, especially in nonhuman primates, and is now in Schedule III of the law enforcement classification. PCP displays a dose-dependent CNS depressant and stimulant action. At low doses (5 to 10 mg inhaled), users appear disoriented to time or place, may exhibit regressive or self-destructive behavior, and are usually anxious and agitated. With moderate doses (10 to 20 mg inhaled) the patient may be comatose or stuporous with open eyes, responding only to deep pain. This usually lasts for one to two hours, after which the low dose effects appear. Higher doses usually produce a comatose state, followed by a prolonged recovery period marked by alternating sleeping and waking, illusions, and hallucinations. Users have expressed feelings of "craziness" and of "being out of control," but in an environment of sensory isolation, the psychopathological and physiological effects of the drug were considerably dampened.

PCP produces signs of muscular rigidity, increased deep tendon reflexes, shivering (myoclonus), facial grimacing and general seizure activity. Surgical analgesia induced by PCP is similar to that produced by ketamine—neither produces good muscle relaxation, unlike most other general anesthetics.

Phencyclidine also causes diaphoresis, flushing, nausea, vomiting, and excess salivation. Although the mode of action of phencyclidine is unknown, it may be that it acts on the sensory cortex, thalamus, and midbrain in such a way as to impair discrimination of stimuli in the body, thereby disrupting vital feedback.

Phencyclidine has potent mind-altering effects and sometimes causes seizures and life-threatening hypertension. Numerous reports have shown PCP to be a major problem on the street. Clandestine labs have synthesized impure PCP. The by-products have caused abdominal cramps, hematemesis, coma, respiratory failure, and death.

FOOD ADDITIVES—DRUGS?

Food additives are "drugs" that we consume daily with little thought as to possible health consequences. Although these have not been known

as psychotropic drugs, they may be misused to the point of causing human disorders.

Due to the expanse of our country and the desire of the population to eat any food regardless of the season, the use of preservatives is now widespread. Preservatives have an obvious nutritional usefulness in that they help make possible a greater abundance and variety of foods. Some chemicals prolong the "life" of food by preventing contamination via bacteria or fungi. Some of these substances (benzoic acid, sulfur dioxide, sulfites, boric acid, and hydrogen peroxide) have ancient beginnings; this does not mean they are safe by any means.

Antibiotics are added to retard the spoilage of fish, meat, and poultry. If this is done, the product is generally chilled or frozen, and the eventual cooking process should destroy any antibiotic that has been authorized as a food preservative. This precaution is taken because unknown doses of antibiotics can kill some of the body's intestinal flora. Another group of preservatives known as antioxidants prevent the spoilage of fat and protect taste by inhibiting the formation of dangerous peroxides. Antioxidants preserve polyunsaturated fatty acids and fat-soluble vitamins.

Aesthetic additives include chemicals, such as nitrites, for glazing confectionery and improving the shine on bakery products, and enzymes for improving the taste and consistency of many foods.

Flavoring additives include acids that give added tartness to certain foods and beverages. Carbonic acid makes beverages effervescent and sparkling.

Bases, which are substances that react with acids, are used in baked goods and to neutralize the increased acidity of certain canned products.

Taste enhancers include monosodium glutamate (MSG), which is the main additive used for taste enhancement. Since dangerous side effects seem to be limited to infant mammals, the three major infant food manufacturers (Beech-Nut, Gerber, and Heinz) have discontinued its use in baby foods. A few adults have been found to be highly sensitive to large doses, which cause headaches, dizziness, a sense of tightness about the head and neck, and gastrointestinal discomfort.

Coloring additives are dyes employed in foods that lose natural coloring when processed. Pale foods tend to discourage appetite – and customers. Synthetic foods are replacing original products, and artificial colors are being introduced to reinforce taste. The use of arbitrary colors in new products can be justified only on purely aesthetic grounds.

Stabilizers are put into food products for practical reasons – to keep jellies in a gel state and to keep ice cream creamy. Pectin, sodium alginate, agar, and vegetable gums and starches are the agents commonly added to jellies and baby foods. Ice cream stays that way with the addition of stabilizers such as agar, vegetable agaroid, sodium alginate, methylcellulose, and sodium caseinate. Emulsifiers prevent oil and water from separating and are added to bakery products and to margarine. Related to emulsifiers are antiseparating agents. Inorganic salts, such as potassium and magnesium carbonates, make up this group. Additives already on the Food and Drug Administration's "Generally Recognized As Safe" list should be subjected to review. It may be pointed out that diseases have existed for millions of years before food additives were available – and even natural foods most likely contain unidentified chemical substances.

Presently, the FDA is considering a total investigatory effort regarding the toxicity of food additives. What do you feel is the answer? What do you propose as a limiting factor?

OVER-THE-COUNTER DRUGS

By the time they begin school, most children have been exposed to thousands of hours of television commercials, and this time will no doubt double before they are of high school age. A large portion of programming today is supported by companies that produce pharmaceuticals available at the local food or drug store. By the age of 10 years, an individual has become aware that there is an available over-the-counter drug for almost any disorder or ailment.

Over-the-counter drugs are drugs that can be purchased without a physician's prescription. They can be grouped into six general categories:

vitamins, analgesics (internal and external), cold remedies, sleep-producing aids, stimulants, and medicinal cosmetics. All have a genuine purpose as well as the potential to be misused to the point of physical damage.

Analgesics are for the most part used to alleviate pain without affecting consciousness; in other words, they are not similar to the mind-altering substances referred to earlier. They are effective in a truly integrated sense; that is, they relieve pain in any area of the body. Aspirin, or acetylsalicylic acid, remains the most popular of the over-the-counter pain relievers. Although the function of aspirin is to relieve pain, researchers are not totally sure what biological mechanism is used to affect the pain. Some points are known. Aspirin does not raise one's pain threshold; it simply alters the internal interpretation of the pain. Its anti-inflammatory action has been useful in treating sprains, and similar problems. In addition to its value as a pain reliever, one of its most beneficial mechanisms is its antipyretic effect (causation of perspiration as a cooling agent). Aspirin and aspirin compounds (1) increase the respiration rate, (2) increase oxygen consumption, (3) are ingested orally, and (4) are absorbed in the gastrointestinal tract. Americans have become habitual in the use of these compounds to relieve minor pain from headaches, infections, fever and now arthritis. Psychosomatic illnesses contribute to the multimillion dollar industry yearly.

An overdose of aspirin or aspirin compounds can cause acetylsalicylic acid poisoning that manifests itself as nausea, diarrhea, and even overstimulation of the respiratory centers to the point of death due to respiratory paralysis; however, this is uncommon. Unknown to most habitual aspirin users is the added effect of internal bleeding and irritation to the stomach walls, resulting in ulcers. Although the capability of interactions and contraindications does exist, the potential for detrimental side effects is low.

The pharmaceutical industry has thrived on our inability to deal with the common cold and the respiratory cough that often accompanies it. Cough suppressants have thus come to the forefront as relievers of such discomfort. Today there are three types of cough remedies: a suppressant of the central cough mechanism, a remedy that thins the mucous sputum along the bronchial linings, and an expectorant that expels the sputum by stimulating cough for a limited period of time. Side effects of these substances are drowsiness and gastrointestinal discomfort. Depending on the formulation of the drug, they can also produce a mild sense of euphoria prior to sedation.

The inability of Americans to relax and fall asleep naturally has brought about an abundance of over-the-counter sleeping aids. Most of these contain an antihistamine to provide the sedative action. Regular use is not encouraged because of such adverse effects as (1) extended drowsiness, (2) "cotton" mouth, (3) nausea, (4) muscle spasms, and (5) headaches.

In the past, numerous over-the-counter sleeping aids contained a chemical derivative of scopolamine. A World War II "truth serum," this depressant has a causal effect on the transmission of electrical impulses. Cardiac impasses have resulted from the incorrect use of these drugs.

Stimulants, as over-the-counter drugs, are less popular. Although caffeine is contained in coffee, tea, and colas, it is rarely regarded as an over-the-counter drug. The nonprescription "stay awake" pills or "diet" pills are the bulk of this industry and prove dangerous only to those suffering from cardiovascular difficulties.

Vitamins are a multimillion dollar industry. The average American consumes twice the amount of vitamins he or she actually needs from vitamin supplements. Special interest groups have, however, convinced the public of a growing need for vitamins as a preventive medicine technique. Vitamin toxicity is rare but can occur when they are taken in great quantities or in conjunction with other drugs.

Probably the fastest growing of all over-the-counter pharmaceuticals purchased by the youth are medicinal cosmetics. Acne preparations are seen as a means of eradicating problems that, although due to individual growth patterns, are no longer acceptable. Abuse or misuse of such preparations is rare. However, there have been reported instances of persons using ointments that reduce swelling around the anal passage as a means of reducing skin wrinkling, particularly among the elder population.

In summary, because of the countless references available regarding the use and abuse of drugs, it would be impossible to encompass all such material in this text. Thus, the foregoing discussion may at least demonstrate the need for us to rationally decide the values of drugs presently used in the United States.

THE FUTURE

It has been said by professionals in all fields that public law often reflects the beliefs of a society. Presently our laws are in a state of flux. The laws of the past seem to be inadequate today. No longer is the drug abuser the stereotypical youth with long hair. All ages are involved and societal laws must reflect this.

The problems that exist today and in the future are the result of public ignorance about specific drugs and their effects. This may be in part due to the overmedication of the not-so-ill. Accompanying ignorance are myths and a lack of understanding among generations with regard to the interpretation of scientific research. Not only has there been disputed interpretation of data, drugs and disease but the validity of drug research studies is often in doubt. Combine this factor with the changing life styles and state of the world, and the use of drugs as a means of escape is understandable. The philosophy of this drug use however, is a more perplexing situation.

Basic philosophies as to the control of legal and illegal substances are as numerous as the individuals who profess them. However, the pill society of the future may encounter increasing controls on drugs that are legal today. With the increasing complexity of drug schedules, our legal system has established regulations that seem inadequate to some and too stringent to others. Laws are not the solution to these problems. People's behavior problems are considered by some to be the drug problem; in fact, there may be no drug problem — just a behavior problem.

MARIJUANA AND ALCOHOL — THE SOCIALLY ACCEPTABLE DRUGS

At a time when there is great public interest in the mood-modifying drugs, which have become substantially identified with the "youth culture" in our country, it is important and useful to remember that the most prevalent and potentially dangerous mood-modifying drug consumed in the Western world is alcohol. Yet alcohol occupies a very distinct place in our society — its use, manufacture, advertisement, and sale are major parts of our environment.

Alcohol use has many different facets. Most Americans find it a pleasant and generally enjoyable part of dinner parties, social gatherings, celebrations, and so on. Unlike most of the hallucinogens and opiates, the use of alcohol in our society is not necessarily questioned or condemned; nor is it illegal. It becomes a legal or social problem only under specific conditions — e.g., driving while under the influence of alcohol, public intoxication, and the tragic personal consequences of alcoholism. The effects of alcohol are part of a complex web. Some are definitely due to problems of body chemistry; some relate more to social control and responsibility. Often, severe psychological problems are involved. In this, alcohol is the same as the drugs mentioned previously — it is difficult to directly predict all its effects or to understand how it affects different individuals.

Ironically, because of the generally freer attitudes toward alcohol use, we are able to see and understand more of its harmful results. With the possible exception of heroin addiction, we know more about the damage done by alcohol than we know about any other drug mentioned so far.

Yet, at the same time, millions of people are able to enjoy alcoholic beverages without ever seriously threatening the well-being of themselves or society. The reasons for the differences between these two groups are not clear, but in this section we have offered the facts known to science and medicine.

EXERCISES FOR THOUGHT

ACTIVITY 1

1. Alcoholism and overeating are both psychological dependencies. In what way, however, is dependence on alcohol more compelling?

2. In what ways does drug "use" differ from "abuse"? Why?

3. Behaviorists represent the alcoholic as someone who, through a series of circumstances that involve drinking, becomes publicly labeled as an alcoholic and begins to behave accordingly. Personality theorists propose that drug-dependent people, including alcoholics, possess essential personality traits that predispose them to extreme dependency states. In what ways do these theories differ?

4. Would it be possible to determine if alcoholism has a genetic basis? How?

5. If you are a problem drinker, what is the difference between your drinking and that of an alcoholic?

Many people say, "I know all about alcohol. I've been using it for years." However, use of alcohol does not automatically mean an understanding of it. How many of the following statements are true?

1. Alcohol is absorbed into the blood stream and is distributed to all parts of the body.
2. The higher centers of the brain, which control judgment and reasoning, are affected first.
3. Inhibitions are removed and emotions begin to dominate behavior.
4. As more alcohol is absorbed, muscular coordination is impaired and speech control becomes upset.
5. Focusing of the eyes becomes difficult.
6. Alcohol is an anesthetic and is capable of producing unconsciousness.
7. Alcohol gives a false sense of security to people.
8. Alcohol acts as a depressant upon the nervous system rather than a stimulant.
9. There is always a possibility that a person may become physically dependent on alcohol.
10. Alcohol interferes with good nutrition.
11. Alcohol irritates the membranes of the stomach.
12. People who drink have less resistance to infection.
13. Medical authorities agree that alcohol is injurious to human beings.

ACTIVITY 2

1. What subcultures presently rate "coke" as their drug of choice?

2. What do you see as an advantage of cocaine over heroin?

ACTIVITY 3

With all the advances made in creating "wonder drugs," why has man not created a "nondrug"; a drug to replace those habitual and addicting substances presently in use?

Some psychiatrists have stated for years that marijuana is the *perfect* drug! By what reasoning can you agree or disagree?

ENDNOTES

1. Carr, Robert: Pot vote. *Human Behavior*, May 1976, pp. 3–7.
2. *Ibid.*, p. 5.

BIBLIOGRAPHY

Andrews, George, and Simon Vinkenoog (Eds.): *The Book of Grass*. New York, Grove Press, 1967

Birdwood, George: *Willing Victim: A Parent's Guide to Drug Abuse*. New York, International Publishers, 1970.

Brean, Herbert: *How to Stop Smoking*. New York, Vanguard Press, 1958.

Brenner, Joseph H., Robert Coles, and Dermot Meagher: *Drugs and Youth*. New York, Liveright, 1970.

Byrd, Oliver: *Medical Readings on Drug Abuse*. Menlo Park, Calif., Addison-Wesley, 1970.

Chayet, Neil: Old laws for new junkies. *Emergency Medicine*, 3(4): 216–217, 221, April 1971.

Dienl, Harold S.: *Tobacco and Your Health*. New York, McGraw-Hill Book Co., 1969.

Fort, Joel: *Pleasure Seekers: The Drug Crisis, Youth & Society*. Indianapolis, Bobbs-Merrill, 1969.

Fort, Joel: *Alcohol: Our Biggest Drug Problem*. New York, McGraw-Hill Book Co., 1973.

Gay, George, David Smith, and Charles Sheppard: The new junkie. *Emergency Medicine*, 3(4):116–216, April 1971.

Gay, John E., and Neil E. Gallagher: *Drugs in Our Culture*. Dubuque, Iowa, Kendall/Hunt, 1976.

Hentoff, Nat: *Doctor Among the Addicts*. Chicago, Rand McNally, 1968.

Jones, Kenneth, Louis Shainberg, and Curtis Byer: *Drugs, Alcohol, and Tobacco*. San Francisco, Canfield Press, 1970.

Jones, Kenneth, Louis Shainberg, and Curtis Byer: Drugs: a personal perspective. In *Age of Aquarius*. Pacific Palisades, Calif. Goodyear Publishing, 1971.

Jones, Kenneth, Louis Shainberg, and Curtis Byer: *Drugs and Alcohol*, 2nd ed. New York, Harper & Row, 1973.

Kaplan, John: *Marijuana: The New Prohibition*. Cleveland, Ohio, World Publishing, 1970.

Lingeman, Richard: *Drugs from A to Z: A Dictionary*. New York, McGraw-Hill Book Co., 1969.

National Commission on Marihuana and Drug Abuse: *Marihuana: A Signal of Misunderstanding*. U.S. Government Printing Office, 1972.

Nowlis, Helen: *Drugs on the College Campus*. Garden City, N.Y., Doubleday, 1968.

Oakley, Ray S.: *Drugs, Society, and Human Behavior*. St. Louis, The C. V. Mosby Co., 1972.

Terry, Luther (Chairman): *Summary: World Conference on Smoking and Health*. New York, American Cancer Society, 1967.

CHRONIC AND COMMUNICABLE DISEASES

INTRODUCTION

Fear will always surround disease for humans; it's only the nature and severity of disease itself that changes. The leading causes of death in the United States in 1900 were all *infectious* diseases — influenza, pneumonia, tuberculosis, and diphtheria. We no longer have great fear of these potential killers, for modern science has made available immunizations and antibiotics to prevent or reduce their threat. Our fear has now turned toward killers such as heart disease, cancer, stroke, and emphysema, all of which are *chronic diseases* with no simple disease agent such as a bacterium to conquer. Are we justified in being as fearful of these chronic diseases as our grandparents were of the infectious ones? Yes and no. Simultaneously, we feel helpless (no simple immunization or antibiotic will prevent or cure coronary heart disease) and hopeful (risk factors have been identified that we can control to a great degree).

Helplessness is also felt when the individual sees the air and water being polluted by industry and automobiles, workers subjected to high noise and chemical substance levels, excessive amounts of chemical additives in the foods, insufficiently tested drugs on the market, and don't-smoke and do-smoke advertisements. These environmental factors, which certainly affect one's health, seem beyond the individual's control. The individual must also face the medical care empire alone — receiving inferior or inadequate care and treatment if he lives too far away from a metropolitan medical complex, if his income or insurance coverage is minimal and therefore doesn't cover regular checkups or catastrophic illness, or if his social background makes him feel alien in the impersonal, white, upper middle class world of medical professionals. And yet the individual himself contributes to this feeling of helplessness. We've come

199

to expect quick cures because of our recent experience with the infectious diseases and because of our exposure to Madison Avenue—an immunization for polio, a shot of penicillin for pneumonia, or a few pills to swallow away headaches, upset stomachs, sleeplessness, tension, or emotional upsets. We put all our blind trust in the almighty being known as the physician—who must know all the answers—and in the magic chemicals that only he can dispense.

As individuals, we can't singlehandedly change the environmental ills and the established medical empire, but *we can change ourselves!* We can learn about our own bodies and the interrelationships between our health and the environment. Physicians are certainly necessary, but we need to assert ourselves in asking relevant questions to understand our own health and illness. Medications are important, but we shouldn't demand them unless there's a real need, and then, we must use them wisely. The real key to conquering these modern chronic diseases is prevention. We must arm ourselves with the proper facts so that we can start preventing heart disease while we're young enough to do something about it. Starting an exercise program at age 65 will hardly prevent a heart attack and might even precipitate one! We must reorient our thinking to prevention, as opposed to crisis cures and treatment that are often little more than palliative. The killers of our time will not be wiped out by easy, short-term measures. Fear need not be pervasive if we learn to take responsibility for our own bodies and health, based on accurate knowledge and recommendations from the medical field. In turn, health professionals must also assume a broadened responsibility toward the patient. The following excerpt from the Task Force on Patient Education for the President's Committee on Health Education sums up this new professional viewpoint: "... hospitals and health professionals should accept the premise that the patient has an inalienable 'right to known' the status of his health; the nature of an existing health problem; what community resources are available to him and his family; and what he can do, if possible, to prevent future recurrences."[1] Perhaps we should add to this statement that the individual should accept the responsibility to understand the status of his health and any existing health problems, and what he can do, if possible, to prevent disease or future recurrences. Knowledge and constructive action are killers of fear.

This section will examine a person's health behavior and provide the basic information necessary to take sound preventive action in securing one's health for the present and future.

---

[1]Benenson, Abram S. (Ed.): *Control of Communicable Diseases in Man,* 12th ed. American Public Health Association, 1975.

CHAPTER 11

CHRONIC DISEASES

CARDIOVASCULAR DISEASES

Cardiovascular diseases account for 60 per cent of all deaths in the United States. Most of us have come to view the chronic and degenerative diseases such as heart attack, stroke and cancer as inevitable results of middle or old age. This is not so. The predisposing factors to the cardiovascular diseases, especially heart attack and stroke, have been identified and can start working against you, even in early childhood. One is never too young to undertake preventive behavior for cardiovascular diseases. We will first examine some of the major cardiovascular diseases and their manifestations and then identify the major risk factors, which can tell you how to prevent or reduce the chance of succumbing to disease.

ATHEROSCLEROSIS

Atherosclerosis is the progressive buildup of fatty materials, or lipids, within the walls of arteries, causing a narrowing or thickening of these walls. Coronary atherosclerosis is the thickening or narrowing of the arteries carrying the blood to the heart muscle. This is the underlying cause of myocardial infarction (heart attack) and angina pectoris. If atherosclerosis occurs in the cerebral arteries, it may be the underlying cause of stroke. Atherosclerosis can occur in any arteries, but it is most serious when it blocks the blood flow, and therefore oxygen, to such vital centers as the heart and brain. Although there's no single cause of atherosclerosis, several of the risk factors will be discussed later.

HYPERTENSION

Blood pressure measurement indicates the pressure behind the powerful left ventricle's contraction as it sends oxygenated blood to all parts of the body; this is followed by the pressure reading maintained during this chamber's relaxation period. The first measurement is called

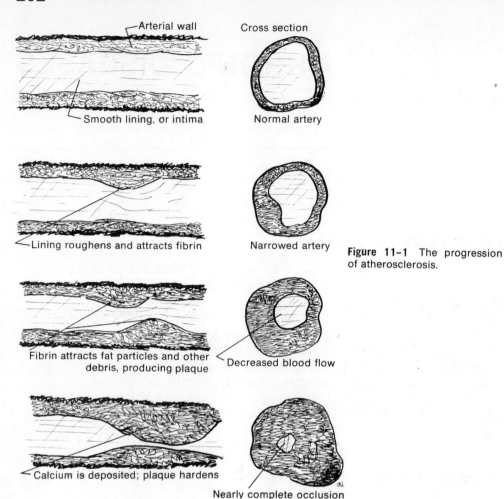

Arterial wall

Cross section

Smooth lining, or intima

Normal artery

Lining roughens and attracts fibrin

Narrowed artery

Figure 11-1 The progression of atherosclerosis.

Fibrin attracts fat particles and other debris, producing plaque

Decreased blood flow

Calcium is deposited; plaque hardens

Nearly complete occlusion

the systolic blood pressure and the latter is the diastolic; they are written as a ratio, such as 120/80, a normal reading for a college age student. Normal systolic blood pressure for young adults ranges from 100 to 120 mm Hg; for older adults it ranges from 120 to 140 mm Hg. Diastolic pressure is usually below 90 mm Hg in healthy individuals. High blood pressure or hypertension is a condition in which a continued reading above approximately 145/95 exists. About 85 per cent of persons with hypertension have *essential hypertension*, which is caused by constriction of the small arteries throughout the body. This constriction decreases the amount of blood flow throughout the body, and therefore, the heart tries to pump harder to overcome this resistance. The cause of this arterial constriction is not yet known, although there seems to be an interrelationship between hypertension and atherosclerosis, each aggravating the other. Hypertension can be controlled through the use of medication or a restricted salt diet or both.

ANGINA PECTORIS

Not actually a disease but a symptom of restricted oxygen flow to the heart muscle, angina pectoris is manifested by mild to severe pain, pressure, or tightness under the breast bone and often radiating to the left shoulder or arm. It is characteristically precipitated by physical exertion or emotion, which requires added blood flow to the body. If the coronary arteries are narrowed (coronary atherosclerosis), the heart is unable to meet this increased demand, being deprived of its oxygen supply. Upon stopping the exertion, the heart rate slows down, the increased work demands on the heart are relieved, and the pain disappears within one or two minutes. A nitroglycerin tablet placed under the tongue also gives prompt relief of angina pectoris. Angina pectoris may precede or follow a heart attack or may exist in persons who never will have a heart attack.

HEART ATTACK

Also called *myocardial infarction, coronary thrombosis* or coronary occlusion, heart attack is the number one killer today in the United States and most Western countries. If atherosclerosis becomes so severe in the coronary arteries (see Fig. 11–1) that the passageway becomes completely closed or a blood clot lodges and blocks the very narrowed passage, then

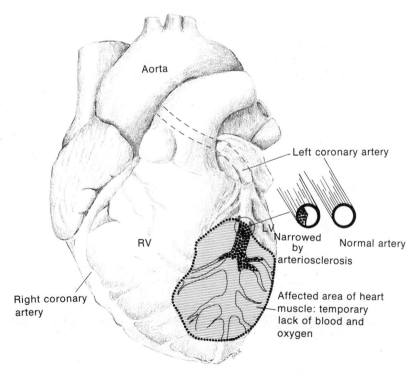

Figure 11-2 The heart: angina pectoris.

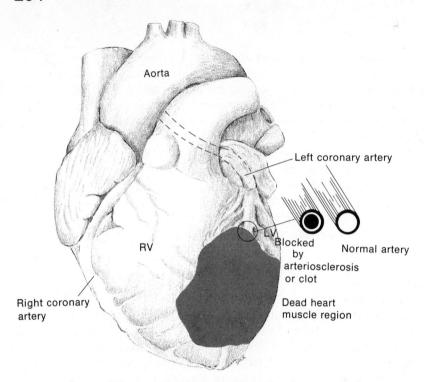

Figure 11-3 The heart: myocardial infarction.

the blood supply is insufficient to maintain heart tissue. This part of the heart muscle that is supplied by the affected artery is then permanently damaged and dies. If the damaged area is extensive enough, then the attack is fatal. Some attacks (and therefore area of damaged heart muscle) are so slight as not to be felt at all. The typical symptoms, however, of heart attack are (1) a pressing or squeezing pain located behind the lower portion of the breastbone, possibly radiating to one or both arms or to the jaw or neck (very similar to angina pectoris, but may last for several hours); and (2) sweating, which is typical and may be accompanied by nausea, vomiting or shortness of breath. Since 40 per cent of deaths from heart attacks occur within the first hour after the onset of these symptoms and 60 per cent of patients who die from a heart attack never reach the hospital, the recognition of symptoms is of great importance. Since hospitals cannot always be reached in time, the average citizen's knowledge and use of the cardiopulmonary resuscitation (CPR) technique has saved thousands of lives. Your local Red Cross chapter or Heart Association can advise you of training classes near you.

STROKE (CEREBROVASCULAR ACCIDENT) OR CEREBRAL THROMBOSIS

The precipitating factors for stroke are quite similar to those for a heart attack, except that the impaired blood flow involves arteries nourishing the brain rather than the heart. When the brain cells are deprived of their blood supply by a stroke, the parts of the body controlled by these nerve centers can no longer function normally — paralysis, speech impairment, memory loss, or death may result. Stroke may also be caused by rupture of a cerebral artery, followed by hemorrhaging. The major underlying factor in stroke is hypertension, which in turn aggravates atherosclerosis by causing fatty substances to be deposited more rapidly in arterial linings. As you can begin to see, it is difficult to divorce one cardiovascular disease factor from another, as they are all interrelated and have reciprocal effects on one another.

Let us now look at the major risk factors to determine what an individual can do to prevent or reduce the risk of cardiovascular disease. A risk factor is some factor that increases the risk of a certain disease; thus, the chances of contracting the disease are lowered if the risk factor can be eliminated or controlled. This is not to be confused with a causal factor, which is much more definitive and would assure one of not contracting the disease if it were eliminated or controlled. Unfortunately, there is no one causal factor (such as a virus or a bacterium) for the cardiovascular diseases under consideration here. Rather, many factors work together on a long-term basis to increase one's chances of succumbing to disease. We have no individual control over some of these factors, such as age and heredity, but most of them are amenable to human alteration.

RISK FACTORS IN HEART DISEASE

HYPERTENSION

Hypertension has been discussed earlier as a disease entity, but it is also a predisposing factor to more serious complications such as heart attack and stroke. Although hypertension is difficult to prevent, it is readily controlled by medication and/or diet. The important thing is to check your blood pressure periodically and see a physician promptly if it becomes elevated.

ELEVATED BLOOD LIPIDS

Chronic high fat levels in the blood can lead to atherosclerosis. Lipids or fats are necessary for body functioning, and some, such as the unsaturated fat linoleic acid, must be obtained from the diet. The majority, however, are synthesized from other nutrients taken into the body, so we don't need to obtain them from our diet. *Cholesterol* is derived from the breakdown of fats in the liver and is manufactured by body cells in small amounts. It is essential to metabolism in all animals and therefore is found in all animal tissues. When we eat animal products high in cholesterol, we are only adding to our own body's supply of cholesterol. Excessive amounts of cholesterol (hypercholesterolemia) can be detected in the blood quite easily. This has now become a routine part of thorough physical examinations in conjunction with other blood analyses. Normal values range from 120 to 250 mg per 100 ml, depending on the individual's age and sex. Restriction of foods high in cholesterol is valuable in reducing the cholesterol blood level. All animal products contain certain amounts of cholesterol, but the major culprits are egg yolks, shellfish, and organ meats such as liver, brain and kidney.

Triglycerides are a type of lipid synthesized by the liver from dietary or endogenous carbohydrates. Recently they have been considered equal to or more important than cholesterol in the etiology of atherosclerosis. Detection of triglycerides is also done through blood analysis; a normal range is 10 to 190 mg per 100 ml, again depending on age and sex. Reduction of triglyceride blood levels can be brought about by lowered carbohydrate and sugar intake in the diet. The American diet is appallingly high in sugar content, especially in regard to convenience foods (e.g., breakfast cereals and flavored drinks.) Because of their high blood sugar levels, diabetics are extremely susceptible to atherosclerosis.

Saturated fats contribute to both atherosclerosis and diabetes. Saturated fats are usually those of animal origin, and in general are solid at room temperature. The unsaturated fats are usually of vegetable origin and are produced from corn, peanuts, soybeans, seeds (e.g., safflower oil), or nuts. Linoleic acid is an unsaturated fatty acid that is necessary in diet, since it helps to break down saturated fats. The unsaturated fats do not produce high blood lipid levels, and in fact, they usually cause a lowering of these levels. Foods high in saturated fats are red meats, butter, cheese, cream, whole milk, coconut oil, chocolate, and lard. On the other hand, skim milk, most fish, and most vegetable oils and products are relatively unsaturated.

One need only compare the coronary heart disease incidence among countries with different dietary habits to get an idea of the role diet can play. The incidence of coronary heart disease is highest in countries, such as the United States and Finland, where dairy and meat products compose a large portion of the diet; also, when persons from low-fat diet areas like Japan move to areas like the United States, their incidence of heart disease increases significantly.

CIGARETTE SMOKING

The risk of heart attack among heavy smokers is almost three times that of nonsmokers; this risk increases with the number of cigarettes consumed daily; it also increases as the age at which one started smoking lowers. Interestingly enough, the death rate drops toward normal after the smoker stops smoking. So it's never too late to quit!

Exactly what is the effect of tobacco on the heart? Nicotine, which is the active drug in tobacco, acts as a stimulant on the central nervous system. In relation to the heart, it is manifested by increased pulse rate (15 to 25 beats per minute faster), increased blood pressure (increased by 10 to 20 mm Hg systolic and 5 to 15 mm Hg diastolic), and constriction of the peripheral arteries. This latter effect usually results in a lowered temperature of the extremities by as much as 5 to 13 degrees centigrade, (Celsius), experienced by many smokers as "cold feet" or "cold fingers." Other detrimental effects of smoking on the heart include accelerated thrombosis (blood clot) formation, which, if accompanied by atherosclerosis, can precipitate a heart attack, and decreased oxygen supply to the body cells and tissues due to the competition of carbon monoxide (in the smoke), which attaches to hemoglobin in the red blood cells instead of the needed oxygen.

The local unit of the American Cancer Society or American Lung Association can provide literature on how to stop smoking or information on the nearest "stop smoking" clinic. The best cure is not to start smoking, but if you already have, it's never too late to quit. The role of smoking in other diseases such as lung cancer and emphysema will be discussed later.

DIABETES

A diabetic's pancreas produces inadequate amounts of insulin, resulting in abnormally high blood sugar levels. This high carbohydrate level stimulates lipid production, which in time, accelerates the progress of atherosclerosis. (See the discussion of elevated blood lipids as a risk factor.) Diabetics can control their carbohydrate metabolism through diet and/or medication; but early detection and treatment are essential to prevent cardiovascular and other diseases. The blood test for diabetes is a fairly simple test that should be part of one's yearly physical examination.

AGE

Although we cannot control our age, it is known that cardiovascular disease incidence rises significantly after age 35 and is the major cause of death for those over this age. For this reason, one is *never too young* to start taking preventive action before the processes of cardiovascular disease become irreversible.

EXERCISE

The five preceding risk factors have been statistically proved to contribute to cardiovascular disease. That is, any one alone does not mean that you will develop heart disease, but it does *increase* the risk of your developing cardiovascular disease. Exercise and the subsequent factors discussed have not been proved to be direct risk factors, but they can aggravate some conditions that have been proved to be risk factors. They don't directly contribute to heart disease, but their value is to be heeded, since they can help control or reduce the negative effects of other risk factors.

The type of exercise that is most beneficial to the cardiovascular system is stamina or endurance training. Using the heart and lungs to provide the maximum amount of oxygen to all body cells has also been called aerobic exercise, a term coined by Dr. Kenneth Cooper in his book *Aerobics*. The reader is referred to that book and the subsequent titles, *The New Aerobics* and *Aerobics for Women*, for excellent directions and explanations for starting or continuing your own endurance-type exercise program. Swimming, jogging, and cycling are the best type of aerobic exercise, but Cooper gives point values to all other types as well, in order for the individual to determine his or her own degree of aerobic exercise and proficiency.

As a result of regular and progressive aerobic or stamina training, one can expect to lower the resting pulse rate by as much as 15 beats per minute in a three-month period, to have the pulse and blood pressure return to normal more quickly after exertion, to lower blood cholesterol and triglyceride levels, and to increase vascularization (greater branching of capillaries). All these results serve to produce a more efficient heart muscle and to counteract atherosclerosis.

Overexertion can be just as detrimental as underexertion, so one must be careful to start out gradually and progress at a regular pace that is suitable to one's age and condition. Unfortunately, Americans have overemphasized contact and team sports at the expense of individual, recreational ones. The exercise habit should be formed early in life, should require little expense and little dependence on others, and should afford pleasure and safety. For those who are really out of shape, it is never too late to start walking!

OBESITY

The term obesity means that one has 20 per cent or more excess body fat. In terms of the heart, this means an extra load to pump blood and therefore oxygen. Although not really an independent risk factor in heart disease, obesity does aggravate high blood pressure, sugar tolerance, and high serum lipid levels and increases the risk of diabetes. A weight reduction program is beyond the scope of this text, but two principles should be kept in mind: (1) in order to lose weight, more calories must be used than taken in (i.e., smaller food portions and exercise), and (2) weight should be lost at the same rate it was gained—slowly! Crash and fad diets, which initially appear to work because of the water weight loss, are unhealthy, as they rarely prescribe a well-balanced intake of food.

SEX

Like age, one's gender is usually not within control, but an interesting fact to note is that the incidence of coronary heart disease is significantly lower in premenopausal women than in men, but it soon catches up to the male incidence after the early menopause years. It is believed that the female hormone estrogen causes lower lipid levels in the blood; during menopause the estrogen level drops, resulting in a greater tendency toward higher blood lipid levels and therefore a greater risk of cardiovascular disease.

STRESS

The relationship of emotional stress to coronary artery disease remains controversial; however, palpitation due to premature beats or to rapid cardiac rhythms is among the most widely recognized symptoms of emotional stress and therefore has been considered a precipitating factor in many heart rhythm disturbances. Dr. J. Friedman describes a relationship between the so-called type A personality and coronary artery disease. This individual has intense ambition, competitive drive, and a sense of urgency; he is constantly preoccupied with deadlines and makes a sustained effort to achieve. This type of stress has been shown to cause the following physiological effects which, if chronic, could aggravate coronary heart disease: increased pulse and blood pressure, increased fatty acids in the blood, and increased coagulability of blood. Other evidence suggests correlation between stress and coronary heart disease: a greater incidence in urban vs. rural areas, white collar vs. agricultural and blue collar workers, persons with greater geographical mobility, and those with greater job mobility. Stress can also aggravate symptoms in patients with advanced heart disease. A certain amount of stress is necessary for life functioning, but chronic, unrelieved emotional stress seems to take its toll on most body systems, including the heart. More direct evidence is needed, however, to define the degree of stress and determine its effects on individual personality types.

HEREDITY

If a history of coronary heart disease exists in one's family, then the chances of that individual developing heart disease do increase if other factors are kept equal. However, the risk may be purely a function of similar life styles (smoking, exercise, eating habits), which can certainly be altered. In the case of heart disease, which is not due to any single gene defect, family history need not dictate any individual's fate.

Although we don't have control over all these heart disease risk factors all the time, we can do something about most of them, and the earlier in life the better. Find your own heart disease risk score by playing

Risk-O at the end of this section. Not to be equated with a physician's diagnosis, Risk-O can help point up some of your weak areas in preventing heart disease.

CANCER

The word cancer refers to more than a hundred different disease entities, but they all have the following characteristics in common: (1) the ability to divide and produce abnormal daughter cells, (2) the ability to displace, invade, and destroy normal tissues, and (3) the ability to grow in the presence of control mechanisms that preserve the orderly growth of normal cells. Since 500 billion body cells must be replaced daily, it is little wonder that all these cell divisions are not perfect, resulting in at least 10,000 abnormal cells a day. A majority of these abnormal cells are so defective that they are unable to divide into daughter cells or even survive. However, of those that do survive and multiply, what factors favor their development as cancer cells? Although we don't know the complete answer to the etiology of cancer, we do know some of the variables that favorably and unfavorably affect cancer development. Presumably, some of the abnormal cells provoke the formation of antibodies against themselves, acting as antigens and being rejected in the same way that foreign biological material is routinely rejected. But even the abnormal cells that do survive the body's immune mechanism are not necessarily cancer cells. Referring to our three-point definition, these cells must also continue to grow despite control mechanisms and must invade and destroy normal tissues. These last qualities are manifested in what scientists call a *neoplasm*, or tumor, which may have the ability to *metastasize*, or spread, to other parts of the body, usually via the blood or lymph system. Not all neoplasms metastasize, and those which do not are called *benign* (noncancerous) neoplasms to distinguish them from the cancerous, or *malignant*, neoplasms which spread.

Cancers are classified according to the type of tissue or cells affected. *Carcinoma*, the most common type, refers to those cancers affecting tissue of epithelial origin, such as the skin, mouth, lung, breasts, liver, intestines, and uterus. Metastasis or secondary growth sites in other tissues and organs may result through passage of cancerous cells in the lymph system and blood stream. *Sarcoma* refers to cancer of the connective tissues — muscle, bone, cartilage — with metastasis through the blood system being fairly common. *Lymphoma* is cancer of the lymph system, e.g., Hodgkin's disease. Unfortunately, lymphomas metastasize rapidly throughout the lymph network. *Leukemia* is cancer of the blood-forming tissues, and *melanoma* is a particular type of skin cancer affecting the pigment-producing cells. The names are endless, depending on how specifically the cancer can be defined in terms of site of origin and degree of spread. Let us now look at some of the more specific types of cancer and their trends.

Cancer is the second leading cause of death in the United States today, and unlike heart disease, the mortality rate due to cancer is on the increase, accounting for almost one-fifth of all deaths. The survival rate is 2 out of 6 persons with diagnosed cancer, but it could be 3 out of 6 if diagnosed early and proper treatment were received in time. A person is considered cured of cancer if he remains free of cancer 5 years after a diagnosis.

In females, the overall cancer death rate has declined, mainly because of the Papanicolaou (Pap) test, which provides early diagnosis of cervical and uterine cancer, and because of a decrease in stomach and rectal cancers. Breast cancer is the most common and the most fatal cancer in women. At present rates, 1 out of every 13 American women will develop breast cancer, but if it is discovered in an early stage before it has spread, the survival rate is 84 per cent. For this reason, breast self-examination and regular medical check-ups are a must. Black women have a lower incidence of breast cancer and uterine cancer than their white counterparts, but they have a higher incidence of cervical cancer.

The overall rate of cancer in men has drastically risen, due mainly to a steady increase in lung cancer, the number one killer. Cigarette smoking is the major cause of lung cancer; the risk of lung cancer is ten times greater in smokers than in nonsmokers. The American Cancer Society estimates that 80 per cent of lung cancer would be prevented if no one smoked cigarettes. Unfortunately, lung cancer has no early warning signals, so when it is discovered, metastasis usually has already occurred, making the survival rate about 10 per cent. The prostate, colon, and rectum are other common sites for cancer in the male, but unlike lung cancer, these types are more easily detected in a thorough physical examination and therefore have better survival rates.

CAUSES OF CANCER

There is no one specific or universal event that occurs in the body and causes cells to become malignant. Certain *carcinogens* (cancer-causing substances) have been identified. Depending on the amount of these carcinogens and the period of exposure to them, a person's chances of developing a given cancer are increased. Exposure alone is not sufficient to assure disease; not all smokers develop lung cancer, for example. Rather, a person's biochemical make-up, environment, and inheritance all interact in a complex way to determine health status. There is no evidence, with two rare exceptions, that cancer is directly transmitted from parent to offspring. However, there are definitely family and ethnic tendencies toward specific types of cancer, such as breast cancer, skin cancer, and leukemia. The environment probably plays as big a role as does inheritance, however. The known carcinogens can be classified as chemical, physical, or biological.

Chemical Carcinogens. Hydrocarbons found in tar, smoke, smog, and automobile exhausts contribute to lung, bladder, and scrotal cancer. Sex hormones have produced cancer in the sex organs of rodents.

Diethylstilbestrol (DES), a synthetic form of estrogen, has been linked to vaginal cancer in female offspring of women who took high doses of DES during pregnancy. Certain dyes used in industry can cause bladder cancer. Liver and brain cancer have been linked with overexposure to vinyl chloride, used in the plastics industry. Arsenic, asbestos, chromates, and nickel, used in certain industries, have contributed to the incidence of lung and other cancers. Alcohol and tobacco have been cited as carcinogens in cancer of the mouth, throat, esophagus, and larynx. The list is quite extensive, with new suspicions being raised every month. However, proof of a carcinogen takes years of testing by several independent laboratories. The biggest risks occur in industry, in urban areas (pollution), and in smokers.

Physical Carcinogens.   All types of radiation can alter the genetic mechanisms of a cell and are therefore potentially carcinogenic. Dosage and duration of exposure are the two important variables to bear in mind when determining degree of risk. Ultraviolet rays from the sun can cause skin cancer, usually in fair or freckled skin. X-rays can cause skin or thyroid-cancer or leukemia. Gamma rays, as in radium paints and dials, can cause bone cancer through prolonged, direct contact; and atomic radiation can cause leukemia and lung, breast, and thyroid cancer. Since some of these types of radiation are used to treat cancer, this evidence seems contradictory. Again, it's a matter of dosage, duration, and ability to direct the radiation to isolated body parts. Properly controlled, x-rays are not yet known to be harmful to the average patient on a once-a-year basis. Overexposure or chronic exposure should be avoided, however, especially in pregnant women.

Biological Carcinogens.   Viruses have been demonstrated to cause several types of cancer (e.g., leukemia) in animals. In human beings, it seems only a matter of time before viruses are isolated and shown to be carcinogens. Indirect evidence has linked the herpesvirus (also the causative agent of chickenpox and cold sores) with cancer of the mouth, cervix, vulva, prostate, kidney, and bladder. Adenoviruses, the cause of the common cold and other upper respiratory tract infections, are another cancer virus suspect. Very recently, the *Clostridium* bacteria, normally found in the bowel, have been linked to bowel cancer by their action on bile acids, in turn forming carcinogens. As soon as these biological carcinogens are fully isolated, the development of a vaccine against them will inevitably follow.

CANCER TREATMENT

Surgical removal of all cancerous tissue is the oldest form of cancer treatment. This is not always possible, as the cancer may have already metastasized or may have overtaken an organ so completely that complete removal would cause imminent death. Two other drawbacks to surgical removal of cancer are the inevitable removal of some normal tissue and the possibility of speeding up cancer cell replication and causing

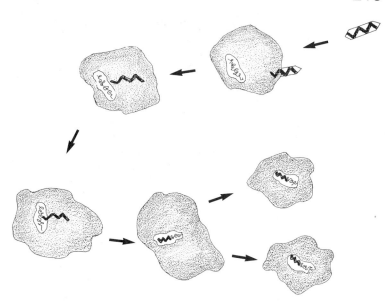

Figure 11-4 The viral theory of cancer. The viral DNA becomes incorporated into the cellular DNA, altering the cell's genetic code and rendering it deviant or abnormal.

metastasis. Still, in early stages of cancer in most body tissues, surgery is the most effective method of treatment. Preceding surgery, a definitive diagnosis of cancer is made with a *biopsy.* A biopsy is a minor surgical procedure in which a small piece of suspect tissue is removed, preserved, thinly sliced, stained, and examined under a microscope by a pathologist, who subsequently pronounces it benign or malignant.

Radiation, such as that from x-rays and cobalt isotopes, destroys cancer cells more quickly than normal cells, and with more recent refinements, radiation can be directed to specific, isolated tissue, minimizing the damage to the normal cell. As in surgery, radiation treatment is most effective in treating unmetastasized lesions. In cases in which surgical excision would cause severe deformity, encased radioactive materials may be implanted directly in tumor tissue and then removed when the desired dosage has been delivered. Radiation is often used jointly with surgery as a cancer treatment both pre- and postoperatively to shrink the malignant neoplasm and kill any residual cancer cells left after surgery.

Chemotherapy is the newest method of cancer treatment, and new drugs are being tested every year. These chemical agents can be classified according to their biological action: (1) cell mitosis interference (alkylating drugs like nitrogen mustard for leukemia), (2) cell metabolism inhibitors (methotrexate for uterine cancer), (3) hormones that inhibit tumor growth (most effective for breast, uterine, kidney, prostate, and thyroid cancers(, (4) immunological agents that increase the resistance of the host to the tumor cells (antibiotics and vaccinations). The difficulty in chemotherapy lies in finding chemicals that will destroy cancer cells but not normal cells. Compounded with this is the difficulty of testing these drugs on human beings, as animals studies are not always applicable. As yet, chemotherapy is not considered a cure for cancer, but as an aid or palliative. Chemotherapy as an adjunct to radiation and surgery is well recognized, however; good results, for example, have been obtained with colon and bladder cancer through the combined use of radiation and 5-fluorouracil.

To date, surgery is the most successful cancer treatment, especially if coupled with radiation and/or chemotherapy. However, successful surgery is limited by the extent and location of the malignant tissues. The key to cancer cure lies in early detection and, more important, in prevention.

The best protection against cancer is to (1) heed the seven danger signals, (2) have thorough, periodic medical examinations, and (3) avoid cancer-producing agents. Consult the American Cancer Society charts for the seven warning signals and the diagnostic methods for each cancer type (Fig. 11–5). And all women, regardless of age, should have an annual Pap smear and perform a monthly breast self-examination (Fig. 11–6). Cancer need not be the dreaded killer if we're armed with the facts and practice preventive and early detection care.

CHRONIC RESPIRATORY DISEASES

Asthma, chronic bronchitis, and emphysema are the three most common and disabling chronic respiratory diseases. Although there is no cure for any of them, avoidance of smoking, air pollution, and long-term dust inhalation can have a profound preventive effect, especially in the case of chronic bronchitis and emphysema. These respiratory disorders have far-reaching effects, as they interfere with the

---

CANCER'S 7 WARNING SIGNALS

Change in bowel or bladder habits
A sore that does not heal
Unusual bleeding or discharge
Thickening or lump in breast or elsewhere
Indigestion or difficulty in swallowing
Obvious change in wart or mole
Nagging cough or hoarseness

If YOU have a warning signal,
see your doctor!

THE 7 SAFEGUARDS URGED BY ACS

Lung: Reduction and ultimate elimination of cigarette smoking
Colon-Rectum: Proctoscopic exam as routine in annual checkup for those over 40
Breast: Self-examination as monthly female practice
Uterus: Pap test for all adult and high-risk women
Skin: Avoidance of excessive sun
Oral: Wider practice of early detection measures
Basic: Regular physical examination for all adults

Figure 11–5 *Left,* Cancer's seven warning signals and seven safeguards urged by the American Cancer Society. *Right,* Chart of the leading cancer sites in 1976. Incidence estimates are based on the rates from the N.C.I. Third National Cancer Survey, 1969–1971. (Courtesy of the American Cancer Society, 1975.)

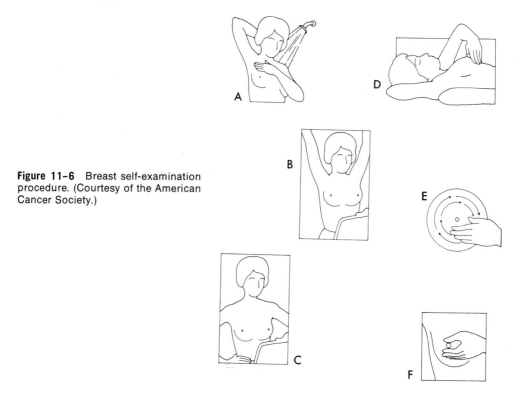

Figure 11-6 Breast self-examination procedure. (Courtesy of the American Cancer Society.)

oxygen supply that is so vital to all living tissues; they therefore put an added strain on the heart, which must pump oxygenated blood to all parts of the body.

ASTHMA

Asthma is characterized by periodic attacks of difficult breathing with varying degrees of wheezing and shortness of breath. This choked breathing is caused by a narrowing of the bronchioles, which are the smaller branches of the bronchi. This narrowing may result from swelling of the bronchiole membrane lining, a spasm of the bronchioles, or mucus blockage of these tubes. Allergic reactions to dust, pollen, animal hair, or certain foods seem to be the predominant cause of asthma, but bacterial infections of the sinuses, nose and throat, or reactions to emotional stress can also play a role in causation.

It is important that asthma sufferers receive early medical treatment, as prolonged or repeated attacks can cause permanent damage to the lungs and heart. These serious effects can be alleviated, depending on the cause. Desensitization shots for allergies, antibiotics for infection, reduction in emotional stress, change of climate, and bronchodilator drugs are among the treatment methods.

REFERENCE CHART: LEADING CANCER SITES, 1976*

Site	Estimated New Cases, 1976	Estimated Deaths, 1976	Warning Signal— If You Have One, See Your Doctor	Safeguards	Comment
Breast	89,000	33,000	Lump or thickening in the breast	Annual checkup Monthly breast self-exam	The leading cause of cancer death in women
Colon and rectum	99,000	49,000	Change in bowel habits; bleeding	Annual checkup including proctoscopy, especially for those over 40	Considered a highly curable disease when digital and proctoscopic examinations are included in routine checkups
Lung	93,000	84,000	Persistent cough, or lingering respiratory ailment	80% of lung cancer would be prevented if no one smoked cigarettes	The leading cause of cancer death among men and rising mortality among women
Oral (including pharynx)	24,000	8000	Sore that does not heal. Difficulty in swallowing	Annual checkup	Many more lives should be saved because the mouth is easily accessible to visual examination by physicians and dentists
Skin	9000†	5000	Sore that does not heal, or change in wart or mole	Annual checkup, avoidance of overexposure to sun	Skin cancer is readily detected by observation: diagnosed by simple biopsy
Uterus	47,000**	11,000	Unusual bleeding or discharge	Annual checkup, including pelvic examination with Pap test	Uterine cancer mortality has declined 65% during the last 40 years with wide application of the Pap test; postmenopausal women with abnormal bleeding should be checked

Kidney and bladder	45,000	17,000	Urinary difficulty; bleeding — in which case, consult doctor at once	Annual checkup with urinalysis	Protective measures for workers in high-risk industries are helping to eliminate one of the important causes of these cancers
Larynx	9000	3000	Hoarseness — difficulty in swallowing	Annual checkup, including laryngoscopy	Readily curable if caught early
Prostate	56,000	19,000	Urinary difficulty	Annual checkup, including palpation	Occurs mainly in men over 60, the disease can be detected by palpation and urinalysis at annual checkup
Stomach	23,000	14,000	Indigestion	Annual checkup	A 40% decline in mortality in 25 years, for reasons yet unknown
Leukemia	21,000	15,000	Leukemia is a cancer of blood-forming tissues and is characterized by the abnormal production of immature white blood cells; acute leukemia strikes mainly children and is treated by drugs which have extended life from a few months to as much as ten years; chronic leukemia strikes usually after age 25 and progresses less rapidly		
Lymphomas	30,000	19,000	These cancers arise in the lymph system and include Hodgkin's disease and lymphosarcoma; some patients with lymphatic cancers can lead normal lives for many years: Five-year survival rate for Hodgkin's disease increased from 26% to 64% in 20 years		

*All figures rounded to the nearest 1000.
†Estimate of new cases of nonmelanoma skin cancer: about 300,000.
**If carcinoma-in-situ is included, cases total over 87,000.

CHRONIC BRONCHITIS

Frequent and prolonged coughing with excessive expectoration is the major symptom of *chronic bronchitis*. Due to chronic irritation by cigarette smoking or heavy air pollution, the mucous membranes lining the bronchioles thicken and produce excess mucus. In addition, the tiny reverberating cilia on the membrane become paralyzed and eventually deteriorate so that they no longer propel the mucus with its trapped foreign particles upward and out of the lung to the throat (Briney, 1970). Thus, this excess mucus begins to accumulate in the bronchioles, obstructing airflow and triggering the coughing reflex to help clear the lungs. The accumulation of mucus and the chronic irritation make the normally sterile bronchioles more susceptible to infection by bacteria, creating a cyclical irritation pattern.

If coughing is severe and prolonged, it may gradually tear the tiny air sacs, the *alveoli*, creating emphysema. Treatment involves removal of the major source of irritation (usually cigarettes), antibiotics for bacterial infections, and use of expectorants and bronchodilators.

For a personal understanding of what having chronic bronchitis means, take a breath and cough deeply 5 or 6 times, then without inhaling again, try to cough 5 or 6 more times before taking a breath. Multiply this by many times a day for years, and you can sense the debilitating effect of this chronic respiratory disorder.

EMPHYSEMA

Emphysema is a deterioration of the lungs that develops gradually over a period of years. It is characterized by shortness of breath and a "barrel-chest" appearance. The alveoli become enlarged, lose their elasticity, and tear, reducing the ability of the lungs to exhale (Fig. 11–7). Air thus becomes trapped, making it difficult for oxygen and carbon dioxide exchange to take place. This in turn puts a great strain on the heart, especially the right ventricle, which must pump all the blood through the lungs before it can circulate to the body. Heart failure is common in emphysema patients.

Over 90 per cent of emphysema patients are heavy smokers, although prolonged exposure to severe air pollution or other chronic respiratory disorders can aggravate or trigger the condition. It is most common in white male smokers between the ages of 50 and 70. Emphysema cannot be diagnosed by a standard chest x-ray, making early detection difficult; a high amount of carbon dioxide in arterial blood, however, may be a sign of this disease. As no cure exists for this debilitating condition, treatment is basically symptomatic: stop smoking; treatment of infections; increased fluid intake; use of expectorants, bronchodilators, and humidifying agents; employment of breathing techniques; and if very severe, use of oxygen and surgical removal of bullae.

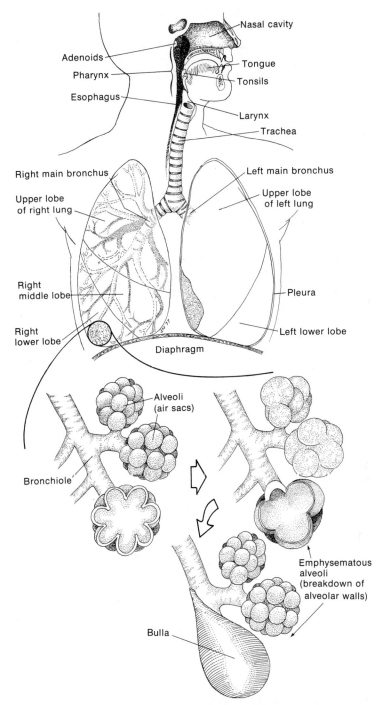

Figure 11–7 The respiratory system: emphysema. (Adapted from Watson, J.: *Medical-Surgical Nursing and Related Physiology.* Philadelphia, W. B. Saunders Co., 1972, p. 258.)

To experience what it's like to have emphysema, breath in deeply, count to 20, then without exhaling, breath in deeply again and hold for a count of 10. Repeat. You'll soon see why the emphysema patient has so much difficulty in breathing—he or she can barely exhale! Multiply this brief experience by many years, and you'll begin to have an understanding of the seriousness of this disorder.

BIBLIOGRAPHY

Briney, Kenneth L.: *Cardiovascular Disease*. Basic Concepts in Health Science Series. Belmont, Calif., Wadsworth Publishing Co., 1970.

Cooper, Kenneth: *Aerobics*. New York, M. Evans & Co., 1968.

Cooper, Kenneth: *The New Aerobics*. New York, M. Evans & Co., 1970.

Cooper, Mildred, and Kenneth Cooper: *Aerobics for Women*. New York, M. Evans & Co., 1972.

Moore, George E.: *The Cancerous Diseases*. Basic Concepts in Health Science Series. Belmont, Calif., Wadsworth Publishing Co., 1970.

Ross, Jolem, and Robert A. O'Rourke: *Understanding the Heart and Its Diseases*. New York, McGraw-Hill Book Co., 1976.

CHAPTER 12

COMMUNICABLE DISEASES

The communicable diseases are those that are caused by a living disease agent or pathogen, such as a bacteria or virus, which can be transmitted from one person to another directly or indirectly. Communicable diseases are usually acute, or of short duration, and most are responsive to drug treatment or immunizations, unlike chronic diseases. We have come a long way in the twentieth century in combating the communicable diseases; influenza and pneumonia have dropped from the top of the mortality list to fifth place in the last 75 years, and no other communicable diseases are among the top ten killers today.

Several factors are responsible for this shift away from communicable disease mortality. The most spectacular achievement was the discovery of the antibiotic drugs such as the sulfa drugs and penicillin during World War II. These drugs have reduced mortality and disability from infections such as syphilis, gonorrhea, and streptococcal infections. Also, the development of immunizations for such viral diseases as poliomyelitis, measles, mumps, and certain influenzas has greatly lowered morbidity (disease incidence) and mortality rates in the United States. Public health measures have perhaps played the largest overall role in the lowering of communicable disease incidence and mortality. Food and meat inspection, dairy inspection, restaurant inspection, water testing, sewage disposal and treatment, rodent and insect control, and discovery and treatment of carriers of disease in populations are the major means that local, state, and federal health agencies have cooperatively used to control and prevent communicable diseases.

Due to our successful record in the past decades, however, we have become complacent in our concern over the communicable diseases. Instead of taking preventive measures, we rationalize our behavior by relying on drugs in a crisis. This has already had noticeable effects. Poliomyelitis, completely preventable through oral immunizations, has seen an increase, as have measles and other childhood diseases. Tuberculosis and the venereal diseases syphilis and gonorrhea are curable with drugs, yet we're in an ever-increasing epidemic of VD throughout the country and TB in certain urban areas. Overuse and misuse of antibiotics, especially penicillin, has led to many drug-resistant strains of bacteria, producing a false sense of security in relying solely on drugs for a cure or control. Many strains of *Neisseria gonorrhoeae*, the gonococcus that causes gonorrhea, are penicillin-resistant due to overreliance and misuse of this drug. International travel of people and animals is a potential source of disease spread, and yet many will try to avoid or falsify immunizations. Governments cannot always assume the responsibility for health, especially for an individual. Let us now examine some basic facts that will arm the reader with at least minimal means to protect himself or herself, as well as others, from the major communicable diseases.

DISEASE AGENTS OR PATHOGENS

Viruses. Despite the fact that viruses are the smallest of pathogens—they can be seen only with an electron microscope—they are the cause of some of the most serious diseases, such as rabies, yellow fever, poliomyelitis, and smallpox, as well as some common ones like colds, influenza, and measles.

Viruses are not classified as true living organisms because they lack the requirements to satisfy the definition of the smallest living entity—the cell. They consist only of an inner core of genetic material, either DNA or RNA, surrounded by a protein coat. The virus is capable of reproducing itself, however, but only through the help of a living cell. The viral genetic material penetrates a host cell, leaving its protein coat outside, and takes over the cell's mechanisms, directing it to make new virus material. When sufficient new virus particles have been made, they burst through the cell, rendering it defunct, and travel to the next host cell to begin the process again (Fig. 12–1). All viruses are *obligate intracellular parasites*.

TABLE 12-1 GROUPS OF LIVING ORGANISMS THAT INCLUDE
IMPORTANT PATHOGENS

Group	Brief Description	Size	Diseases
1. Viruses	Subcellular, intracellular parasite	10–250 millimicrons	Colds, poliomyelitis, measles, rabies, smallpox
2. Rickettsia	Single-celled, intracellular parasite, transmitted by arthropods	Under 1 micron	Rocky Mountain spotted fever, typhus
3. Bacteria	Single-celled, plant-like organisms	1–10 microns	Syphilis, gonorrhea, TB, "strep" throat, tetanus
4. Fungi	Single-celled or multicellular plant-like organisms	A few microns to several inches	Athlete's foot, vaginal yeast infection, ringworm
5. Protozoa	Single-celled animals	A few microns to 250 microns	Amebic dysentery, malaria
6. Parasitic worms	Multicellular animals, flat or round	1/32 inch to 20 or 30 feet	Hookworm, trypanosomiasis, trichinosis

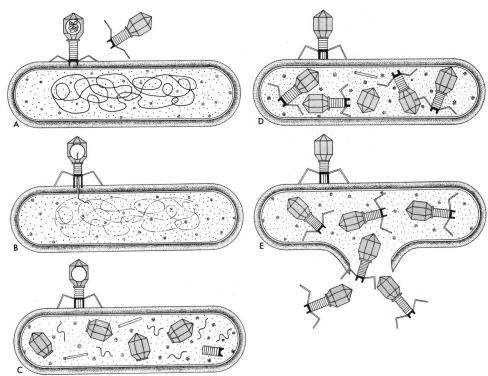

Figure 12-1 Viral replication. The virus attaches to the cell to allow the viral DNA to enter. Replication of the virus occurs within the cell, finally causing it to burst, releasing many new virions. (From Frobisher, M., et al.: *Fundamentals of Microbiology*, 9th ed. Philadelphia, W. B. Saunders Co., 1974, p. 234.)

Viruses are not affected by antibiotics, despite the popular belief that penicillin will cure a cold. Immunizations and natural body defenses are the major individual means of protection, with some public sanitation methods helpful in certain viral diseases.

Rickettsia. Rickettsiae are one-celled microorganisms that resemble very small bacteria but have in common with viruses the dependency on a host cell for multiplication. Uniquely, rickettsiae are usually transmitted from one host body to another by arthropods, such as ticks, fleas, mites, lice, and flies. As a whole, rickettsiae do not cause significant morbidity or mortality in the United States.

Bacteria. Bacteria are microscopic single cells that have cell walls and cell membranes like plants, but no chlorophyll to carry on photosynthesis. Since they are dependent on an external food source, we find them growing on or in just about anything that can provide some sort of nourishment, from soil to food to plants to human tissues. They have an undeserved bad reputation, since the large majority of bacteria are harmless to human beings, and many are beneficial and necessary. Of the few that do cause disease, most do so only when weakened or malnourished conditions exist in the host.

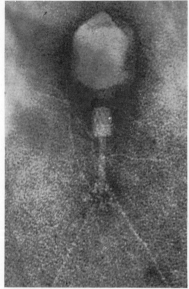

A

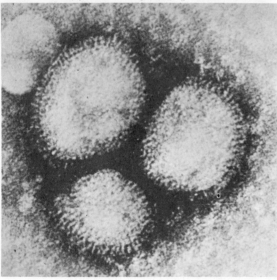

B

Figure 12–2 *A,* Electron micrograph (left) and model (right) of a T-phage virus. (From Frobisher: *Fundamentals of Microbiology,* 9th ed., pp. 220 and 232.) *B,* A flu virus. (From Raphael, S. S.: *Lynch's Medical Laboratory Technology,* 3rd ed. Philadelphia, W. B. Saunders Co., 1976, p. 851.)

Bacteria come in many different shapes and sizes; the cocci, bacilli, and spirilla are three common and distinctive shapes (Fig. 12–4). Some bacteria thrive well in aerobic conditions (oxygen present) and some do best in anaerobic environments. The relative acidity or alkalinity of an environment also affects certain bacteria, as do temperature and amount of moisture.

Most bacteria are susceptible to antibiotics and sulfa drugs, provided that they haven't already become resistant. If treatment is prompt, bacteria rarely cause serious or fatal diseases; it is when treatment is delayed and they have time to multiply and spread throughout the body that bacterial diseases become serious.

Fungi. Fungi come in many different forms, some visible to the

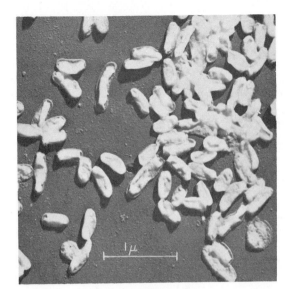

Figure 12-3 Rickettsiae. (From Burrows, W.: *Textbook of Microbiology*, 20th ed. Philadelphia, W. B. Saunders Co., 1973, p. 833.)

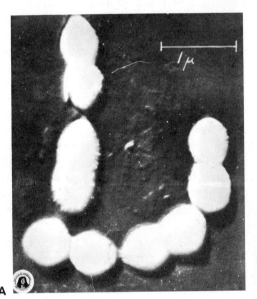

A

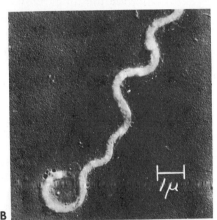

B

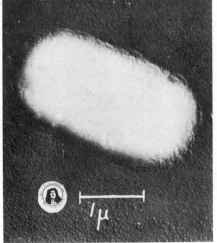

C

Figure 12-4 Bacteria. *A*, Cocci. *B*, Spirilla. *C*, Bacilli. (From *Dorland's Illustrated Medical Dictionary*, 25th ed. Philadelphia, W. B. Saunders Co., 1974, Plate VII.)

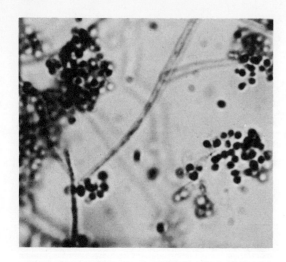

Figure 12-5 Athlete's foot fungus. (From Burrows: *Textbook of Microbiology*, 20th ed., p. 705.)

human eye and some not. Mushrooms, bread and cheese molds, mildew, and plant rusts are some of the more apparent fungi. In human beings, microscopic fungi, which consist of thread-like strands and reproduce by forming spores, usually cause disease of external body parts, like the skin, scalp, and nails. Although annoying, fungal infections are rarely serious or life-threatening and can be controlled or cured by topical application of fungicides.

Personal cleanliness in bathing and use of clean clothes, as well as thorough drying of the body after exercise or bathing, is effective in preventing fungal infection. Not using others' shoes, socks or clothing and wearing shoes on cold, wet locker room-type floors is necessary in preventing athlete's foot. Women often experience vaginal yeast infections, especially after intercourse with an infected partner or after taking antibiotics for bacterial infections. Yeast normally live in balance with bacteria in the vagina, but if that balance is upset, the infection can result. A physician should be sought for a definitive diagnosis and recommendation of an antifungal drug.

Protozoa. Protozoa are microscopic one-celled animals, such as the

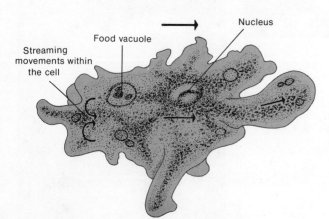

Streaming movements within the cell

Food vacuole

Nucleus

Figure 12-6 Amoeba. (From Villee, C. A., and Dethier, V. G.: *Biological Principles and Processes*, 2nd ed. Philadelphia, W. B. Saunders Co., 1976, p. 354.)

ameba, plasmodium, and trichomonad. Protozoan diseases of man are most prevalent in tropical areas and regions with poor sanitation. Malaria, amebic dysentery, and African sleeping sickness are some protozoan diseases of concern outside the United States; trichomoniasis, however, is a common vaginal infection in women in this country and is caused by *Trichomonas*. Drugs are available for treatment of protozoan diseases.

Parasitic Worms. The largest pathogens are the multicellular parasitic worms, which can vary from a fraction of an inch to 60 feet long! As with the protozoa, parasitic worms are not a major health problem in nontropical areas with good sanitation. Some of the parasitic flatworms are the fluke and tapeworm; trichinosis and pinworm infection are caused by parasitic roundworms.

MODES OF DISEASE TRANSMISSION

The mode of disease transmission is important to know in order to determine control measures; if the disease transmission mechanism can be blocked or altered, prevention or control can be readily achieved. There are several acceptable ways to classify disease transmission, but we

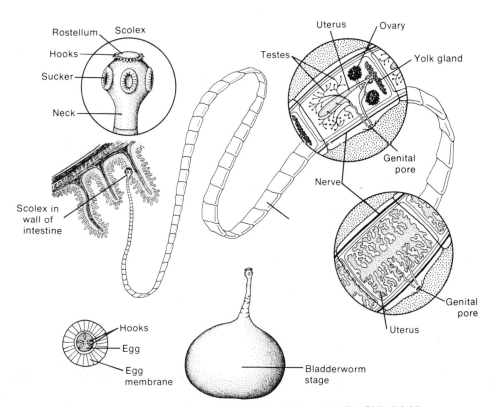

Figure 12-7 Metazoan: tape worm. (From Villee, C. A.: *Biology*, 7th Ed. Philadelphia, W. B. Saunders Co., 1977, p. 291.)

shall use the one which best describes four major modes: (1) fecal-oral, (2) respiratory, (3) direct contact, and (4) arthropod.

1. Fecal-Oral. This route is also called enteric or alimentary, all names implying ingestion of fecally contaminated matter. The feces may be human or animal. The transmission may be direct, from hands to mouth, or indirect from a contaminated water supply or food source. Examples of diseases transmitted in this manner include cholera, dysentery, typhoid, poliomyelitis, and infectious hepatitis. The method of control is good treatment of human sewage and water supplies, and good personal hygiene by food handlers. Immunizations are available for most of these diseases.

2. Respiratory. Respiratory transmission involves the inhalation of respiratory droplets or secretions from another's cough, sneeze or talking spray. Depending on air currents and temperature, droplet nuclei (residues after moisture evaporates) may remain suspended in the air for hours. Diphtheria, pneumonia, meningitis, influenza, colds, measles, smallpox, and chickenpox are some common examples of respiratory-transmitted diseases. Control of this mode is relatively difficult, but ultraviolet lights, disinfectant aerosals, and air-conditioners as well as immunizations and avoidance of others' respiratory secretions all contribute to prevention and control.

3. Direct Contact. Direct contact involves transmission of an infectious agent from one host to another through touching, kissing, or sexual intercourse; direct exposure of susceptible tissue to an agent in the soil or decaying matter; or by the bite of an animal. Impetigo, leprosy, venereal diseases, "strep" infections, tetanus, and rabies are some of the better known direct contact diseases. Control is especially difficult here, but avoidance of contact with infected persons (not always obvious) is essential.

4. Arthropod. Rocky Mountain spotted fever, yellow fever, malaria, plague, and typhus are examples of disease in which a vector is the intermediate carrier of the disease agent from one human or animal host to another. This vector is usually an arthropod, which includes all insects and arachnids. Ticks, fleas, mites, mosquitoes, and lice are the more common arthropod vectors. Control obviously involves elimination or reduction of the arthropod vector. Mosquito spraying campaigns have met with varying results due to eventual buildup of immunity to a particular pesticide by a given mosquito population. Rodent control has been fairly effective in elimination of pathogen-carrying fleas, and wearing of protective clothing in wooded areas is very beneficial in tick avoidance.

STAGES OF INFECTION

Once a pathogen gains entry into a susceptible host, infection begins and, depending on the virulence of the pathogen and health status of the host, may progress into full-blown clinical disease.

The first stage of infection is termed the *incubation period*; this is the interval of time between initial infection by the pathogen and the appearance of the first symptoms of a disease. During this time the pathogen is multiplying until its numbers are sufficient to overcome the body's defenses and produce disease. Depending on the disease, incubation periods vary from a few hours, as with the common cold, to a few weeks, as with infectious hepatitis. Most diseases become contagious during the latter part of this period.

The *prodromal* period is a short stage characterized by general symptoms such as headache, fever, malaise, and overall aches and pains. Diagnosis of the particular disease is difficult at this stage because the symptoms are so similar for most diseases. Most diseases are highly contagious during this time.

The *typical illness* or *clinical disease* stage occurs when the disease is at its height and characteristic symptoms appear, making a specific diagnosis more possible. Some infections fail to progress to typical illness and are termed subclinical; they may remain undiagnosed and therefore carry a greater potential for transmission to an unsuspecting host.

The *decline* is characterized by subsiding symptoms, indicating that the body's defenses are overpowering the pathogens. Although the patient is starting to feel a lot better, it is important to not become too active yet, in order to avoid a relapse (a return of disease symptoms).

Convalescence is the recovery stage, but the disease may still be communicable. If the patient no longer has any symptoms of disease, but still gives off disease-causing organisms, he/she then becomes a *carrier* of that disease. People don't always know if they're carriers, and until this has been diagnosed, they are a potential threat to disease control.

PROTECTION AGAINST COMMUNICABLE DISEASES

Other than individual characteristics of the pathogenic agent itself, what determines the progression of infection in an individual's body? How does our body defend itself against the millions of bacteria, viruses, and other pathogens it encounters daily? Let us now describe the various body defenses, bearing in mind that the strength with which these defenses operate is greatly influenced by the health condition of the whole body or of the involved body system.

Skin and Mucous Membranes.   The unbroken skin acts as a physical barrier to most pathogens, and the mucous membranes lining the respiratory, digestive and urogenital tracts provide a physical and chemical barrier to underlying organs and tissues.

Tears, Sweat and Urine.   These secretions can flush bacteria away as well as chemically inhibit bacterial growth.

Enzymes.   Enzymes and stomach acid secretions destroy many pathogens in the gastrointestinal tract.

Cilia.   These fine, short, moving hairs—cilia—line the respiratory passages and, in conjunction with mucus, trap disease organisms and other foreign particles and transport them upward to the throat where they're swallowed or coughed out.

White Blood Cells and Macrophages. Pathogens that get beyond these first lines of defense face a second line of defense in the blood and the tissues. The blood contains some chemicals that kill bacteria and viruses, but most important, it contains a variety of white blood cells that have the ability to engulf bacteria and foreign particles and digest them. Although these *phagocytes* normally circulate in the blood, they can also squeeze through the blood vessel walls and migrate to the tissue site where microorganisms have entered. Here they are joined by the tissue's own larger phagocytic cells — macrophages — and the battle is waged. Due to the large concentration of these phagocytic cells, the injured area usually is swollen and painful from added pressure on surrounding nerves.

Interferon. Interferon is a chemical released by virus-infected cells which in turn protects other cells from invasion by virus particles. Although the mechanism is only partially understood, it is thought to be very important in our recovery from virus diseases and as a future basis for an antiviral drug.

Antibodies. A final line of defense is called into play while the local battles are being waged. Over a period of several days to several weeks certain types of lymphoid cells produce substances called *antibodies*. Antibodies are proteins that destroy the foreign substances, called *antigens*, that produced them. Antibodies are specific in that they only destroy the agent that evoked the antibody or one closely related chemically to it. Antibodies are the basis of *immunity*. Immunity is acquired naturally in the course of a disease, such that the person will usually be immune to that disease upon a second exposure. Due to specificity, however, measles antibodies, for example, will do the body no good against a mumps virus antigen.

Antigens are any foreign bodies that have a protein and/or carbohydrate component, such as viral protein coats, bacterial capsules and cell walls, pollen, animal hair, and certain foods. Unfortunately, antigenic components of viruses and bacteria can mutate over a period of time, thus bypassing the attack by the previously formed specific antibodies. The influenza virus is a good example of how antigenic structure changes in a year's time; thus we can catch the "flu" more than once. There are over a hundred different cold viruses known, and our antibodies for one type don't protect us against the many others we may subsequently encounter.

This antigen-antibody immune mechanism has been used to great advantage by man through artificial immunizations. Instead of actually encountering the disease, an immunization or vaccination exposes the body to a small amount of the specific antigen, but not enough to cause clinical disease. As a result, the body's immune system manufactures antibodies against this specific antigen. This is called *artificial, active* immunity; immunity as a result of having had the disease itself is called *natural, active* immunity. *Passive* immunity occurs in a crisis situation in which exposure to the antigen has already occurred and therefore it's too late to get a vaccination and wait many days for it to take effect. Instead, antibodies from another person's or animal's blood serum are injected into the individual's body to fight the antigen. Since these are not the host's antibodies they are effective for only a short time, eventually being destroyed by the host's own immune system. Passive immunity is usually *artificial*, in that it is induced by a medical procedure, but there does exist a case of *natural, passive* immunity in the newborn infant for the first few months of life. Here the maternal antibodies travel across the placenta and protect the child until its own immune system matures a few months after birth.

Active immunity, artificial or natural, is the most effective type of immunity, usually lasting many years to a lifetime. However, in diseases without any developed vaccine, such as hepatitis, or in emergency cases of exposure when the person has not been previously vaccinated, artificial passive immunization is invaluable, despite being short-lived.

Levels of immunization of young children in the United States have begun to fall in past years, especially in urban poverty areas, despite the fact that immunizations are free from health departments. Even states that require proof of certain immunizations before a child enters school cannot ensure that preschool age children are also protected. Public education must assume responsibility of informing all parents of the necessity of immunizations for themselves and their children. Another area of concern is immunizations for foreign travel. Your physician or local health department can advise you of the latest international requirements for immunizations for specific countries. See Table 12–2 for the recommended immunization schedule for home and abroad.

SOME IMPORTANT COMMUNICABLE DISEASES

VENEREAL DISEASES

Venereal diseases (VD) are those communicable diseases which are transmitted directly from person to person through sexual contact, including kissing and oral, anal, and vaginal intercourse. Although epidemics can be traced back as far as Columbus' time, this country is presently experiencing an epidemic of syphilis and gonorrhea. The discovery of penicillin brought a reprieve from these two curable venereal diseases during the World War II era, but not for long. Several factors have contributed to the steadily rising incidence of VD: (1) more widespread use of effective contraceptives, and therefore greater sexual freedom; (2) increase in use of the birth control pill and a subsequent decline in use of the condom—the Pill alters the chemical environment in the vagina making it easier for the gonococci to grow, and the condom is a prophylactic, preventing direct skin-to-skin contact; (3) appearance of more drug-resistant strains of the causative microorganisms, especially in Indochina. Despite these factors all genitally transmitted diseases are

TABLE 12-2   RECOMMENDED IMMUNIZATION SCHEDULES

Disease	Age of First Dose	Boosters
Diphtheria, whooping cough, and tetanus	6 weeks to 2 months; series of 3 injections, 1 month apart	At 1 year and before entering school; tetanus every 4 years
Poliomyelitis, Sabin vaccine (oral)	6 weeks to 3 months; three doses 6 to 8 weeks apart	At 12 to 15 months and on entering school
Measles	1 vaccination at 12 months	As yet, no recommendation
Mumps	1 vaccination in preadolescence	As yet, no recommendation
Influenza	Any age past 3 months, series of 2 shots 1 month apart for persons exposed to "flu" in their work	Annually for person exposed or endangered
German measles	1 vaccination at 12 months	As yet, no recommendation
Typhoid and paratyphoid and B	After 3 months; series of 3 shots 1 to 4 weeks apart for persons taking trips where water supply is questionable	1 shot every 3 years if visiting frequently or living in typhoid area
Tuberculosis	After 3 months; 1 shot BCG vaccine for selected persons unavoidably exposed to continuous contact with TB	BCG only on recommendation of the U.S.P.H.
Rabies	Any age; series of up to 14 injections after being bitten by a rabid animal or one suspected of being rabid	None
Yellow fever	After age 6 months; 1 shot if going to yellow fever area	One, if remaining in a yellow fever area for prolonged period
Cholera	After age 6 months; series of 2 shots 7 to 10 days apart if traveling to cholera area	Boosters 4 to 6 months apart if living in cholera area; after 4 years repeat immunization
Smallpox	1 vaccination for travelers to smallpox areas, and those in health and sanitation industries	Every 3 to 10 years

Source: Adapted from U.S. Public Health Service, Communicable Disease Center, Atlanta, Ga.

quite curable, and therefore, anyone who is sexually active should be aware of the symptoms.

Gonorrhea. Gonorrhea is the most common bacterial disease in the United States and Europe; only the common cold, a viral disease, outranks it. Several characteristics account for this high incidence. An attack gives no immunity, and since few antibodies are formed, no reliable blood test exists for diagnosis. The incubation period is short, from three to five days, and 80 per cent of female victims show no outward signs initially of harboring the gonococci microorganisms.

The majority of males, however, do exhibit symptoms a few days after sexual contact. Frequent and painful urination often accompanied by a thick, yellow-green discharge from the penis are the distinctive characteristics. Correct and prompt treatment with an antibiotic from your physician is essential to avoid further complications.

Women usually must rely on communication from their male sex partner(s) before suspecting the disease. Then, a specific pelvic examination for gonorrhea, involving cultures taken from several genital sites, must be sought from a physician immediately to avoid further complications.

If gonorrhea goes untreated in the male or female, the gonococci can invade further into the reproductive tracts causing painful inflammation and scarring. Sterility is the usual result for both, and mortality is not uncommon in the female. Complications for both sexes can occur in other parts of the body, resulting in blindness, arthritis, meningitis, inflammation of the heart, kidney infections, and liver abscesses.

Gonorrhea is easily cured if treated early. Treatment is available free of charge in most local health departments, and confidentiality is assured at any medical facility. Most states have laws allowing treatment of minors for VD without parental consent or knowledge. By prompt treatment you protect not only your own health but also the health of those you care about.

Syphilis. Although not as prevalent as gonorrhea, syphilis is a far more serious disease if left untreated. Late syphilis can cause blindness, heart disease, paralysis, insanity, and death.

Primary, or *early*, *syphilis* is characterized by a small, painless, raised sore that can appear ten days to three months after exposure. This sore, or *chancre*, as it's usually called, lasts four to six weeks, and is usually found on the genitals or wherever contact took place with a partner's infected area. It is easily seen on the penis, but difficult to locate in the vagina. Since it is painless, women are usually less cognizant of syphilis infection than men, as with gonorrhea.

If you suspect that you've been exposed to syphilis, go to any available medical facility, either free clinic or private physician. Fluid from the chancre will be extracted and examined under a dark-field microscope to determine the presence of the syphilis spirochete, *Treponema pallidum*. Primary syphilis is easily curable with an adequate dose of penicillin or alternative antibiotic. Unfortunately for the individual, the chancre will disappear after a few weeks even if treatment has not occurred, rendering a false sense of cure to the victim.

In *secondary syphilis*, the result of untreated primary syphilis, the spirochete has invaded the blood system. A generalized, nonitching rash may develop one to six months after the appearance of the chancre. Large, moist sores that are loaded with spirochetes may develop on or around the sex organs or in the mouth; these are extremely contagious. Sore throats, headaches, fever, red eyes, joint pain, and patchy hair loss may also occur.

The symptoms of secondary syphilis may last from several weeks to several months. Unfortunately, they mimic many other diseases, so it is important to mention suspicion of syphilis infection when seeking treatment. Like primary syphilis, the second stage symptoms eventually disappear whether treated or not. Also like the primary stage, secondary syphilis is easily cured with penicillin. A blood test is used for diagnosis.

Latent syphilis begins when the symptoms of secondary syphilis disappear, and it lasts for a few months or a lifetime. There are usually no outward symptoms of the disease during this time, and thus, the only way it can be detected is through a blood test. As long as no secondary syphilis symptoms reappear the person is not contagious to a sexual partner. However, a pregnant woman can infect her unborn child, causing congenital syphilis.

Late or tertiary syphilis begins when the spirochetes invade specific body organs, resulting in permanent disability or death. The cardiovascular and nervous systems are the most susceptible to attack. Cure is difficult but possible; however, it cannot reverse any of the damage already incurred.

Congenital syphilis is acquired in the fetus from the mother during the last half of pregnancy. The syphilis spirochetes pass across the placenta into the blood of the unborn, endangering the chances of survival. If the child is born alive, he or she will exhibit symptoms similar to secondary syphilis. If the disease is allowed to progress, it will lead to serious permanent damage to the brain and circulatory system, as in tertiary syphilis.

Congenital syphilis can be prevented by giving all pregnant women a blood test for syphilis early in pregnancy and again in the seventh month. A cure of mother and child is possible at any stage, although permanent damage is irrevocable.

Like gonorrhea, primary and secondary syphilis do not confer immunity on the patient, so reinfection can always occur. Likewise, no vaccination exists, making prompt diagnosis and treatment essential. Every infected person owes it to himself or herself and his or her sexual partners to seek early treatment from a private doctor, clinic or health department. Embarrassment should not be allowed to stand in the way of preventing serious disease.

Venereal Warts (Condyloma Acuminatum).   Venereal warts are soft, pink, cauliflower-shaped growths appearing on the glans of the penis or in the vagina. They may also form around the anus. They are not painful, but psychologically they can cause discomfort due to their unattractive appearance. These warts are sexually transmitted. Caused by a virus, they can be treated by topical application of a 20 per cent solution of podophyllin until they disappear.

Yeast Infections. Characterized by an intolerable itching around the vulva, yeast infections (*moniliasis*) have become more prevalent in the era of the Pill. The Pill changes the acidity of the vaginal mucosa, making it more favorable for yeast growth. A vaginal discharge that is white and lumpy with a yeasty odor also accompanies the itching.

Moniliasis can be sexually transmitted to males; the penis, anus, skin and oral mucosa are vulnerable areas. Transmission can also take place from mother to infant during childbirth.

In women treatment may involve discontinuation of the Pill and/or antibiotics until topical and oral nystatin, a fungicide, takes effect. Nystatin is used for males also.

Herpesvirus Type II. A first cousin to the causative viral agent in cold sores or fever blisters, herpesvirus type II causes similar types of sores on the genitalia of males and females. These painful sores are clear, and within a few days crust and heal; however, they are usually recurrent and chronic.

The real danger lies in female infection. Chronic herpes infection of the cervix may be a precursor to cancer of this structure. Another risk is placental transmission of the virus to the fetus, which is highly fatal. A cesarean section is usually indicated before a spontaneous abortion occurs.

Topical applications of anesthetic ointments help relieve the pain, but unfortunately, there is no drug or vaccine providing a cure. Chronic female carriers must have a Pap smear every six months, and pregnancy may not be advisable.

Trichomoniasis. The protozoan *Trichomonas vaginalis* causes this common chronic disease of the vagina and urinary tract in women. It is characterized by a reddening of the vulva and a profuse, thin, foamy, yellowish discharge of foul odor. Men are also susceptible to this sexually transmitted disease. The urethra, prostate, and seminal vesicles are common sites, but rarely are symptoms or demonstrable lesions produced.

Diagnosis is through identification of the motile parasite by microscopic examination of the discharges. The drug metronidazole (Flagyl) is given orally to the infected person and his/her sexual contacts. A condom should be used until the infection is terminated, and alcoholic drinks should be avoided during drug treatment. Metronidazole interferes with alcohol metabolism, producing unpleasant side effects.

Crab Lice. Not really a disease, but an infestation by the tiny arthropod *Phthirus pubis*, "crabs" cause annoying itching in the pubic hairs. Transmission is usually through sexual contact but contact with infected clothing or bedding may be an indirect source. Treatment is with an insecticide powder or shampoo, Lindane or Kwell, obtainable without prescription from a pharmacy. Washing of clothes in hot, soapy water is a good preventive measure.

Chancroid. Also known as *soft chancre*, this bacterial venereal disease is rare in the United States and is most common in tropical countries or those with low standards of cleanliness. About three to five days after exposure, a patch of tiny, clear, blister-like spots appears, usually on the sex organs. These spots soon break open, forming a painful ulcer that oozes pus and bleeds easily. The lymph nodes around the genitalia usually become swollen and painful. Treatment with sulfa drugs is very effective.

Granuloma Inguinale. Granuloma inguinale is a chronic venereal disease caused by a tiny bacteria known as *Donovania granulomatis*, or Donovan bodies. The characteristic raised spots on the penis or vulva are similar to those of chancroid or syphilis. These spots can break down and become ulcers, which can invade and severely damage surrounding tissues. Permanent damage and disfigurement of the sex organs may result from chronic infection. Antibiotics provide a cure. Incidence is low in this country.

Lymphogranuloma Venereum. Lymphogranuloma venereum (LGV) occurs primarily in warmer climates, including the southern United States. Small, raised blisters may appear, followed by a more noticeable swelling and tenderness in the lymph nodes near the sex organs. Fever, chills, headache, and joint pains may also occur. Once the lymph system becomes blocked, fluid cannot drain from the tissues. Swelling of the genitals and blockage of the anus ensue, the latter sometimes requiring surgery if chronic. Although caused by a virus, LGV is susceptible to some antibiotics.

OTHER IMPORTANT COMMUNICABLE DISEASES

TUBERCULOSIS

Although not the great killer that it used to be in this country, tuberculosis (TB) still ranks high as a serious communicable disease. Some urban areas, such as Baltimore, have seen a significant upsurge in the last three years.

Tuberculosis is caused by a rod-shaped bacterium which has an amazing ability to survive for a long time outside the human body. Heat, drying, and many disinfectants have little effect on this sturdy organism. Usually the bacteria are inhaled into the lungs where infection may ensue, but any part of the body can be infected with TB. Respiratory discharges from infected persons, released in coughing, sneezing, singing, or talking, is the main source of infection. Occasionally, infection may occur from drinking the raw milk of TB-infected cows.

Very few TB infections result in clinical disease. However, the bacteria may remain dormant inside the lungs, to become active later if the physical condition of the person is weakened through malnutrition, alcoholism, excess fatigue or another disease. The pathogens in the inactive state in the lungs are walled off with a layer of special cells, producing a nodule or *tubercle*. It is important that persons with these tubercles be checked periodically and take medication to prevent a reactivation of disease and spread to others.

Screening of the general population for TB is now done by a tuberculin skin test. Some killed tuberculosis bacteria is injected or scratched into the skin. If a person is infected or *has ever been infected* with TB bacteria, a significant redness and swelling will develop at the point of inoculation. This test just demonstrates presence of TB antibodies in the body and does *not* mean the person has active, contagious TB. Chest x-rays and sputum cultures can further diagnose active tuberculosis.

Modern drug therapy can treat active TB, rendering it noninfective within six months. A complete cure can take longer, depending on the compliance level of the patient in following a rigorous medication program. A vaccine (BCG) exists for TB, but since it is not completely effective and is sometimes hazardous, use of it in the United States is limited to high-risk groups. Some medical personnel and children in contact with active cases are vaccinated. Most state and local laws require TB screening of teachers and other personnel working with children on a daily basis.

INFECTIOUS AND SERUM HEPATITIS

Hepatitis is a viral infection of the liver; though seldom fatal, it can be quite debilitating and chronic. Jaundice, a yellowing of the skin, is the characteristic symptom. This indicates that the liver is not removing enough bile pigment from the blood, so it is deposited in the skin.

Transmission is usually fecal-oral, with the virus found in feces, blood, and urine. Blood transfusions and contaminated injection needles from infected persons also play a role in transmission, especially in serum hepatitis or hepatitis B. Infectious hepatitis or hepatitis A outbreaks are usually related to contaminated water and food, including milk, sliced meats, salads, raw or undercooked clams and oysters, and bakery products.

Personal and public hygiene in the disposal of human wastes is essential in preventing outbreaks. All food handlers should be properly advised of sanitary methods in food preparation. Blood transmission can be prevented by proper selection of blood donors and the use of disposable or properly sterilized needles and syringes. Heroin addicts run a high risk of contracting hepatitis through use of contaminated needles.

Neither of these viral hepatitis diseases has an active vaccine, but infectious hepatitis can be treated or temporarily prevented through passive immunization with serum immune globulin (ISG) or gamma globulin. Travelers to highly endemic areas in Africa, Middle East, Asia, and parts of South America should be given prophylactic doses of ISG. Infants and preschool children are less susceptible to these viruses than are school-age children and young adults.

INFECTIOUS MONONUCLEOSIS

Taking its name from the characteristic proliferation of monocytes, a type of white blood cell, this viral disease is characterized by sore throat, fever, swollen lymph glands, and a lingering fatigue. This severe fatigue is caused by liver function impairment.

Like hepatitis, this disease is rarely fatal, but it can cause disability from several weeks to several months. "Mono" has also been called the "kissing disease" because kissing is one of its modes of transmission; but any means of contact with nasal or throat discharges from an infected person can spread the virus.

Blood tests can quickly diagnose mononucleosis, but unfortunately, there is no drug or vaccine available to cure or prevent it. Incidence of clinical disease is highest among older children and young adults.

THE COMMON COLD

Although the common cold is not a very serious disease, it causes more discomfort, inconvenience and lost time from work and school than any other disease. It is the most widespread infectious disease in the United States.

Colds are caused by as many as 89 different viruses. The initial symptoms include nasal congestion, scratchy throat, fatigue and chills. A high fever is not a typical symptom of a cold, and usually indicates a more serious secondary infection requiring prompt treatment.

Contrary to popular belief cold temperatures do not cause colds; rather, the presence of one of the cold viruses transmitted via the respiratory tract from an infected person to others is the cause. Winter temperatures facilitate person-to-person contact by increased indoor congregation.

Despite the thousands of cold remedies on the market, there is no cure for the common cold. Vaccines for each of the viruses is impractical, and penicillin only has an effect on the secondary bacterial infections, not on any cold viruses. Megadoses of vitamin C have not been proved to be effective in either preventing or curing the cold. The best treatment is to take it easy during the early stages and avoid infecting others.

INFLUENZA

True influenza or "flu" has a sudden onset accompanied by fever, massive general aching, headache and eye ache. The acute stage usually lasts three to five days, during which time the patient is extremely susceptible to other infections. Many other types of viral and bacterial infections are incorrectly labeled as "flu." Influenza is a seriously debilitating disease, especially for those who already have heart disease, lung disease, diabetes, liver disease or hormonal deficiency. It ranks as the fifth leading cause of death when complicated by pneumonia.

Influenza is transmitted through viruses present in nasal and oral discharges of infected persons; massive epidemics often occur. There are three basic types of viruses—A, B, and C—with strains of these changing slightly every year. The best protection is a flu vaccine, especially for the high-risk groups. Due to the change in antigenic structure each year, a yearly or current vaccine must be obtained.

Age	10 to 20	21 to 30	31 to 40	41 to 50	51 to 60	61 and over
	1	**2**	**3**	**4**	**6**	**8**
Heredity	No known history of heart disease	1 relative with cardiovascular disease over 60	2 relatives with cardiovascular disease over 60	1 relative with cardiovascular disease under 60	2 relatives with cardiovascular disease under 60	3 relatives with cardiovascular disease under 60
	1	**2**	**3**	**4**	**6**	**7**
Weight	More than 5 lbs. below standard weight	−5 to +5 lbs. standard weight	6-20 lbs. overweight	21-35 lbs. overweight	36-50 lbs. overweight	51-65 lbs. overweight
	0	**1**	**2**	**3**	**5**	**7**
Tobacco Smoking	Nonuser	Cigar and/or pipe	10 cigarettes or less a day	20 cigarettes a day	30 cigarettes a day	40 cigarettes a day or more
	0	**1**	**2**	**4**	**6**	**10**
Exercise	Intensive occupational and recreational exertion	Moderate occupational and recreational exertion	Sedentary work and intense recreational exertion	Sedentary occupational and moderate recreational exertion	Sedentary work and light recreational exertion	Complete lack of all exercise
	1	**2**	**3**	**5**	**6**	**8**
Cholesterol or Fat % in Diet	Cholesterol below 188 mg.% Diet contains no animal or solid fats	Cholesterol 181-205 mg.% Diet contains 10% animal or solid fats	Cholesterol 206-230 mg.% Diet contains 20% animal or solid fats	Cholesterol 231-255 mg.% Diet contains 30% animal or solid fats	Cholesterol 256-280 mg.% Diet contains 40% animal or solid fats	Cholesterol 281-300 mg.% Diet contains 50% animal or solid fats
	1	**2**	**3**	**4**	**5**	**7**
Blood Pressure	100 upper reading	120 upper reading	140 upper reading	160 upper reading	180 upper reading	200 or over reading
	1	**2**	**3**	**4**	**6**	**8**
Sex	Female under 40	Female 40-50	Female over 50	Male	Stocky male	Bald stocky
	1	**2**	**3**	**5**	**6**	**7**

The purpose of this game is to give you an estimate of your chances of suffering a heart attack. The columns—from left to right—represent the *coronary risk factors*. The risk factors are some of the medical conditions and habits associated with your chances of suffering a heart attack. Not all risk factors are measurable enough to be included in this game; see next page for other risk factors.

HOW TO PLAY

Study each risk factor then find the item applicable to you and circle the large number in it. For example, if you are 37, circle the number in the column labeled 31-40.

After checking out all the rows, add the circled numbers. This total—your score—is an estimate of your risk.

If you Score
6–11—Risk well below average
12–17—Risk below average
18–24—Risk generally average
25–31—Risk moderate
32–40—Risk at a dangerous level
41–62—Danger urgent. See your doctor now.

THE RISK FACTORS
Heredity
Count parents, grandparents, brothers, and sisters who have had heart attack and/or stroke.

Tobacco Smoking
If you inhale deeply and smoke a cigarette way down, add one to your classification. Do NOT subtract because you think you do not inhale or smoke only a half inch on a cigarette.

Exercise
Lower your score one point if you exercise regularly and frequently.

Cholesterol or Saturated Fat Intake Level
You should obtain a cholesterol blood level from your doctor. If you can't get one from your doctor, then estimate honestly the percentage of solid fats you eat. These are usually of animal origin—lard, cream, butter, and beef, and lamb fat. If you eat much of this, your cholesterol level probably will be high. The U.S. average—40 percent—is too high for good health.

Blood Pressure
If you have no recent reading, get one. In the meantime, consider yourself to be normal (120 for upper reading) if you are under 30.

Sex
This line takes into account the fact that men have from six to ten times more heart attacks than women of childbearing age.
Because of the difficulty in measuring them, these RISK FACTORS are not included in RISKO:
1. Diabetes, particularly when present for many years.
2. Your character or personality, and the stress under which you live.
3. Vital Capacity—determined by measuring the amount of air you can take into your lungs in proportion to the size of your lungs. The less air you can breathe, the higher your risk.

4. Electrocardiogram—if certain abnormalities are present in the record of the electrical currents generated by your heart, you have a higher risk.
5. Gout—caused by a higher than normal amount of uric acid in the blood. Persons with gout have an increased risk.

If you have a *number of risk factors, for the sake of your health, ask your doctor to check your medical conditions* and quit your risk-factor habits.
Note: The fact that various habits or conditions may be rated similarly in this test does not mean these are of equal significance. The reaction of individual human beings to risk factors—as to many other things—is so varied it is impossible to draw valid conclusions for any individual.
This scale has been developed only to highlight what the Risk Factors are and what can be done about them. It is not designed to be a medical diagnosis.

Enter your score in the heart, cut out this section, and send it to the:
Michigan Heart Association
13100 Puritan
Detroit, Michigan 48227

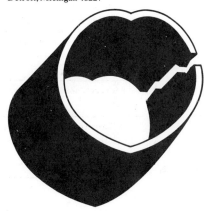

SUSCEPTIBILITY TO LUNG CANCER (for females and males)

	A	B	C	D
1. Age (at present)	50-60	61+ or 40-49	Other	Other
	10	5	0	0
2. Number of years smoking cigarettes (or as ex-smokers)	10+ Years	5-9 Years	1-4 Years	Few Months or Don't Smoke
	40	30	15	0
3. Number of cigarettes you now smoke per day	30-40	11-29	5-10	Don't Smoke or Ex-smoker
	20	15	5	0
4. Age you started smoking	10-14	15-19	20-24	25+ or Don't Smoke or Ex-smoker
	10	7	3	0
5. Number of years working in coal mine or rock quarry	20 Years	10-19 Years	1-9 Years	Few Months or Never
	10	7	4	0
6. Number of years working in asbestos factory	20 Years	10-19 Years	1-9 Years	Few Months or Never
	20	15	5	0
7. Number of years working in other jobs such as sandblasting, tunneling, fiberglass, grain elevator	20 Years	10-19 Years	1-9 Years	Few Months or Never
	5	3	1	0
8. Number of years working in chromium plating factory	20 Years	10-19 Years	1-9 Years	Few Months or Never
	5	3	1	0
9. Unexplained chronic coughing	Yes	—	—	No
	5	—	—	0
10. Repeated episodes of respiratory infections (flu, pneumonia, bronchitis) in past year	5+	3-4	1-2	None
	5	3	1	0

	Always	Often	Sometimes	Never
11. Feeling shortness of breath	5	3	1	0
12. Feeling tired or exhausted	5	3	1	0
13. Wheezing (chest) while breathing	5	3	1	0
Total				

SUSCEPTIBILITY TO BREAST CANCER (for females only)

	A	B	C	D
1. Age	45–64	25–45 or 65–75	21–24	Other
	10	7	4	0
2. Frequency of self-examining your breasts	Never	Qnce Per Year	2–3 X's Year	Each Month
	25	20	10	0
3. Heredity—relatives who had or were treated for breast cancer	Grandmother	Mother	Sister or Aunt	None
	10	10	5	0
4. Frequency of doctor examining your breasts	Never	Less than Every 3 Years	Every 2–3 Years	Yearly
	10	7	4	0
5. Income—check *one* only (a) *Family* income per year	$9000	$10,000–$14,000	$15,000–$19,000	$20,000
(b) *Singles* income per month	$400 or less	$500–$700	$800–$900	$1000+
	5	3	1	0
6. Your religion	—	Jewish	—	Other
	—	3	—	0
7. Discharge or fluid and/or blood from nipple	Yes	—	—	No
	5	—	—	0
8. Lump in breast not examined by doctor	Yes	—	—	No
	5	—	—	0
Total				

BIBLIOGRAPHY _____

Benenson, Abram S. (Ed.): *Control of Communicable Diseases in Man*, 12th ed. American Public Health Association, 1975.

Jones, Kenneth, Louis Shainberg, and Curtis Byer: *Communicable and Noncommunicable Diseases*. San Francisco, Canfield Press, 1970.

Mausner, Judith, and Anita Bahn: *Epidemiology, An Introductory Text*. Philadelphia, W. B. Saunders Co., 1974.

Richards, Ruth, and Howard Kalmer (Eds.): Patient education. *Health Education Monographs*, Vol. II, No. 1, Spring 1974.

THE AGING PROCESS

CHAPTER 13

AGING: THE LAST
FRONTIER OF LIFE

THE AGING POPULATION

In 1976 the United States celebrated its 200th birthday. During those first 200 years many changes were recorded. One significant change was the increase in the elderly population. At the beginning of the twentieth century 3.1 million men and women were 65 years of age and older. By 1970 there were 6.6 million elderly, and projected estimates indicate that the beginning of the twenty-first century will show around 28.8 million (see Table 13–1). Elderly blacks composed about 8.2 per cent of the older population in 1974, an increase of 2.3 per cent from 1930.[1]

The increase in the number of older people has been attributed to three factors:

1. Birth rates have dropped. The total population of the United States grew by 17 per cent between 1960 and 1974, but the number of preschool children declined by 20 per cent.

2. Death rates have declined. In 1974 the rate was 9 per 1000 people.

3. There have been fewer immigrants. Since World War I, the number of immigrants who were primarily of child-bearing age has decreased.[2]

The life expectancy for a white male born in 1969 is 67.9 years. White females born in 1969 have a life expectancy of 75.1 years. Black males

TABLE 13–1   THE OLDER POPULATION: 1900–2000

Year	Men	Women	Total	Female/Male Ratio
1900	1,555,000	1,525,000	3,080,000	98/100
1930	3,325,000	3,309,000	6,634,000	99/100
1970	8,416,000	11,503,000	20,066,000	138/100
2000	11,650,000	17,338,000	28,842,000	150/100

Source: U.S. Department of Health, Education and Welfare, Office of Human Development, Administration on Aging: *New Facts about Older Americans,* 1973.

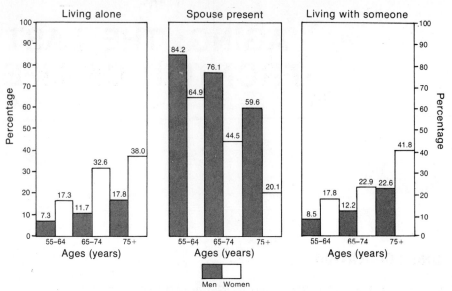

Figure 13-1   Living arrangements of men and women, ages 55 to 75+ years. (From U.S. Department of Health, Education and Welfare: *Epidemiology of Aging,* 1972, p. 75.)

born in 1969 can expect to live to the age of 60.7 and black females to the age of 68.4.[1, 2]

Contrary to popular belief, most older people do not live in institutional settings. Most older men are married and live in a family setting, whereas most older women are widowed and live either alone or in a family setting (Figs. 13–1 and 13–2). The highest proportion of older people reside in Florida, Arkansas, Iowa, Kansas, Nebraska, South Dakota and Missouri.[1]

Some elderly are financially secure where others are not. In 1971, 5 million couples with the head of the household over 65 years of age had the following annual income distribution:

$10,000 or more	17%
$5000–$10,000	32%
$3000–$ 5000	30%
$1000–$ 3000	20%
Under $1000	1%

The annual financial income of the 6.1 million persons aged 65 and over, living alone or with nonrelatives in 1971, was as follows:

$5000 or more	13%
$3000–$5000	18%
$2000–$3000	24%
$1500–$2000	19%
$1000–$1500	16%
Under $1000	10%

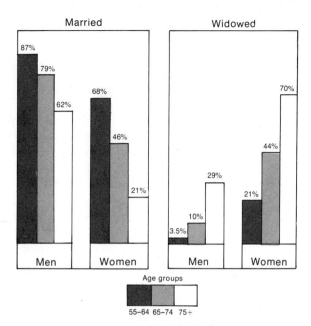

Figure 13-2 Distribution of population 55 years of age and older by marital status. (From U.S. Department of Health, Education and Welfare: *Epidemiology of Aging*, 1972, p. 75.)

One out of every five elderly persons has an income of $58 a week ($3000 a year). These elderly make up 16 per cent of the 26 million poor people of all ages. Some older men and women continue to remain in the labor force; however, male labor force participation rates have steadily decreased from 2 out of 3 older men in 1900 to 1 in 4 in 1972. One in ten females are now working, compared to a past record of 1 in 12.[1]

THREE BASIC TYPES OF AGING

What does it mean when we hear, "That person is old"? The answer depends upon who is asking the question. To a young child, any person in

Determining who is old depends on one's frame of reference.

his late teens or early twenties will probably be considered old. The young adult will probably consider his parents to be old. The general criterion used to determine who is old is chronological age. However, there are other factors.

Each individual ages biologically, psychologically and sociologically. The degree to which each person ages is determined by hereditary and environmental factors. *Biological aging* is most generally associated with chronological age and longevity because this is the most reliable method of determining it. For years scientists have been searching for an explanation of the process of biological aging. Does the human body change with age because of the loss of irreplaceable, long-lived cells, molecular changes in the DNA, an accumulation of somatic mutations, immunological changes, or hormonal changes, or is it just the rate at which one lives? No one knows for sure, but as each theory of biological aging is developed and studied scientists get closer to an answer.

Biological aging.

Psychological aging.

Psychological and sociological aging are closely related and more difficult to measure. *Psychological aging* generally refers to an individual's capabilities of adapting to age-related tasks. We can see, then, that psychological aging is also closely related to biological and chronological age. In measuring psychological age, an individual is compared with established norms in terms of his capacity to adapt to familiar as well as unfamiliar environments. Behavioral scientists have studied personality in all stages of human development and have established theories about psychological aging. Some theories suggest that in extreme old age people tend to return to behaviors seen at younger ages. Other theories suggest that later life is seen as more complex and dangerous; thus, the older person moves from an outer world to an inner world.

Sociological aging refers to an individual's social status and social roles. It is generally measured by developing a composite index of an individual's performance of social roles that are expected at a specific age

Sociological aging.

and within a specific culture or social group. As one can see, social aging is closely related to psychological, biological and chronological aging.

Sociologists wonder if an individual ages socially because he disengages from society, because of negative psychological perceptions, or because of physiological dysfunctioning or economic deprivation. These are a few of the theories that have been examined in the past.

It is generally acknowledged in all fields of science that, regardless of the theory one accepts in relation to how a person ages, there does exist a reciprocity between the physical, mental and social dimensions of life. The degree of this reciprocity will continuously be under investigation until the questions about the aging process are answered.

PHYSICAL CHANGES THAT OCCUR AS THE BODY AGES

For most people physiological change is inevitable. These changes may be the result of normal decline, a disease process, nutrient deficiency, a lack of exercise or any combination of these factors.

NORMAL DECLINE

Let us look first at those changes which might be considered normal and not directly related to a disease process.

The integumentary system, since it is easily observed, exhibits several changes. The skin becomes progressively more dry, wrinkled, lax,

Are skin changes due to normal aging, nutritional deficiencies, lack of exercise, or environmental influences?

inelastic, and thinner. For many individuals these changes are a traumatic experience. We appear to be living in a society that pursues youth and ignores maturity and age. For the most part, these changes in the skin and surrounding tissues are inevitable.

Possible Changes in the Integumentary System	Probable Cause
1. Wrinkling and loss of resiliency	Changes in collagen and elastic fiber; dryness and loss of moisture; less efficient sweat and oil glands
2. Fissures and deep grooves, particularly around the mouth	Atrophy of the epidermal layer of skin
3. Angiomas and keratoses (types of warts)	Reduced secretions of the sebaceous glands
4. Changes in hair color	Atrophy of hair cells
5. Thinning and loss of hair on body (head, underarms, pubic area); increased body hair (face)	Atrophy of hair follicle; elevated cholestrol levels; hormonal imbalance; possible changes in sebaceous glands
6. Inefficient temperature maintenance	Atrophy of eccrine sweat glands

"Garnet! A hair! I think I'm on the road back!"

The most evident changes in the muscular and skeletal systems are stooped posture, stiffened joints and loss of muscle power. Physiological changes in these systems affect appearance and movement. They may also influence the adequate functioning of other body systems. For example, adequate supplies of oxygen are necessary for all cells to function properly. Removal of carbon dioxide is also important. These functions occur as the exchange of gases takes place in the respiratory system. The respiratory system functions in part by the contraction and expansion of specific sets of muscles. If muscle power is reduced, then the process of respiration is also reduced.

All muscles seem to be affected equally. Reduced power in voluntary muscles in the abdomen and pelvis may create problems in urination and defecation. Muscles also provide a major site for glycogen storage, used to provide energy in emergency situations. When muscles become impaired, meeting an emergency situation such as running to catch a bus, involvement in an automobile accident, or recovery from illness becomes much more difficult.

Of all changes in body systems, those associated with the special senses are generally overlooked because even a total loss of any of these processes will still be compatible with life. For some people a loss or severe impairment of any of the special senses may have profound

"Harvey's decided to go out for the 15-yard waddle this season."

Possible Skeletal and Muscular Changes	Probable Cause
1. Loss of muscle strength	Thinning of individual muscle fibers; loss of muscle cross striations; disappearance of muscle fibers replaced by fibrous tissue (nonfunctional scar tissue), which does not have the ability to expand and contract at will
2. Postural changes; bent hips and knees, stooping back	Structural changes in ligaments, joints and bones; ligaments calcify; joints stiffen as a result of erosion of the cartilaginous joint surfaces and their ossification; degenerative changes in soft tissue (synovium), calcification and ossification of the ligaments of the vertebrae; atrophy and thinning of discs between vertebrae; bones become porous and lighter, losing much of their elasticity

personality effects and may create serious problems in coping with the environment. Vision impairment, for example, interferes with shopping, reading, television viewing or traveling. Hearing impairment limits social relationships, church activities, listening to the radio, going to concerts or television viewing. Reduced sensitivity to smell may create a hazardous situation if a person cannot smell a gas leak or smoke from a fire. It also reduces many pleasures we take for granted, such as eating and appetite.

Possible Sense Impairment	Probable Cause
1. Presbyopia (farsightedness) or the inability to see objects from a near point may develop around the age of 40	Progressive rigidity of the lens and reduced ability of muscles to accommodate
2. Glaucoma (intraocular pressure in the eyeball) can result in asymptomatic destruction of the optic nerve, leading to gradual loss of vision	Unknown if not directly related to a disease process
3. Presbycusis (hearing loss with age) generally begins about age 30; high frequencies lost first, followed by progressive loss of lower frequencies	Aging brain, aging auditory system, trauma, noise, or a combination of these factors
4. Loss of the sense of taste and smell	Reduced sensitivity in the olfactory nerves; diminished number of taste buds

In the absence of any type of disease process there is little change in the heart and only minor changes in the vascular system. Because heart disease is a leading adult health problem, any impairment of these systems may induce fear and apprehension.

Possible Cardiovascular Changes	Probable Cause
1. Decline in cardiac output	Increase in the interstitial fibrous tissue, but the atrophy seen in voluntary muscle fibers does not occur; muscle cells progressively accumulate brown pigment; excessive deposits of a starch-like material which occurs even in the absence of significant narrowing of the coronary arteries
2. Increase in peripheral resistance to the flow of blood; increased systolic blood pressure	Arteries elongage with advancing age and sometimes calcify; fibrosis of the inner channel of the artery

If changes occur in the respiratory system an individual's mobility and participation in various activities become limited. Performing routine daily tasks such as climbing steps, walking, shopping, vacuuming or

"There was a time I used to call him 'Tiger'!"

visiting friends often produces shortness of breath, breathing difficulties, apprehension and fear.

Possible Respiratory Problems	Probable Cause
1. Ventilation (breathing)	Weakness of muscles, skeletal changes, diminished resiliency of lungs due to changes in elastic fibers
2. Diffusion (exchange of oxygen and carbon dioxide)	Reduction in alveolar capillaries; mild maldistribution of inspired gases
3. Decreased pulmonary circulation	Changes in arteries, arterioles and capillaries as noted under cardio-vascular system

Enjoyment and satisfaction of food is important to everyone. The loss of smell affects appetite and generally tends to reduce food intake. Some experts believe that a combination of factors such as food fads, poor diet, dental health problems and impairment of gastrointestinal tract brings about digestive problems.

Possible Gastrointestinal Problems	Probable Cause
1. Achlorohydria (loss of digestive acids); reduction in gastric volume; impairment of absorption	Atrophy of mucosal lining of the entire gastrointestinal tract; thickening of the basement membrane and submucosal connective tissue; age-related vascular changes
2. Diminished peristalsis	Generalized weakness of muscles

Problems of the urinary tract often do not develop until the middle years. A person in his twenties will generally have 50 per cent more renal blood flow and filtration rate as compared to a person in his eighties.

Possible Urinary Tract Problems	Probable Cause
1. Polyuria (excessive urination) 2. Nocturia (night-time urination)	In a male either problem is generally related to an enlarged prostate gland; in both sexes problems may be due to obsolescence of kidney filters, interstitial fibrosis with some loss of tubules in the cortex; atrophy of collecting tubules

In both sexes changes occur in the reproductive structures. In the female these changes generally occur earlier and to a much greater degree than in the male. Scientists have not yet been able to completely answer the question as to whether these physiological tissue changes are due to intrinsic aging factors or simply due to the reduction of hormones. Regardless of why the changes occur, most women successfully progress through menopause and the climacteric with the aid of supplementary hormones.

The climacteric is a period in life characterized by clear morphological and physiological changes in the body. Menopause is the cessation of the menstrual cycle subsequent to the loss of ovarian functions. The climacteric and menopause occurs in both sexes.

Women begin to experience menopausal symptoms in their late forties and early fifties. However, malnutrition, overwork and poor general health can prematurely begin the process. Most men do not experience menopausal symptoms that are comparable to those of a woman, and spermatogenesis and androgenic hormone production may continue into the seventieth, eightieth and sometimes ninetieth decades.

The symptoms of menopause are both objective and subjective and generally are placed in the following categories:

1. Autonomic and vascular: "Hot flashes," chills, sweats, and hypertension

2. Neurologic: Headaches, dizziness, irritability, emotional and nervous instability, impairment of memory, loss of a sense of well-being, and periods of depression

3. Direct somatic origin: Changes in reproductive system, disturbances of bones and joints, diabetes, changes in skin especially on face and neck, graying and drying of hair and general muscle weakness.

Reproductive Changes in the Female

Ovarian Function. Beginning around the age of 30 there is a progressive reduction in egg production as well as graafian follicle development. There is increasing evidence that eggs released just before and during menopause are less viable and perhaps have chromosomal aberrations. The formation of functional corpora lutea begins to decline in premenopausal years and this may partially account for a lower incidence of miscarriage.

Hormonal Changes. The estrogen level generally remains fairly constant until the age of 40. This is closely related to the decline in follicular characteristics. After menopause small amounts of estrogen are secreted from the adrenal cortex and any remaining estrogen-producing cells in the ovary. Progesterone may be reduced by as much as 50 per cent in women between the ages of 30 and 80 as a result of the decline of functional corpus luteum. Gonadotropic hormone production seems to increase slightly in premenopausal women and increases markedly during and after menopause until the age of 80.

Genital Tract. The maintenance and physiological functioning of the internal and external genitalia depend on estrogen and progesterone. A shrinkage and decrease in the size of the genitalia and the atrophy of epithelial lining are generally associated with the loss of these hormones.

Reproductive Changes in the Male

The male climacteric is somewhat different from that of the female. Spermatogenesis does not stop as does gametogenesis, and there is no abrupt decline in androgenic hormones. Some men have reportedly experienced abnormal hypofunctioning of the testes. This may influence potency, libido, cardiovascular changes (flushes, chills and sudden perspiration) and emotional instability. When these symptoms have occurred, they generally appear in men who are in their sixties.

Testicular Function. In a healthy male there appears to be very little significant change in the size of the testes. There may be some changes in the Leydig cells, which are responsible for the production of testosterone and other androgenic hormones.

Hormonal Changes. Beginning about the age of 25 or 30 there is a gradual decline in androgenic hormones which continues until age 90. As in the female, there is a slight increase in gonadotropic hormones following the decrease in androgenic hormones.

Genital Tract. The accessory glands that produce semen may experience change in the absence or decline of androgenic hormones. The seminal vesicles decrease in weight after the age of 60. Between 40 and 50 years of age, the epithelium of the prostatic tubes may atrophy. Between 50 and 60 years there may be some atrophy of muscle tissue.

PHYSICAL CHANGE RESULTING FROM DISEASE

Almost all older people have one or more chronic conditions. Some of these conditions interfere with mobility, create difficulties in getting around alone, require a mechanical aid to get around, keep the older person homebound or interfere with other body processes. The four most

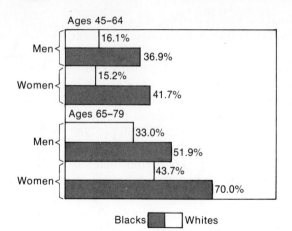

Figure 13-3 Prevalence of heart disease in the United States. (From The National Center for Health Statistics: *Health in the Later Years of Life*, 1971, p. 18.)

common chronic diseases of the elderly are heart disease, hypertension, diabetes and arthritis.

Heart Disease. The prevalence of heart disease increases from age 45 to 79 and is more prevalent in black men and women. After the age of 65, heart disease in white females surpasses that of white males (Fig. 13–3).

In older people disease of the heart may be attributed to (1) coronary atherosclerosis, a thickening of the coronary arteries, (2) cor pulmonale, heart disease secondary to a pulmonary embolism and infarction of the lungs, (3) valvular heart disease due to rheumatic infection, syphilitic aortic insufficiency, or arteriosclerosis, (4) bacterial endocarditis due to severe bacteria infections beginning in the upper respiratory tract, teeth, genitourinary system or biliary tract, and (5) thyroid heart disorders due to disturbances in thyroid glands, especially hypothyroidism and myxedema.

Hypertension. High blood pressure or hypertension is generally diagnosed as a problem when the diastolic pressure is over 95 mm Hg and

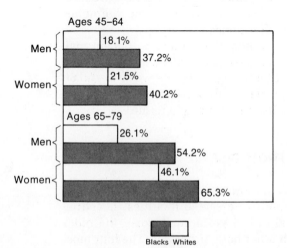

Figure 13-4 Prevalence of hypertension in the United States. (From The National Center for Health Statistics: *Health in the Later Years of Life*, 1971, p. 19.)

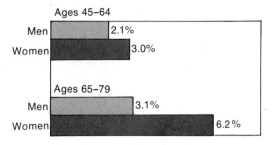

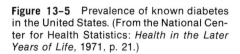

Figure 13-5 Prevalence of known diabetes in the United States. (From the National Center for Health Statistics: *Health in the Later Years of Life*, 1971, p. 21.)

the systolic pressure is over 170 mm Hg and is repeatedly found during several visits to the doctor. In the older patient blood pressure will fluctuate widely.

Hypertension affects many parts of the body. Impaired circulation to the brain, heart and kidneys precipitates congestive failure of these organs and aggravates arteriosclerosis. Each of these structures have important functions in the maintenance of health and life. As in heart disease, hypertension is found more frequently in black men and women. After the age of 65, women of both races have a higher incidence of hypertension (Fig. 13-4).

Several factors that may contribute to the development of hypertension are changes in blood viscosity and blood volume, changes in cardiac output, loss of elasticity in arterial walls, changes in peripheral resistance, advancing age, race, environment, individual heritage, state of activity and emotional stress.

Diabetes. Diabetes is not a problem of great magnitude in the older adult. However, as more known diabetics survive to old age, these figures will increase (Fig. 13-5). One important factor in the older diabetic is that of obesity. At least one-half of older diabetics are overweight. This is an important symptom because doctors report that in adult diabetes weight gain often appears shortly before the symptoms of the disease become manifest. Other symptoms include thirst, polyuria and glycosuria. These symptoms, along with positive laboratory tests, easily diagnose the disease. Often, though, the onset of adult diabetes is gradual and mild, and the symptoms displayed are not characteristic of the disease but rather of the complications which often occur in older adults. In adult diabetes, these complications include the following:

1. *Vascular complications* are often seen in the form of peripheral vascular disease, particularly in the lower extremities. Often there is a decrease in sensory perception. In nonhypertensive females before age 60, atherosclerosis is uncommon. Middle-aged diabetic females lose this immunity and in the absence of hypertension, coronary artery disease is greatly influenced by disorders of carbohydrate metabolism.

2. *Renal complications*, such as lesions in the intercapillary glomerulus, generally require a long period of time to develop. With diabetes these lesions develop much more rapidly.

3. *Ophthalmic complications*, such as retinopathy, are believed to be indicative of diabetes. Cataracts and glaucoma are normal developments

"I do belong to Weight Watchers. I watch my weight go up 2 pounds every week."

in the elderly and are almost always seen in the diabetic. Therefore, any older person who develops these problems should also be tested for diabetes.

Neurological complications—particularly neuritis, which is associated with a loss of reflex in the Achilles tendon—develop in the diabetic person as well as in the nondiabetic. Diagnosis of peripheral neuritis should be followed by tests for diabetes.

Arthritis.   Arthritis may be seen in two forms: osteoarthritis and rheumatoid arthritis. Osteoarthritis is a noninflammatory disorder of movable joints. It is characterized by deterioration and abrasion of articular cartilage and by formation of new bone at the joint surfaces. Most often it affects the weight-bearing joints (knees, hips, lumbar spine), shoulders, cervical spine and terminal joints of the fingers.

The main symptom of osteoarthritis is pain when the joint is in motion or bearing weight. The pain is usually aching and rarely intense and is relieved by rest. Many times changes in the weather will increase the pain. Osteoarthritis is seen much more frequently in obese individuals.

Rheumatoid arthritis is an inflammatory systemic disease of connective tissue and is chronic and progressive, leading to characteristic deformities and disabilities. The exact cause is still unknown. It is characterized by an inflammation of the synovial membrane, exudation

Using the hands can become a painful task for the arthritic person.

(effusion), cellular infiltration (mainly lymphocytes) and proliferation of granulation tissue. As the synovial membrane thickens it spreads over the cartilage and erodes it along with the bone.

The main symptoms of rheumatoid arthritis are joint pain, especially on motion but also at rest, swelling, stiffness after inactivity, especially in the morning, and limited motion due to pain. The typical joint appears spindle-shaped, with thickening of the soft tissues and atrophy of the contiguous muscles. The joints may be hot, red and tender. The typical rheumatoid arthritic may display fatigue, malaise, low-grade fever, tachycardia, weakness, wasting and weight loss and mild or moderate anemia.

Mild osteoarthritis is a common ailment beginning in the middle forties. Older men between the ages of 65 and 79 have a higher incidence

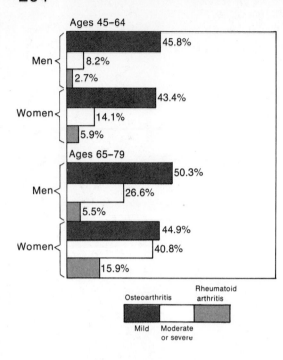

Figure 13-6 Prevalence of osteoarthritis (by severity) and rheumatoid arthritis in the United States. (From The National Center for Health Statistics: *Health in the Later Years of Life,* 1971, p. 20.)

of osteoarthritis, while older women ages 65 through 79 have a higher incidence of rheumatoid arthritis (Fig. 13-6).

OTHER HEALTH PROBLEMS

Only the most prevalent chronic conditions have been discussed but this does not mean that the elderly have no other chronic health problems. The list of diseases are innumerable and many are inter-related.

The ten leading causes of death in the older population in 1968 are listed below in rank order:

1. Diseases of the heart
2. Malignant neoplasms
3. Cerebrovascular diseases
4. Influenza and pneumonia
5. Arteriosclerosis
6. Accidents

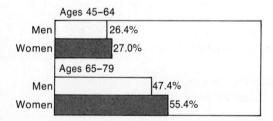

Figure 13-7 Prevalence of persons who have lost all their natural teeth. (From U.S. Department of Health, Education and Welfare: *Health in the Later Years of Life,* 1971, p. 22.)

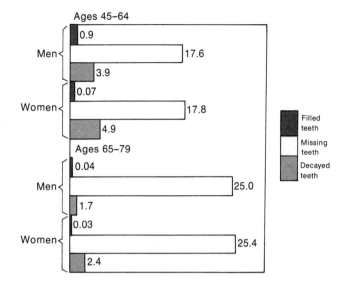

Figure 13-8 Decayed, missing or filled teeth per person at ages 45 to 64 years and 65 to 79 years. (From U.S. Department of Health, Education and Welfare: *Health in the Later Years of Life,* 1971, p. 24.)

7. Diabetes mellitus
8. Bronchitis, emphysema and asthma
9. Cirrhosis of the liver
10. Infections of the kidneys

Men have a much higher death rate from heart disease, cancer, influenza and pneumonia, accidents and lung problems. Women have a higher death rate for cerebrovascular diseases, arteriosclerosis and diabetes. At ages 65 through 74 blacks have a much higher death rate for every major disease except those of the lungs. The opposite appears to be the case after the age of 75.[3]

Another disease worth mentioning, although it is not incapacitating or life-limiting, is that of poor dental health. Dental disease is progressive in nature and is the most prevalent health problem found in this country. Practically no one, regardless of age, goes without dental impairment.

As age increases, so do dental health problems, particularly loss of teeth and periodontal disease (Figs. 13–7 to 13–9). By the middle years a little over one-fourth of the men and women in this country have lost all their teeth, and about one-half have lost all their teeth by the time they are 65 to 79 years old.[4] Fortunately, a majority of these people have satisfactory artificial dentures.

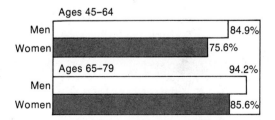

Figure 13-9 Prevalence of periodontal disease among persons with one or more natural teeth. (From The U.S. Department of Heath, Education and Welfare: *Health in the Later Years of Life,* 1971, p. 23.

"Remember the tooth fairy? Tonight you can collect for all 32 teeth!"

Tooth loss may be due to the progressive nature of tooth decay or to periodontal (gum) disease. Periodontal disease is an inflammatory disease of the tissues surrounding and supporting the teeth. In the middle years 76 per cent of the women and 85 per cent of the men with any natural teeth have periodontal disease. The percentages are even higher in the older age group.[4]

For most people periodontal disease develops because of deposits of calculus, malocclusion of the teeth, food impacted between the teeth and gums and mouth breathing. In the older person systemic diseases may have oral manifestations. Alveolar bone changes may occur with hyperparathyroidism, Cushing's syndrome, diabetes mellitus, syphilis, postclimacteric hormonal deficiencies and any diseases that cause a faulty protein metabolism. Severe hemorrhage, leukemia, scurvy, herpes infection, drug therapy and many other factors also affect the gum tissue.

NUTRITION, AGING AND DISEASE

Regardless of age, the achievement and maintenance of good health is partly dependent upon a well-balanced diet containing all of the

Milk Group
Children—3 or more glasses daily
Teenagers—4 or more glasses daily
Adults—2 or more glasses daily
Cheese, ice cream, and other milk products
can supply part of the milk

Fruits and Vegetables
4 or more servings daily of dark green and yellow
vegetables, citrus fruits, or tomatoes

Meat Group
2 or more servings daily of meats, fish, poultry,
eggs, or cheese—with dry beans, peas, or nuts as
alternatives

Breads and Cereals
4 or more servings daily of enriched or whole
grain products

TABLE 13-2   RECOMMENDED DAILY DIETARY ALLOWANCES FOR MEN
AND WOMEN, AGES 23–51 YEARS

Dietary Factor	Men, 23–50 Years		Men, 51+ Years		Women, 23–50 Years		Women, 51+ Years	
Energy	2700	kcal	2400	kcal	2000	kcal	1800	kcal
Protein	56	g	56	g	46	g	46	g
Vitamin A	5000	IU	5000	IU	4000	IU	4000	IU
Vitamin D	400	IU	400	IU	400	IU	400	IU
Vitamin E	15	IU	15	IU	12	IU	12	IU
Vitamin C	45	mg	45	mg	45	mg	45	mg
Folacin	400	g	400	g	400	g	400	g
Niacin	18	mg	16	mg	13	mg	12	mg
Vitamin B_2	1.6	mg	1.5	mg	1.2	mg	1.1	mg
Vitamin B_1	1.4	mg	1.2	mg	1.0	mg	1.0	mg
Vitamin B_6	2.0	mg	2.0	mg	2.0	mg	2.0	mg
Vitamin B_{12}	3.0	mg	3.0	mg	3.0	mg	3.0	mg
Calcium	800	mg	800	mg	800	mg	800	mg
Phosphorus	800	mg	800	mg	800	mg	800	mg
Iodine	130	g	110	g	100	g	80	g
Iron	10	mg	10	mg	18	mg	10	mg
Magnesium	350	mg	350	mg	300	mg	300	mg
Zinc	15	mg	15	mg	15	mg	15	mg

Source: Adapted from Food and Nutrition Board, National Academy of Sciences–
National Research Council. *Recommended Daily Dietary Allowances.*

nutrients. The primary difference in the diet of a young person and that of an older person is the number of calories needed each day. Older people generally are less physically active than their younger counterparts and need fewer calories. Men and women between the ages of 55 and 75 need between 150 and 200 fewer calories a day than they did between 35 and 55.[5] A balanced diet should include foods from each of the four food groups, thus assuring that the essential nutrients—protein, fats, carbohydrates, water, minerals and vitamins—are consumed (Table 13–2).

For some elderly persons, the motivation for preparing and eating an adequate diet is lost, and for others special health problems interfere with the utilization of adequate diet. Regardless of the motivation, neglecting nutritional intake eventually results in poor health.

In a country where foods are plentiful, we might wonder why malnutrition and nutrient deficiency pose a special problem for the older population. At the 1971 White House Conference on Aging several factors were identified. Food habits are strongly influenced by childhood experiences and ethnic, religious, cultural and social forces. Food costs, inflation and the higher cost of living on a reduced and fixed income enhance malnutrition and nutrient deficiency, as does living in housing that hampers carrying packages of groceries up stairs because of special health impairments or housing that is not conveniently located near stores. Some housing areas have inadequate kitchen facilities for food preparation and storage. A lack of transportation to grocery stores and restaurants also poses a problem for some elderly, and poor health status

Nutrient Deficiency	Possible Related Health Impairment
Caloric requirements in excess	Overweight and/or obesity
Carbohydrates	Low energy levels
Fats	Low energy levels; saturated fats may contribute to atherosclerosis; failure for the body to utilize fat-soluble vitamins A, D, E, K
Protein	Failure of the body to synthesize hormones, enzymes, plasma proteins and hemoglobin of blood; fatigue; muscle weakness
Iron	Low hemoglobin levels and anemia
Magnesium	Disorders in soft tissues and bones
Sodium	Excessive or deficient body fluid volume; imbalance of osmotic equilibrium
Vitamin A	Vision problems
Vitamin D	Failure of absorption and utilization of calcium; related to osteoporosis
Vitamin E	Red blood cells more susceptible to hemolysis
Vitamin K	Problems in blood clotting
Vitamin C (ascorbic acid)	Fragility of capillary walls; swollen spongy gums; changes in dentine structure of teeth
Vitamin B_1 (thiamine)	Failure of carbohydrate metabolism; loss of appetite, nausea, muscle tenderness in legs
Vitamin B_2 (riboflavin)	Skin problems; digestive upsets
Niacin	Lassitude, loss of appetite; mild digestive disturbances; emotional changes
Vitamin B_6	Consequences not yet identified
Vitamin B_{12}	Abnormal functioning of cells of bone marrow, nervous system and gastrointestinal tract; failure to metabolize protein, fat and carbohydrate
Folacin	Megaloblastic anemia, glossitis, diarrhea; impaired absorption and utilization of other nutrients; increased demands of body tissue
Pantothenic acid	Impaired metabolism of fats and carbohydrates
Water	Impairment of all body functions; failure to utilize water-soluble vitamins

There are many motivations for eating empty calorie foods.

such as a physical handicap, restricted diets, a lack of teeth or ill-fitting dentures, slower absorption rates and other digestive problems contributes to this situation. Some elderly are not informed about community resources, programs and counseling that are available to them. Food fads, quackery and a lack of nutrition education also influence the problem.[5]

PHYSICAL EXERCISE AND AGING

Much has been reported on the role of regular exercise and the achievement and maintenance of good health. Age-related losses of functional capacity occur, but some wonder whether these losses are due to intrinsic factors of normal aging, disease processes, or poor nutrition or if they result from losses in physical fitness.

The loss of vigor experienced by most older people is the result of losses in aerobic capacity. These losses can be expected as the cardiovascular system, respiratory system, skeletal musculature and body composition begin to change.

Two questions need to be explored: (1) Can physical exercise bring about vigor and changes in the body of an older person? (2) Is it possible for older people who have been relatively inactive to begin regular exercise safely? The answer to both questions is yes.

So long as no disease is present, many of the somatic and mental changes brought about by inactivity are reversible. Numerous studies have demonstrated that vigorous physical training of the older adult can

The older adult needs rhythmic activities involving large body segments.

bring about significant improvements. These improvements include increased oxygen transport capacity, increased resting heart rate, increased vital capacity of the lungs, lowered body fat, increased physical work capacity, improved diastolic and systolic blood pressure and greater ability to relax from emotional stress. In other words, regular physical training improves the heart, lungs, musculature, body composition and psyche.

The percentage of improvement in physical conditioning of middle-aged and older healthy individuals is equivalent to that of younger individuals, although the older person generally starts from a lower achievement level. The achievement of physical conditioning is not dependent upon a previous history of physical conditioning. A person who has been relatively inactive most of his life can achieve a relatively high level of conditioning through a carefully planned, graduated exercise program.

Any exercise program in which the inactive middle-aged or older adult begins to participate should be closely supervised by professionally trained personnel. To produce maximum benefits with a minimum of hazard, a vigorous exercise program will be prescribed, which increases the heart rate more than 40 per cent from resting to maximal. Only a trained professional can determine this.

Under conditions of static (isometric) muscular contraction and high activation levels of small muscle masses, the heart must work harder. These types of exercises are not beneficial to the body as a whole and can raise the systemic blood pressure. The best types are rhythmic exercise involving large body segments such as in walking, jogging, running, swimming or bicycling.

ENDNOTES

1. National Center for Health Statistics: *New Facts About Older Americans*. Washington, D.C., U.S. Department of Health, Education and Welfare, Administration on Aging, 1973.
2. Fowles, Donald J.: U.S. 60+population may rise 31 per cent to 41 million by year 2000. *In Aging*. Washington, D.C., U.S. Department of Health, Education and Welfare, Clearinghouse on Aging, June–July 1975, pp. 14–17.
3. Ostfeld, Adrin M., and Don D. Gibson (Eds.): *Epidemiology of Aging*. Bethesda, U.S. Department of Health, Education and Welfare, National Institute of Health, 1972.
4. National Center for Health Statistics: *Health in the Later Years of Life*. Rockville, Maryland, U.S. Department of Health, Education and Welfare, Public Health Service, 1971.
5. Fowles, Donald J.: *Food Is More Than Just Something to Eat*. Rockville, Maryland, U.S. Department of Health, Education and Welfare, Public Health Service, 1969.
6. Todhunter, E. Neige: *Nutrition — Background and Issues*. Washington, D.C., The White House Conference on Aging, 1971.

BIBLIOGRAPHY

A list of suggested readings may be found at the end of Chapter 14.

THE PSYCHOSOCIAL FORCES OF AGING

A reciprocity exists between the physical, mental and social dimensions of aging. Sometimes it is difficult to assess which comes first. Poor health, reduced incomes, poverty, social loss and changes in the family unit are examples of psychosocial forces in later life (Fig. 14–1).

Reduced income, for example, is a social dimension of aging. It encourages inadequate diet, which may lead to specific kinds of health problems. This is the physical dimension of aging. This dimension encourages crisis-oriented health care, a psychological dimension of aging. Crisis-oriented health care aggravates economic strain, and the circle continues.

The overt behavior displayed by some elderly persons is accepted and often attributed to senility. Many times one hears: "You'll have to overlook her behavior. She's senile." True cases of senility that are seen in very old people are almost always associated with pathological condi-

Figure 14-1 Which comes first?

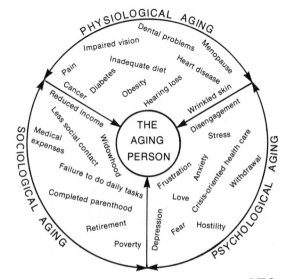

tions such as arteriosclerosis and other vascular diseases that result in nutritional and dynamic inefficiencies of the blood supply to the brain. According to figures from the National Center for Health Statistics, a majority of the older people residing in nursing and personal care homes have no mental disability. Complete disability increases with age, and only 21 per cent of those people 85 and older are completely disabled.[1]

Throughout life, everyone has problems and must make adjustments to them. The important thing at any age is how problems are handled—realistically or unrealistically, with a sense of personal responsibility or a tendency to blame others, with confidence or a feeling of failure and defeat. The pattern of handling problems is firmly established in youth and generally follows throughout life.

The older person is confronted with many situations that require adjustments. The "normal" physical changes, those not associated with disease, have been discussed in Chapter 13. The older a person becomes, the more he or she must learn to adjust and cope with wrinkled skin, graying hair, changing body, deficient vision, and so forth. Positive coping involves the acceptance of these changes and making the most of life with what is available. Some people have difficulty in coping with these changes and may engage in continuous dieting, health clubs, using wrinkle creams, using hair coloring, wearing extremely youthful clothes or procuring cosmetic surgery.

"Why am I being punished? My wife reads *Ms.* magazine, my kid smokes pot, and I gained weight on diet cola!!"

Adult roles begin to change as one gets older. For most men and women, earning a living and raising a family are the two principal jobs. As these roles change, men and women must find other activities and interests to feel useful.

Adjustments must also be made when death takes a spouse or friend. Death is inevitable, and the older a person becomes, the more easily one accepts death, although it is still painful. The widowed have had more time to psychologically prepare themselves after having gone through the grieving process with friends and relatives. They have, in a sense, placed themselves in the role of the widowed, and mentally have gone through the process of funeral arrangements, financial arrangements, housing arrangements and the many other aspects of widowhood.

One of the most difficult aspects of growing older is giving up one's home. To some, this means giving up independence and privacy, especially if they live with married children. Reduced income and health often prohibit the care and maintenance required in owning a home.

In *Preparation for Retirement*,[2] 10 rules for positive mental health have been suggested. The book suggests that the older person should

1. Face reality
2. Take responsibility
3. Take an interest in other people
4. Have varied interests
5. Be interested in new things as well as old
6. Look forward to the future
7. Watch health
8. Maintain a neat appearance
9. Know how to relax
10. Adapt to changing circumstances

The adjustments to life may vary from youth to old age but the principles of achieving and maintaining positive mental health are much the same throughout life.

POSITIVE HEALTH STATUS DEPENDS UPON VARIOUS HEALTH BEHAVIORS

Getting old is a universal process, but growing older is highly personal and is dependent upon specific health behaviors. In other words, the way a person thinks, feels and acts influences how and to what degree he ages. The aging process cannot be prevented, but many premature, detrimental physiological and psychosocial changes can be altered by applying sound principles of health.

Skin. Many changes in the skin which occur prematurely can be slowed by avoiding excessive sun rays. Excessive sun exposure dries the skin and may predispose a person to skin cancer. Increasing evidence also indicates that tobacco use and excessive wrinkling of the skin are related.

Regular exercise helps supply the tissues of the skin with oxygen. A balanced diet is also necessary for healthy skin. Adequate amounts of water, fats, and vitamins A and B are very important. Water and fats are important because without them vitamins A and B cannot be utilized by the body.

Muscles and Bones. To prevent premature changes in the muscles and bones, sound nutritional practices as well as regular exercise are of utmost importance. Regular exercise helps to maintain adequate supplies of oxygen, removes waste products and builds and maintains the power of the muscle tissue. Adequate supplies of protein are necessary in order to build muscle tissue and provide strength to work. Minerals, such as calcium and phosphorus, are needed for both bone and muscle tissue. Vitamin D helps to strengthen bones by promoting deposition of calcium.

Special Senses. Here, again, nutrition is extremely important. Adequate supplies of vitamin A are very important in the functioning of the eyes, and the B complex vitamins help to maintain proper functioning of the nervous system. Another important consideration are those environmental factors which enhance hearing loss, such as the high levels of noise found in a factory. Routine eye examinations are important if problems such as cataracts, glaucoma and retinal detachment are to be found early. Good light is important when reading and working with the eyes, and the eyes should also be protected from bright sunlight. Regular physical examinations are necessary in detecting diabetes and arteriosclerosis, since both can impair vision.

The Cardiovascular System. Regular exercise keeps the cardiovascular system operating properly. Although there is still some controversy, there appears to be a causal relationship between heart disease, arteriosclerosis and hypertension and a high-fat diet, high-carbohydrate diet, sedentary life-style, tension and cigarette smoking. Therefore, maintenance of good health depends upon eliminating or reducing these risk factors.

The Respiratory System. Because adequate functioning of the respiratory system depends so heavily on healthy tissues, energy and muscle strength, such factors as diet and exercise are important in maintaining this system. Also important are the reduction or cessation of tobacco use and avoidance of heavily air-polluted areas.

The Digestive System. In order for the digestive tract to absorb and utilize nutrients and eliminate waste products, a good diet, regular exercise and adequate circulation must be present. Water is necessary in the process of digestion and utilization of water-soluble vitamins. The vitamin B complex is particularly important in proper functioning of the digestive system. Regular exercise keeps muscles strong so that food and wastes are moved through the digestive tract. Excessive emotional stress, alcohol and tobacco use are detrimental to the digestive system.

The Reproductive System. Even though an individual experiences menopausal changes, all the structures necessary for sexual intercourse are still functioning. It simply takes a longer period of time to go through the stages of sexual response. Intercourse is a complex process that depends on the proper functioning of the cardiovascular and respiratory systems as well as the endocrine and nervous systems. Therefore, if health is relatively positive, there is no physiological reason for a man or woman not to participate in sexual activities well into his or her eighties, nineties or even longer.

The feelings and attitudes of many older people about sexual activity are directly related to the expectations of the society in which they live. Our society still continues to consider sexual activities in old age to be taboo. The nature of this taboo stems from three factors: (1) A hangover from the Victorian Age still exists. Many in our society still hold that sexual activities should be engaged in primarily for procreation and only secondarily for recreation. (2) Some adult children of older adults still cannot imagine mom and dad having a sexual relationship. (3) Many perceive the older adult as being asexual. In other words, many people feel that when a person reaches a particular age, he or she is no longer interested or able to participate in a sexual relationship.

Many studies indicate that the older adult is not only interested in sex but continues to remain relatively sexually active. Because of society's attitudes, though, it is not uncommon for the older adult to feel guilty and ashamed of his or her sexual feelings, attitudes and behavior. Researchers have found a remarkable constancy in sexual drive in individuals throughout life. If a person has a strong sexual drive in youth, it will more than likely be seen in older age. If a person has a weak sexual drive in youth, it will more than likely be weak in older age.[3, 4, 5]

"Forget it, Agnes!"

Dental Health Problems. Heredity and environment play a role in dental problems. Scientists now believe that a person inherits a degree of resistance toward tooth decay. The oral environment of each person varies. Persons with a high incidence of tooth decay have a higher bacterial count, deeper fissures and different tooth structure, which makes them more susceptible to tooth decay.

Three very important factors in preventing dental diseases are proper nutrition, proper tooth-brushing and flossing techniques, and regular visits to the dentist. Carbohydrates are sources of energy, but excessive quantities, particularly sugars, combine with specific bacteria to form acid. This acid destroys the enamel of the tooth if it is not removed. Vitamin C is helpful in maintaining the cementing materials that hold cells together. Vitamin D helps to build strong teeth, as do calcium and phosphorus. Fluorine, which is available in most water supplies, helps strengthen the enamel of the tooth.

Regular and proper methods of tooth-brushing and flossing are necessary to remove food particles trapped between the teeth and to remove dental plaque.

Regular visits to the dentist are important at any age. Dental diseases are progressive in nature and most can be easily detected and corrected. However, many adults feel that only children need go to the dentist. This, of course, is incorrect.

Developing positive health practices early in life has tremendous carry-over value. Positive behaviors concerning exercise, diet, dental health practices, dealing positively with stress, and obtaining routine physical, dental and visual examinations should be established and practiced throughout life.

RETIREMENT

One of the values seen in our society is related to productive work, and there are many advantages to work—financial, social and psychological. This is particularly true for men after the age of 65. Because a lifetime has been devoted to work and routine schedules, it is important for the well-being of many men to continue some type of productive work after formal retirement. Others look forward with great anticipation to the day when they no longer must go to work, when they can escape competitive stress and when they will have time for their family.

Women seem to progress through retirement a little easier than do men. Long before formal retirement women gradually begin making adjustments in their lives. They give up roles of child-bearing and child-rearing, and their home responsibilities are lessened. Perhaps one of the greatest adjustments for some women is becoming accustomed to having a retired husband around the house.

Planning for retirement, whether a person is married or single, should begin in the middle years. Consideration should be given as to where to

In retirement there is time for leisure activities.

live, what to do after retirement, financial matters, community resources and health maintenance.

Reduced income and lessened health sometimes make the maintenance of a home very difficult. This may be particularly true for the newly widowed. A part-time job adds to income and may either hamper or enhance the chances of travel or use of leisure time. Many people find that their Social Security payments and the modest retirement funds set aside while they were working are not enough to meet the continually spiraling costs of living. Careful financial planning with the family lawyer, banker or accountant during the middle years will assist in the expenses of living.

Within each community many resources are available to assist the older adult in meeting their physical, mental and social needs. Being aware of these resources may be of great benefit in meeting specific needs.

SERVICES AVAILABLE FOR OLDER ADULTS

Since aging is of a multidimensional nature, the services found within each community have been established to meet some of the physical, mental or social needs of the older adult. These services vary from community to community.

Sound planning to provide services depends on the number of older adults living in the community, the community's knowledge of itself, the probability of delivering services without sacrificing dignity, the manpower needs, the availability of manpower and financial resources. Services for the older adult range from financial counseling to legal counseling, from health maintenance to recreation.

HEALTH CARE SERVICES

When it is medically feasible, every effort should be made to allow the older adult to remain in his home. Home is a part of a person's identity. It is a place where things are familiar and unchanging; it provides a sense of freedom and independence and is a place for autonomy and control. Of course, there are more practical advantages to home care. Family members tend to get more involved, and families do not have to be separated; earlier intervention is possible, since the patient does not have to wait until hospitalization for treatment to begin; more community services are utilized and it generally costs less. The one disadvantage to home health care is finding a physician who will make a house call. In 1972 less than 50 per cent of physicians made house calls and those who did practiced mostly in rural areas.[6] Most physicians feel it takes too much of their time to make a house call.

Health care services include nursing, homemaker–home health aides, physical, occupational and speech therapies, dental services, local health centers, day-care centers, outpatient clinics, mental health clinics, hospitals and nursing homes.

Nursing services include those provided by the registered nurse, the licensed practical nurse, the Visiting Nurse Association and home health aides. The area of nursing found in the community setting with a specialty pertinent to the older adult is that of public health nursing. The registered nurse and licensed practical nurse work for the tax-supported city or county health departments. Their responsibilities include home visits, nursing care, health guidance, communicable disease control and public health clinics. Of particular importance is the instruction they can give about the community health and social resources which are available. The patient load of the public health nurse is obtained by referrals from public health clinics, hospitals or other community agencies.

Another group that works with the older adult is the Visiting Nurse Association. This is a voluntary organization supported by private funds and patient fees. These nurses generally have a smaller case load and can devote more time to patient care. The duties are the same as those of the public health nurse.

The licensed practical nurse performs many nursing skills and is supervised by the registered nurse. Individuals who become homemaker –home health aides are selected, trained and supervised by an agency, organization or administrative unit. Their responsibilities include home-making tasks, such as cooking and cleaning and simple nursing tasks which are medically prescribed, such as taking vital signs, applying simple dressings, giving massages, baths, grooming and physical therapy.

Physical and speech therapists are used following bone and joint diseases and strokes. The occupational therapist is concerned with helping an individual improve his functioning. This is generally done through activities which encourage self-expression. Unfortunately, these services are only partially reimbursable under Medicare, and this often restricts their use in rehabilitating a patient.

Visiting dentists are available in some communities and take care of many of the dental needs of the older adult. Again, these services are not covered by Medicare.

Larger cities have community health centers that provide preventive and maintenance health care to individuals who live within a short distance from the center. Older ambulatory patients can utilize these facilities without having to travel long distances.

Outpatient clinics are available 24 hours a day at most hospitals and generally deal with medical or psychiatric emergencies. Many hospitals also offer clinical care; however, many of these facilities do not offer the type of services needed by most older adults.

Mental health clinics are designed to provide four types of clinical activities: inpatient care, outpatient care, partial hospitalization such as in a day-care program and 24-hour emergency service.

Nursing homes are commercial homes that provide nursing care for people who are ready to leave the hospital but are not yet able to be at home and for those people who need constant nursing and medical assistance.

ECONOMIC SERVICES

The two major sources of income for the retired adult are private pension plans and Social Security benefits. Only about one-fourth of all older people are receiving benefits from private pension plans because of the many limitations to the program. Social Security is much more prominent and accounts for about one-third of the total income. Social security payments are based upon past yearly income. If a man retires and had an average income of $8000 between 1950 and 1975, at age 65 he could receive $402 a month. If married, his wife at age 65 would be eligible for $201 a month.[7]

Another source of income for the older adult who is considered poor or is blind or disabled is the Supplemental Security Income (SSI) program, which went into effect January 1, 1974. This program replaced all state-administered assistance programs which provided welfare relief for the elderly poor, blind and disabled. The program guarantees a minimum income ranging from $1752 for an eligible individual to $2628 for eligible couples. Any individual can receive benefit information for Social Security or Supplemental Security Income by contacting the local Social Security office.

Expenses for medical care are provided through another program of social security called Medicare. This is a health insurance program with two parts. Medicare Part A helps pay for inpatient hospital care and certain follow-up care. It is financed through contributions from employers, employees and self-employed people. Medicare Part B helps pay for doctors' services, outpatient hospital services and many other medical items and services not covered under Part A. This part of Medicare is financed by monthly premiums paid by people enrolled in it and an equal amount contributed by the federal government. Medicaid is another program which provides medical assistance payments for the poor, many of whom are also older adults.

In addition to these major programs older people from low incomes are eligible for food stamps and surplus food programs.

NUTRITIONAL PROGRAMS

Many programs have been developed to provide nutrition education and meet daily nutritional needs. One educational program operating through the Cooperative Extension Service of the U.S. Department of Agriculture is the Expanded Food and Nutrition Education Program (EFNEP). It is directed toward low-income homemakers of all races and reaches the older homemaker either directly or indirectly.

The program is designed to help women manage better with what they have available. It is implemented in the home of participants and utilizes the services of community volunteers and part-time paid workers who are trained and supervised by an extension home economist.

Home-Delivered Meals, also called Meals-on-Wheels, provides portable meals and mobile meals and is a nonprofit system of delivered meals to the home-bound elderly, ill and handicapped. Usually these programs are sponsored by private or public organizations and utilize the services

Community-sponsored feeding programs can fulfill some of the physical, mental, and social needs of the older adult.

of volunteers. Participants who receive meals pay a minimum charge. Those unable to pay have meals funded by some community group.

One Full Hot Meal Daily program also provides food and is implemented through various groups within the community. In some of these programs participants are encouraged to assist in the preparation of meals. Other programs provide informal instruction on food and nutrition. One important benefit, in addition to the meal, is the socialization that takes place during the time everyone is together.

LEGAL SERVICES

The older adult, like any other person, has legal rights, but many of them do not have access to or know how to utilize legal services. A lawyer can be of great value in cases dealing with protective custody.

The older adult has legal needs but may not have access to or know how to utilize such services.

There have been instances in which elderly persons have been committed to an institution or have been classified as incompetent by relatives and lawyers who stood to gain financially from the commitment.

In some instances programs designed to aid the older adult are undermined because of technicalities that the older person either does not understand or does not know how to use to his advantage. If a person is dissatisfied with an administrative decision about a benefit payment, he is entitled to a hearing, but administrative procedures sometimes deter the older person from exercising this right.

There are many who feel that existing laws and programs contain inequities; for example, the practice of mandatory retirement at a certain age, or the federal age discrimination law which pertains only to workers under 65. Most older drivers have excellent safety records, yet some have difficulty in getting a driver's license and automobile insurance. Health, life and other insurances are generally higher for the older adult. Two-thirds of older adults are homeowners and pay high property tax to support local governments. This may place an unfair burden on the elderly. Concern has also been voiced that as the community becomes more dependent upon property taxes, they also become less receptive to the development of tax-free public and nonprofit housing for the elderly.

SERVICES INVOLVING THE OLDER ADULT

Some older adults do not need special services but are able and willing to participate in programs which utilize their services. In some instances they volunteer their services, and in others they are paid for their services.

Senior citizen centers provide a variety of activities.

Retired Senior Volunteer Program (RSVP) works in public and nonprofit institutions. Their services range from teaching delinquent boys how to cook to providing transportation to visiting nursing home patients. They receive no pay but do get reimbursed for travel and meal expenses.

Service Corps of Retired Executives (SCORE) is made up of retired businessmen who provide advice to novices in business.

Volunteers in Service to America (VISTA) are volunteers who commit one to two years to community projects in the United States. Small salaries are provided to cover living expenses.

International Executive Service Corps (IESC) is an independent organization supported by government and nongovernment funds. The volunteers in this program are retired executives who go overseas.

The expertise of the older adult can be used in community service programs.

Foster Grandparents are those individuals who provide relationships and care to orphans and mentally retarded children in institutions. They devote 20 hours per week and are paid an hourly rate of $1.60.

The Senior Opportunities and Service (SOS) program is sponsored by the Office of Economic Opportunity. Volunteers in this program provide service in programs designed to meet special needs of older people, such as nutrition, consumer education and outreach services.

Operation Mainstream is a series of four community service–oriented programs that involve older adults. Green Thumb and Green Light are two programs sponsored by the National Farmers Union. Green Thumb involves men and is concerned with conservation and landscape. Green Light involves women and is concerned with community service. The National Council of Senior Citizens sponsors two programs for community service: Senior Aides and Senior Community Service. The National Retired Teachers Association sponsors Senior Community Service Aides and is also concerned with community service.

EXERCISES FOR THOUGHT

ACTIVITY 1

Below are 17 sentence fragments. Complete each sentence according to your beliefs and feelings about each item.

1. Older adults get lonely when _____

2. To an older adult, religion_____

3. Later life marriages_____

4. To an older adult, happiness_____

5. For an older adult, death_____

6. To an older adult, youth_____

7. In later life, health is_____

8. The greatest worry the older adult may have is_____

9. The older adult views social change_____

10. My greatest fear in getting older is_____

11. I would like to live to the age of _____ because _____

12. When I am old I_____

13. During my life, the greatest contribution I could make_____

    _____

14. The health problem(s) I would least like to acquire in older age____

    _____

15. When I am old, the place I want to live is_____

16. When I retire I plan to_____

17. To me aging means_____

When you have completed this exercise, share your responses with your classmates.

ACTIVITY 2

Record your daily consumption of food for one week. Write down everything you eat. Compute the number of calories you consumed for that week.

1. How many calories did you consume for one week?

2. Compare your caloric intake with what is recommended for your age. Is there a difference?

3. Do you have excessive body fat?

4. Study your list of foods. Identify your major food source for each nutrient.

Carbohydrate:	Vitamin E:

Fats:
  Saturated
  Unsaturated
	Vitamin K:
	
	Vitamin C:

Protein:	Vitamin B_1 (thiamine):
Iron:	Vitamin B_2 (riboflavin):
Calcium:	Niacin:
Iodine:	Vitamin B_6:
Magnesium:	Vitamin B_{12}:
Sodium:	Folacin:
Vitamin A:	Pantothenic acid:
Vitamin D:	Water:

5. List all the physical activities you participated in during the past week. Indicate the amount of time you spent in each activity.

6. Were any of the activities you listed in item 5 suitable for cardio-vascular strengthening?

7. Identify the type and quantity of tobacco products you use in an average week.

8. List the type and quantity of any alcoholic beverage you consume in an average week.

9. Do you have diabetes? Do you have a family history of diabetes?

10. Identify those situations you have experienced in the past year which you view as being stressful or anxiety-producing.

11. What is your blood pressure? Is this normal for you?

12. Do you have a family history of heart disease?

13. When was the last time you had a complete physical examination?

14. Complete each of the following sentence fragments, based upon the preceding information:

I do/do not overeat because ⎯⎯⎯⎯⎯⎯⎯⎯⎯⎯⎯

I am/am not overweight or fat because ⎯⎯⎯⎯⎯⎯⎯⎯

My diet is/is not high in saturated foods ⎯⎯⎯⎯⎯⎯⎯⎯

I am/am not physically active because ⎯⎯⎯⎯⎯⎯⎯⎯

I do/do not use tobacco because ⎯⎯⎯⎯⎯⎯⎯⎯⎯

I do/do not consume alcoholic beverages because ⎯⎯⎯⎯⎯

Since diabetes is/is not a problem for me or my family, I ⎯⎯⎯

⎯⎯⎯⎯⎯⎯⎯⎯⎯⎯⎯⎯⎯⎯⎯⎯⎯⎯⎯⎯⎯⎯⎯⎯⎯⎯⎯

Since high blood pressure is/is not a problem for me, I ⎯⎯⎯

⎯⎯⎯⎯⎯⎯⎯⎯⎯⎯⎯⎯⎯⎯⎯⎯⎯⎯⎯⎯⎯⎯⎯⎯⎯⎯⎯

I do/do not have routine physical examinations because ⎯⎯⎯

⎯⎯⎯⎯⎯⎯⎯⎯⎯⎯⎯⎯⎯⎯⎯⎯⎯⎯⎯⎯⎯⎯⎯⎯⎯⎯⎯

15. How would you describe to your prospective mate your overall attitude and behavior concerning preventive health care?

ACTIVITY 3

Below are eight categories of commercial products. For each category, respond to the following questions:

1. Have you ever used a product in the category? If so, name it (be specific). If not, identify a product you have seen advertised.
2. What are the ingredients in the product? What are the functions of these ingredients?
3. Is the product scientifically sound? Why or why not?
4. What is the motivation for purchasing the product?
5. Were you satisfied with the result you received from the product?
6. What health practices could have been applied in place of the product?

Categories of Commercial Products:
1. Skin care (lotions, creams, soaps, make-up, etc.)
2. Hair products (shampoo, coloring, rinse, etc.)
3. Exercise devices
4. Stop-smoking devices
5. Laxatives
6. Arthritis cures
7. Dental products
8. Vitamin supplements

Study your responses for each of the categories. How would you describe your behavior in using commercial products?

In relation to this exercise, complete the following sentence fragments:

I learned _____

I relearned _____

I was surprised to see _____

I will probably _____

Would you say that the results of this exercise will be indicative of your behavior as an older adult? Why Why not? Share this exercise with your classmates.

ACTIVITY 4

What kinds of services are available for the older adult living in your community?

1. Select one of the following areas: health care, economics, recreation, nutrition, community agencies that utilize the services of the elderly. In the area you have selected, survey the community and identify such programs that are in operation. (You might begin by contacting the local community services council or the United Fund Office.)
2. Select and interview a representative working in one agency or program.
3. Report your findings to the class.

ENDNOTES

1. National Center for Health Statistics: *Health in the Later Years of Life.* Rockville, Maryland, U.S. Department of Health, Education, and Welfare, Public Health Service, 1971.
2. Hunter, Woodrow W.: *Preparation for Retirement.* Ann Arbor, Institute of Gerontology, The University of Michigan–Wayne State University, 1973.
3. Busse, Ewald W., and Eric Pfeiffer (Eds.): *Behavior and Adaptation in Later Life.* Boston, Little, Brown and Co., 1969, pp. 151–162.
4. Palmore, Erdman (Ed.): *Normal Aging—Reports from the Duke Longitudinal Study, 1955–1969.* Durham, Duke University Press, 1970, pp. 277–299.
5. Spinazzola, Angelo J.: Sexual patterns in the process of aging. Health Education, 6(4): 11–13, July–August 1975.
6. Butler, Robert N., and Myrna I. Lewis: *Aging and Mental Health.* St. Louis, The C. V. Mosby Co., 1973.
7. Todhunter, E. Neige: *Your Social Security.* Washington, D.C., U.S. Department of Health, Education and Welfare, Social Security Administration, 1975.

BIBLIOGRAPHY

Atchley, Robert C.: *The Social Forces in Later Life.* Belmont, Calif., Wadsworth Publishing Co., 1972.
Binstock, Robert: *Planning—Background and Issues.* Washington, D.C., The White House Conference on Aging, 1971.
Birren, James E. (Ed.): *Handbook of Aging and the Individual.* Chicago, University of Chicago Press, 1971.
Burdman, Robert, and Geraldene Burdman: The Media and Health Needs of the Elderly. Health Education, 6(4):14–15, July August 1975.
Chen, Young-Ping: *Income—Background and Issues.* Washington, D.C., The White House Conference on Aging, 1971.
Chinn, Austin B. (Ed.): *Working with Older People: A Guide to Practice,* Vol. IV. Rockville,

Maryland, U.S. Department of Health, Education and Welfare, Public Health Service, 1974.

Chinn, Austin B.: *Health Aspects of Aging.* Chicago, American Medical Association, 1965.

Huyck, Margaret Hellie: *Growing Older.* Englewood Cliffs, N.J., Prentice-Hall, 1974.

Kastenbaum, Robert (Ed.): *Contributions to the Psycho-biology of Aging.* New York, Springer Publishing Co., 1965.

Kawabari, Chisato: The aged: An opportunity for the educator. Health Education, 6(4):6–7, July–August 1975.

Keelor, Richard: Physical fitness and health. *In Aging.* Washington, D.C., U.S. Department of Health, Education and Welfare, National Clearinghouse on Aging, May–June 1976, pp. 8–11.

Kent, Donald P., and Margaret B. Matson: The impact of health on the aged family. The Family Coordinator, 21(1):29–36, January 1972.

Kreuger, Esther S.: Freedom to age . . . graciously. Health Education, 6(4):2–3, July–August, 1975.

Leaf, Alexander: *M. D. Youth in Old Age.* New York, McGraw-Hill Book Co., 1975.

Maddox, George L., and Edwin L. Bierman: *Research and Demonstration — Background and Issues.* Washington, D.C., The White House Conference on Aging, 1971.

Manney, James D., Jr.: *Aging in American Society.* Ann Arbor, Institute of Gerontology, The University of Michigan–Wayne State University, 1975.

McKain, Walter C.: A new look at older marriages. The Family Coordinator, 2(1):61–70, January 1972.

Morris, Robert, and Ruth Lauder: *Facilities, Programs and Services — Background and Issues.* Washington, D.C., The White House Conference on Aging, 1971.

Proceedings of the 1971 White House Conference on Aging: *Toward a National Policy on Aging,* Vols. I and II. Washington, D.C., 1971.

Ramoth, Janis: A plan for aging education. Health education, 6(4):4–5, July–August 1975.

Revis, Joseph S.: *Transportation — Background and Issues.* Washington, D.C., The White House Conference on Aging, 1971.

Robbins, Ira S.: *Housing the Elderly — Background and Issues.* Washington, D.C., The White House Conference on Aging, 1971.

Timiras, P. S.: *Developmental Physiology and Aging.* New York, The Macmillan Co., 1972.

Vivian, Valerie, and Wallace Ann Wesley: Report from the congress on the quality of life — the later years. Health Education, 6(4):16–18, July–August 1975

Wallace, Bill C.: Aging: Health education's responsibility. Health Education, 6(4):8–10, July–August 1975.

Woodruff, Diana S., and James E. Birren (Eds.): *Aging — Scientific Perspectives and Social Issues.* New York, D. Van Nostrand Co., 1975.

Work Group Reports from the 16th Annual Conference on Aging: *No Longer Young — The Older Woman in America.* Ann Arbor, Institute of Gerontology, The University of Michigan–Wayne State University, 1974.

Working with Older People — Guide to Practice, Vol. I. Arlington, Va., U.S. Department of Health, Education and Welfare, Division of Health Care Services, 1969.

Working with Older People — A Guide to Practice, Vols. II and III. Rockville, Maryland, U. S. Department of Health, Education and Welfare, Bureau of Health Services Research, 1974.

INDEX

Page numbers in *italics* indicate illustrations.